Contents

THE MECHANICS OF WRITING

CORRECT WORD USAGE

HOW IT IS WRITTEN

Foreword

Using language effectively is the sum of skills in several areas: grammar and meaning, spelling and style, syntax and usage are some of the main ones.

The Written Word is divided into three parts each focusing on a general aspect of the written language. In "The Mechanics of Writing" the overall structural aspects of writing are analyzed; this section provides you with the appropriate tools to use style, grammar, and syntax correctly. The section "Choice of Words" helps you choose the best of all possible words. The main feature of this section is a "Usage glossary" based upon the recommendations of *The American Heritage Dictionary's* unique Usage Panel. The last section "How it is Written" gives you various samples of styles of writing and types of written materials ranging from social notes to business letters and research papers. The library and reference materials are discussed at length; this section also provides guidance on basic research procedures.

People use language to communicate with each other and the ability to write effectively has a great deal to do with what you want to say about a subject, what your feelings about it are, and how you are going to present it to others. The editors hope that the materials contained in this book will help you express yourself more clearly to others.

The Mechanics of Writing

Guide to spelling

To write correctly you must have (or find) the word. You must also know how to syllabicate it, because it is often necessary to divide the word at the end of a line. Words are divided only at the end of a syllable, and there are rules covering division for different situations that may arise.

It is always preferable to avoid division, but often this is not possible. Certain divisions are even done purposely: for example, in legal documents words are sometimes divided at the end of one page and carried over to the beginning of the next page to show the authenticity and continuity of that document.

Words are often divided according to pronunciation. Words that look alike may be syllabicated differently, and in other cases the syllabication may change according to the context of the sentence in which the words are used: for example, the words *project, progress, refuse, present, re-collect* and *recollect*.

If you do not know the syllabication of a word, look it up in your *Word Book* (Houghton Mifflin Company, 1976) which lists most of the words you will need. If the word is not there, you should then turn to your *American Heritage Dictionary* (Houghton Mifflin Company, 1976).

Words must of necessity be divided in order to justify the right-hand margin of printed material: this prevents a ragged right margin and presents a pleasing and

attractive appearance to a typewritten (business) letter. In the preparation of manuscript or copy for printing or publication and in transcription the following rules are generally followed and will aid you in this preparation.

Rules for dividing words, dates, and numbers

The rules that follow are intended to offer writers, editors, secretaries, and proofreaders a guide to traditional practice in word division. The general principles stated here reflect conservative practices followed by printers and publishers and not the comprehensive syllabication indicated in *The American Heritage Dictionary* and *The Word Book,* which reflects the phonetic structure of the word. However, word breaks indicated here will always coincide with one or more syllable divisions as shown in these other books.

1. Never divide a word of one syllable or a word that is pronounced as one syllable:

breadth	mashed	point	cough
horde	yipes	fringe	vibes

2. Words beginning or ending with a single-letter syllable should never be divided before or after the single letter:

   ane-mia, *not* a-nemia *or* anemi-a
   uto-pia, *not* u-topia *or* utopi-a

3. Words like *area, Ohio, ego, ogre* should not be divided at all, because no matter how the word is

4

divided there will be a single vowel either at the end of a line or the beginning of the next line:

abash	idea	oozy
abet	idler	open
abide	idyll	ozone
able	iota	unique
above	Iowa	unit
easy	ivy	unite
echo	oblige	Ural
Eden	oblique	usurp
ibis	ocean	uric
icy	oleo	yeasty

4. A word with an internal single-syllable vowel should be divided after the vowel:

>visi-tation, *not* vis-itation
>oxy-gen, *not* ox-ygen
>maxi-mum, *not* max-imum

5. The preceding rule does not apply to the suffixes *-able* and *-ible* or to words in which the vowel standing alone is the first syllable of a root word. Then the division is *before* that vowel, not *after* it.

>account-able
>answer-able
>prob-able
>collaps-ible
>divis-ible

However there are many words ending in *-able*

and *-ible* where the *a* and *i* do not stand alone as a single syllable. They are divided after the vowel:

> capa-ble
> horri-ble
> charita-ble
> ineligi-ble

When in doubt about any of the *-able, -ible* words, look them up in your *Word Book* where the syllabication can guide you in the proper division.

6. The following suffixes are never divided, although in poetry especially, they are sometimes pronounced as if they had two syllables. In editing, proofreading, and transcription do not divide the following:

-ceous	(herba-ceous)	*-gious*	(egre-gious)
-cial	(cru-cial)	*-sial*	(controver-sial)
-cion	(coer-cion)	*-sion*	(tor-sion)
-cious	(deli-cious)	*-tial*	(bes-tial)
-geous	(gor-geous)	*-tion*	(ra-tion)
-gion	(reli-gion)	*-tious*	(adventi-tious)

7. When a final consonant of a word is doubled in the formation of inflected forms by the addition of a suffix, the division is between the consonants:

red-der	thin-nest	bar-ring
control-ling	dim-mer	regret-ted

But if the root word ends in a double or single con-

sonant, division is after the consonants or consonant:

fall-en   coerc-ing
confess-ing   confid-ing

When there are double interior consonants the
division is between the first two consonants:

foun-tain   hin-drance
ter-res-trial   confes-sion
recom-mend   bat-tlement
expres-sive *but*
express-way

When *-ing, -ed,* or *-er* are added to a verb ending
in *-le,* the division comes before one or more of
the consonants, as in the preceding rule:

gig-gled
daw-dled
whis-tler
fiz-zling
crum-bling

8. Hyphenated words are divided at the hyphen:

all-fired   window-dressing
self-control   public-spirited
strait-laced   wash-and-wear
make-believe   tam-o'-shanter *(divide at*
ready-made   *either hyphen)*

7

Compound words, if possible, are divided between their elements:

steel-worker	under-cover
barn-yard	over-estimate
wing-span	hail-fellow

Many words are made up of a prefix plus a word. Division is always after the whole prefix.

The most commonly used prefixes are:

all-	infra-	pro-
ante-	inter-	pseudo-
anti-	intra-	re-
bi-	micro-	self-
co-	mid-	semi-
contra-	neo-	sub-
counter-	non-	super-
de-	out-	trans-
extra-	over-	tri-
hyper-	post-	ultra-
hypo-	pre-	un-

9. Do not divide abbreviations or acronyms:

UNESCO	FAA
WAVES	Ph.D.
OCS	p.m.
D.A.R.	D.D.S.

10. Do not divide numbers of less than five numerals. If a number has five or more digits, divide after

8

a comma:

346,-422,898 *or* 346,422,-898   10,-000

In business correspondence numbers should never be divided.

11. Do not divide dates between the month and the day, but between the day and year in text.

      October 12,   *not*   October
      1984   12, 1984

In business correspondence these should never be divided.

12. The division of proper nouns follows the rules for division of common nouns. In business correspondence, however, the division of proper nouns should not be necessary and well might result in confusion or error.

13. If it is necessary to divide a proper name formed of initials and a last name, divide after the initials:

    T. S.   *not*   T.
    Eliot   S. Eliot

    e. e.   *not*   e.
    cummings   e. cummings

Try to avoid separating a name from a title:

    Dr. Martin   Ms. Jones
    John Martin, M.D.   Rev. Smythe

In business correspondence these should not be divided.

14. The division of contractions is to be avoided if possible. If it is necessary to divide a contraction, it should be done according to the syllabication:

> should-n't
> have-n't
> Hallow-e'en

In business correspondence these should never be divided.

15. Do not divide years, time, temperatures, latitudes, longitudes, compass directions, or similar units.

> A.D. 19   4:30 p.m.   40°28′
> NNW   28°C

Commonly misspelled words

Some words are more difficult to spell than others and are often misspelled by many people. These commonly misspelled words, each followed by its correct syllabic division according to the preceding rules, are listed below.

Word	*Correct division*
abscess	ab-scess
absence	ab-sence
accede	ac-cede
accept	ac-cept
acceptance	ac-cep-tance
accessible	ac-ces-si-ble
accessory	ac-ces-so-ry
accidentally	ac-ci-den-tal-ly
accommodate	ac-com-mo-date
accordance	ac-cord-ance
according	ac-cord-ing
accrued	ac-crued
accumulate	ac-cu-mu-late
accuracy	ac-cu-ra-cy
accustomed	ac-cus-tomed
achievement	achieve-ment
acknowledgment	ac-knowl-edg-ment
acquaintance	ac-quain-tance
acquiesce	ac-qui-esce
acquire	ac-quire
across	*none*
adapt	*none*
address	ad-dress
adequate	ade-quate
adjourned	ad-journed
adjustment	ad-just-ment
admirable	ad-mi-ra-ble
advertisement	ad-ver-tise-ment
advice (*noun*)	ad-vice

11

Word	Correct division
advisable	ad-vis-able
advise (*verb*)	ad-vise
adviser	ad-vis-er
advisor	ad-vis-or
advisory	ad-vi-so-ry
affidavit	af-fi-da-vit
aggravate	ag-gra-vate
agreeable	agree-able
allotment	al-lot-ment
allotted	al-lot-ted
allowable	al-low-able
allowance	al-low-ance
all right	*none*
almost	al-most
already	al-ready
altogether	al-to-geth-er
amendment	amend-ment
among	*none*
analysis	analy-sis
analyze	ana-lyze
anesthetic	an-es-thet-ic
announcement	an-nounce-ment
annoyance	an-noy-ance
annual	an-nu-al
antarctic	ant-arc-tic
anticipate	an-tici-pate
anticipation	an-tici-pa-tion
anxiety	anxie-ty *or* anxi-ety
anxious	anx-ious
apologize	apolo-gize
appearance	ap-pear-ance
appetite	ap-pe-tite
appliance	ap-pli-ance
applicable	ap-pli-ca-ble
applicant	ap-pli-cant
appointment	ap-point-ment
appraisal	ap-prais-al
appreciable	ap-pre-cia-ble
appropriate	ap-pro-pri-ate
approximately	ap-proxi-mate-ly
architect	ar-chi-tect

Word	Correct division
arctic	arc-tic
argument	ar-gu-ment
arrangement	ar-range-ment
article	ar-ti-cle
artificial	ar-ti-fi-cial
ascertain	as-cer-tain
assassin	as-sas-sin
assess	as-sess
assessment	as-sess-ment
assessor	as-ses-sor
assignment	as-sign-ment
assistance	as-sis-tance
associate	as-so-ci-ate
assured	as-sured
athletics	ath-let-ics
attendance	at-ten-dance
attention	at-ten-tion
attorneys	at-tor-neys
authorize	au-thor-ize
auxiliary	aux-il-ia-ry
available	avail-able
bankruptcy	bank-rupt-cy
bargain	bar-gain
basis	ba-sis
beginning	be-gin-ning
believe	be-lieve
beneficial	bene-fi-cial
beneficiary	bene-fi-ci-ary
benefit	bene-fit
benefited	bene-fit-ed
bookkeeper	book-keep-er
bough	*none*
bouillon	bouil-lon
brief	*none*
brilliant	bril-liant
brochure	bro-chure
budget	budg-et
bulletin	bul-le-tin
bureau	bu-reau
business	busi-ness
businessman	busi-ness-man

Word	Correct division
businesswoman	busi-ness-wom-an
busy	*none*
cafeteria	cafe-te-ria
calendar	cal-en-dar
campaign	cam-paign
cancelable	can-cel-able
canceled	can-celed
cancellation	can-cel-la-tion
candidate	can-di-date
canister	can-is-ter
cannot	can-not
capacity	ca-paci-ty
capital (*city*)	capi-tal
capitol (*building*)	capi-tol
career	ca-reer
casserole	cas-se-role
casualty	casu-al-ty
catalogue	cata-logue
census	cen-sus
cessation	ces-sa-tion
challenge	chal-lenge
characteristic	char-ac-ter-is-tic
choice	*none*
choose	*none*
circuit	cir-cuit
circumstances	cir-cum-stances
civilized	civi-lized
client	cli-ent
clientele	cli-en-tele
collateral	col-lat-er-al
colloquial	col-lo-qui-al
colonel	colo-nel
column	col-umn
coming	com-ing
commission	com-mis-sion
commitment	com-mit-ment
committee	com-mit-tee
comparable	com-pa-ra-ble
comparatively	com-para-tive
comparison	com-pari-son
compelled	com-pelled

14

Word	Correct division
compelling	com-pel-ling
competent	com-pe-tent
competitor	com-peti-tor
complaint	com-plaint
compliment	com-pli-ment
compromise	com-pro-mise
concede	con-cede
conceivable	con-ceiv-able
concern	con-cern
concession	con-ces-sion
concurred	con-curred
concurrence	con-cur-rence
condemn	con-demn
condescend	con-de-scend
conference	con-fer-ence
confident	con-fi-dent
confidential	con-fi-den-tial
congratulate	con-gratu-late
conscience	con-science
conscientious	con-sci-en-tious
conscious	con-scious
consensus	con-sen-sus
consequence	con-se-quence
consequently	con-se-quent-ly
consignment	con-sign-ment
consistent	con-sis-tent
continuous	con-tinu-ous
controlling	con-trol-ling
controversy	con-tro-ver-sy
convenience	con-ven-ience
convenient	con-ven-ient
cordially	cor-dial-ly
corporation	cor-po-ra-tion
correlate	cor-re-late
correspondence	cor-re-spon-dence
correspondent	cor-re-spon-dent
corresponding	cor-re-spond-ing
council (*group*)	coun-cil
counsel (*advice*)	coun-sel
counterfeit	coun-ter-feit
courteous	cour-te-ous

Word	Correct division
courtesy	cour-te-sy
coverage	cov-er-age
creditor	credi-tor
crisis	cri-sis
criticism	criti-cism
criticize	criti-cize
curiosity	cu-ri-osi-ty
current	cur-rent
customer	cus-tom-er
cylinder	cy-lin-der
debtor	debt-or
deceive	de-ceive
decide	de-cide
decision	de-ci-sion
deductible	de-ducti-ble
defendant	de-fen-dant
defer	de-fer
deferred	de-ferred
deferring	de-fer-ring
deficit	defi-cit
definite	defi-nite
definitely	defi-nite-ly
delegate	dele-gate
dependent	de-pend-ent
depositors	de-posi-tors
descend	de-scend
description	de-scrip-tion
desirable	de-sir-able
despair	de-spair
deteriorate	de-te-rio-rate
develop	de-vel-op
development	de-vel-op-ment
device (*tool*)	de-vice
devise (*make, give*)	de-vise
diaphragm	dia-phragm
diarrhea	di-ar-rhea
difference	dif-fer-ence
dilemma	di-lem-ma
dining	din-ing
director	di-rec-tor
disappear	dis-ap-pear

Word	Correct division
disappoint	dis-ap-point
discipline	dis-ci-pline
discrepancy	dis-crep-an-cy
dissatisfied	dis-sat-is-fied
dissipate	dis-si-pate
distinguish	dis-tin-guish
dormitory	dor-mi-to-ry
eagerly	ea-ger-ly
economical	eco-nomi-cal
ecstasy	ec-sta-sy
edition	edi-tion
effect	ef-fect
effervescent	ef-fer-ves-cent
efficacy	ef-fi-ca-cy
efficiency	ef-fi-cien-cy
efficient	ef-fi-cient
eligible	eli-gi-ble
eliminate	elimi-nate
ellipse	el-lipse
embarrass	em-bar-rass
emergency	emer-gen-cy
emphasis	em-pha-sis
emphasize	em-pha-size
employee	em-ploy-ee
enclose	en-close
encouraging	en-cour-ag-ing
endeavor	en-deav-or
endorsement	en-dorse-ment
enterprise	en-ter-prise
enthusiasm	en-thu-si-asm
envelop (*surround*)	en-vel-op
envelope (*paper cover*)	en-ve-lope
environment	en-vi-ron-ment
equipment	equip-ment
equipped	*none*
especially	es-pe-cial-ly
essential	es-sen-tial
esteemed	es-teemed
etiquette	eti-quette
exaggerate	ex-ag-ger-ate
exaggerating	ex-ag-ger-at-ing

17

Word	Correct division
exaggeration	ex-ag-geration
exceed	ex-ceed
excellence	ex-cel-lence
excellent	ex-cel-lent
except	ex-cept
exceptionally	ex-cep-tion-al-ly
excessive	ex-ces-sive
executive	ex-ecu-tive
exercise	ex-er-cise
exhibition	ex-hi-bi-tion
exhilarate	ex-hila-rate
exhilaration	ex-hila-ra-tion
existence	ex-is-tence
expedite	ex-pe-dite
expenditure	ex-pen-di-ture
expense	ex-pense
experience	ex-pe-ri-ence
explanation	ex-pla-na-tion
extension	ex-ten-sion
extraordinary	ex-traor-di-nary
extremely	ex-treme-ly
facilities	fa-cili-ties
fallacy	fal-la-cy
fascinate	fas-ci-nate
fascinating	fas-ci-nat-ing
favorable	fa-vor-able
favorite	fa-vor-ite
feasible	fea-si-ble
February	Feb-ru-ary
fictitious	fic-ti-tious
finally	fi-nal-ly
financier	fin-an-cier
foliage	fo-li-age
forcible	for-ci-ble
forego (*precede*)	fore-go
foreign	for-eign
forfeit	for-feit
forgo (*relinquish*)	for-go
formerly	for-mer-ly
fortunately	for-tu-nate-ly
forty	for-ty

Word	Correct division
forward	for-ward
fourth	*none*
freight	*none*
friend	*none*
fulfill	ful-fill
fulfilling	ful-fill-ing
fulfillment	ful-fill-ment
furthermore	fur-ther-more
gauge	*none*
genuine	genu-ine
government	gov-ern-ment
governor	gov-er-nor
grateful	grate-ful
grievance	griev-ance
guarantee	guar-an-tee
guerrilla	guer-ril-la
gypsy	gyp-sy
handkerchief	hand-ker-chief
handled	han-dled
haphazard	hap-haz-ard
harass	har-ass
hardware	hard-ware
hazardous	haz-ard-ous
height	*none*
hemorrhage	hem-or-rhage
hesitant	hesi-tant
hoping (*expect*)	hop-ing
hopping (*jump*)	hop-ping
hydraulic	hy-drau-lic
hygiene	hy-giene
hypocrite	hypo-crite
hypocrisy	hy-poc-ri-sy
icicle	ici-cle
identical	iden-ti-cal
illegible	il-leg-ible
immediately	im-me-di-ate-ly
immense	im-mense
imperative	im-pera-tive
impossible	im-pos-si-ble
inalienable	in-al-ien-able
inasmuch as	in-as-much (as)

Word	Correct division
incidentally	in-ci-den-tal-ly
inconvenience	in-con-ven-ience
incurred	in-curred
indebtedness	in-debt-ed-ness
indelible	in-del-ible
independent	in-de-pend-ent
indictment	in-dict-ment
indispensable	in-dis-pen-sa-ble
individual	in-di-vidu-al
inducement	in-duce-ment
inevitable	in-evi-ta-ble
inferred	in-ferred
influential	in-flu-en-tial
initial	ini-tial
inoculate	in-ocu-late
inquiry	in-quiry
installation	in-stal-la-tion
intellectual	in-tel-lec-tu-al
intelligence	in-tel-li-gence
intention	in-ten-tion
interfere	in-ter-fere
intermittent	in-ter-mit-tent
interrupted	in-ter-rupt-ed
intimate	in-ti-mate
investor	in-ves-tor
iridescent	iri-des-cent
irrelevant	ir-rele-vant
irresistible	ir-re-sis-ti-ble
itemized	item-ized
itinerary	itin-er-ary
it's	*none*
jeopardize	jeop-ard-ize
journal	jour-nal
judgment	judg-ment
justifiable	jus-ti-fi-able
knowledge	knowl-edge
laboratory	labo-ra-to-ry
legible	leg-ible
legitimate	le-giti-mate
leisure	lei-sure
length	*none*

Word	Correct division
letterhead	letter-head
liaison	li-ai-son
library	li-brary
license	li-cense
lieutenant	lieu-ten-ant
lightning	light-ning
likable	lik-able
liquefy	liq-ue-fy
livelihood	live-li-hood
loose	*none*
lose	*none*
magazine	maga-zine
maintenance	main-te-nance
manageable	man-age-able
management	man-age-ment
manufacturer	manu-fac-tur-er
manuscript	manu-script
marshal	mar-shal
mathematics	mathe-mat-ics
maximum	maxi-mum
medical	medi-cal
memorandum	memo-ran-dum
menus	men-us
merchandise	mer-chan-dise
mileage	mile-age
miniature	minia-ture
minimum	mini-mum
minuscule	min-us-cule
miscellaneous	mis-cel-la-ne-ous
mischievous	mis-chie-vous
modernize	mod-ern-ize
molecule	mole-cule
monotonous	mo-noto-nous
mortgage	mort-gage
murmur	mur-mur
mutual	mu-tu-al
necessarily	nec-es-sari-ly
necessary	nec-es-sary
negligible	neg-li-gi-ble
negotiate	ne-go-ti-ate
neighborhood	neighbor-hood , neigh-bor-hood

Word	Correct division
nevertheless	never-the-less
	nev-er-the-less
nickel	nick-el
niece	*none*
noticeable	no-tice-able
oblige	*none*
occasion	oc-ca-sion
occasionally	oc-ca-sion-al-ly
occupant	oc-cu-pant
occurred	oc-curred
occurrence	oc-cur-rence
occurring	oc-cur-ring
offense	of-fense
offering	of-fer-ing
official	of-fi-cial
omission	omis-sion
omitted	omit-ted
opportunities	op-por-tu-ni-ties
opportunity	op-por-tu-ni-ty
ordinarily	or-di-nari-ly
ordinary	or-di-nary
organization	or-gani-za-tion
organize	or-gan-ize
original	origi-nal
overdue	over-due
paid	*none*
pamphlet	pam-phlet
paradise	para-dise
parallel	par-al-lel
paralleled	par-al-leled
parallelled	par-al-lelled
parentheses	pa-ren-the-ses
parenthesis	pa-ren-the-sis
partial	par-tial
participant	par-tici-pant
participate	par-tici-pate
particularly	par-ticu-lar-ly
patronage	pa-tron-age
peaceable	peace-able
peculiar	pe-cu-liar
perceive	per-ceive

Word	Correct division
peril	per-il
permanent	per-ma-nent
permissible	per-mis-si-ble
permitted	per-mit-ted
perpendicular	per-pen-dicu-lar
perseverance	per-se-ver-ance
personal	per-son-al
personnel	per-son-nel
persuade	per-suade
petition	pe-ti-tion
phase	*none*
Philippines	Phil-ip-pines
philosophical	philo-sophi-cal
philosophy	phi-loso-phy
physician	phy-si-cian
planning	plan-ning
plateau	pla-teau
plausible	plau-si-ble
pleasant	pleas-ant
pleasure	pleas-ure
pneumonia	pneu-mo-nia
politician	poli-ti-cian
Portuguese	Por-tu-guese
possess	pos-sess
possession	pos-ses-sion
practical	prac-ti-cal
practically	prac-ti-cal-ly
practice	prac-tice
precede	pre-cede
precisely	pre-cise-ly
precision	pre-ci-sion
predecessor	prede-ces-sor
preferable	pref-er-able
preference	pref-er-ence
preferred	pre-ferred
prejudice	preju-dice
preliminary	pre-limi-nary
premium	pre-mi-um
previous	pre-vi-ous
price list	*none*
principal (*main*)	prin-ci-pal

23

Word	Correct division
principle (*rule*)	prin-ci-ple
prior	pri-or
privilege	privi-lege
probability	proba-bili-ty
probably	proba-bly
procedure	pro-ce-dure
proceed	pro-ceed
professor	pro-fes-sor
prominent	promi-nent
prosecute	prose-cute
psychology	psy-cholo-gy
purchase	pur-chase
pursue	pur-sue
quantity	quan-ti-ty
questionnaire	ques-tion-naire
quiet	qui-et
quite	*none*
realize	re-al-ize
reasonable	rea-son-able
receipt	re-ceipt
receive	re-ceive
receiving	re-ceiv-ing
recipe	reci-pe
recognize	rec-og-nize
recognized	rec-og-nized
recommend	rec-om-mend
recurrence	re-cur-rence
reference	ref-er-ence
referred	re-ferred
referring	re-fer-ring
regrettable	re-gret-ta-ble
reign	*none*
reimburse	re-im-burse
relevant	rele-vant
remember	re-mem-ber
remembrance	re-mem-brance
reminisce	remi-nisce
remiss	re-miss
remittance	re-mit-tance
rendezvous	ren-dez-vous
renewal	re-new-al

Word	*Correct division*
repetition	*none*
representative	repe-ti-tion
requirement	rep-re-sen-ta-tive
requisition	re-quire-ment
resistance	req-ui-si-tion
respectfully	re-sis-tance
respectively	re-spect-ful-ly
response	re-spec-tive-ly
responsibility	re-sponse
responsible	re-spon-si-bili-ty
restaurant	re-spon-si-ble
restaurateur	res-tau-rant
reticence	res-tau-ra-teur
ridiculous	reti-cence
route	ri-dicu-lous
salable	sal-able
salary	sala-ry
saleable	sale-able
satisfactorily	sat-is-fac-to-ri-ly
schedule	sched-ule
scissors	scis-sors
scurrilous	scur-ri-lous
secretary	sec-re-tary
securities	secu-ri-ties
seize	*none*
seized	*none*
separate	sepa-rate
sergeant	ser-geant
serviceable	serv-ice-able
shepherd	shep-herd
sheriff	sher-iff
shipment	ship-ment
shipping	ship-ping
siege	*none*
significant	sig-nifi-cant
similar	simi-lar
simultaneous	si-mul-ta-ne-ous
sincerity	sin-ceri-ty
skiing	ski-ing
skillful	skill-ful
solemn	sol-emn

25

Word	Correct division
someone	some-one
somewhat	some-what
sorority	so-rori-ty
specialize	spe-cial-ize
specific	spe-cif-ic
spontaneity	spon-ta-nei-ty
spontaneous	spon-ta-ne-ous
stationary (*still*)	sta-tion-ary
stationery (*supplies*)	sta-tion-ery
statistics	sta-tis-tics
statutes	stat-utes
strength	*none*
strictly	strict-ly
submitted	sub-mit-ted
subscriber	sub-scrib-er
substantial	sub-stan-tial
succeed	suc-ceed
succeeded	suc-ceed-ed
successful	suc-cess-ful
succession	suc-ces-sion
sufficient	suf-fi-cient
superintendent	su-per-in-ten-dent
supersede	su-per-sede
supervisor	su-per-vi-sor
supplement	sup-ple-ment
surprise	sur-prise
surveillance	sur-veil-lance
survey	sur-vey
suspicion	sus-pi-cion
sustenance	sus-te-nance
sympathy	sym-pa-thy
synchronous	syn-chro-nous
tariff	tar-iff
temporarily	tem-po-rari-ly
temporary	tem-po-rary
tentative	ten-ta-tive
terrestrial	ter-res-tri-al
their	*none*
there	*none*
thoroughly	thor-ough-ly
through	*none*

Word	Correct division
throughout	through-out
too (*also*)	*none*
tournament	tour-na-ment
tourniquet	tour-ni-quet
tragedy	trage-dy
tranquillity	tran-quil-li-ty
tranquilizer	tran-quil-iz-er
transferred	trans-ferred
typing	typ-ing
ultimately	ul-ti-mate-ly
unanimous	unani-mous
undoubtedly	un-doubt-ed-ly
unfortunately	un-for-tu-nate-ly
unique	*none*
unison	uni-son
unmanageable	un-man-age-able
unnecessary	un-nec-es-sary
until	un-til
urgent	ur-gent
usable	us-able
usually	usu-al-ly
utilize	util-ize
vacancy	va-can-cy
vacuum	vacu-um
vague	*none*
valuable	valu-able
various	vari-ous
vehicle	ve-hi-cle
veil	*none*
vendor	ven-dor
vicinity	vi-cini-ty
vilify	vili-fy
visible	vis-ible
volume	vol-ume
voluntary	vol-un-tary
volunteer	vol-un-teer
warehouse	ware-house
warrant	war-rant
warranty	war-ran-ty
weather (*meteorology*)	weath-er
weird	*none*

Word	Correct division
whether (*if*)	wheth-er
wholesale	whole-sale
withhold	with-hold
worthwhile	worth-while
wretched	wretch-ed
writing	writ-ing
wrought	*none*
yield	*none*

Punctuation

Apostrophe

1. Indicates the possessive case of nouns, proper nouns, and indefinite pronouns:

   > her aunt's house
   > the children's toys
   > Keats's "Ode to Psyche"
   > someone's bright idea
   > one's own home

2. Indicates the plurals of figures, letters, or words used as such:

   > 42's and 53's
   > in the 1700's
   > *x*'s, *y*'s, and *z*'s
   > an article with too many *however*'s

3. Indicates the omission of letters in contractions:

   > isn't   that's
   > couldn't   o'clock

4. Indicates the omission of figures:

   > the class of '12

Brackets

1. Enclose words or passages in quotations to indicate the insertion of material written by someone other than the original writer:

   > . . . On these two commandments hang [are based] all the Law and the Prophets.
   > And summer's lease [allotted time] hath all too short a date [duration]; . . .

2. Enclose material inserted within matter already in parentheses:

> (Washington [D.C.], January, 1972)

Colon

1. Introduces words, phrases, or clauses that explain, amplify, exemplify, or summarize what has preceded:

> Suddenly I knew where we were: Paris.
>
> The army was cut to pieces: more than fifty thousand were killed or captured.
>
> The lasting influence of Greece's dramatic tradition is indicated by words still in our vocabulary: *chorus, comedy,* and *drama.*
>
> She has three sources of income: stock dividends, interest from savings accounts, and salary.

2. Introduces a long quotation:

> In his Gettysburg Address, Lincoln said: "Four score and seven years ago our fathers brought forth on this continent, a new nation, conceived in Liberty, and dedicated to the proposition that all men are created equal. . . ."

3. Introduces lists:

> Among the conjunctive adverbs are the following: *so, therefore, hence, however, nevertheless, moreover, accordingly,* and *besides.*

4. Separates chapter and verse numbers in references to biblical quotations:

> Esther 2:17

5. Separates hour and minute in time designations:

> 1:30 P.M.
>
> a 9:15 class

6. Follows the salutation in a formal letter:

> Dear Sir or Madam:
> Gentlemen:

Comma

1. Separates the clauses of a compound sentence connected by a coordinating conjunction:

> There is a difference between the musical works of Mozart and Haydn, and it is a difference worth discovering.
> He didn't know where she got such an idea, but he didn't disagree.

The comma may be omitted in short compound sentences in which the connection between the clauses is close:

> She understood the situation and she was furious.
> He got in the car and he drove and drove.

2. Separates *and* or *or* from the final item in a series of three or more:

> Lights of red, green, and blue wavelengths may be mixed to produce all colors.
> The radio, television set, and records were arranged on one shelf.
> Would you rather have ice cream, cake, or pie for dessert?

3. Separates two or more adjectives modifying the same noun if *and* could be used between them without changing the meaning:

> a stolid, heavy gait
> a large, high-ceilinged room
> a polished mahogany desk

4. Sets off a nonrestrictive clause or phrase (one that if eliminated would not change the meaning of the sentence):

> The thief, who had entered through the window, went straight to the safe.

The comma should not be used when the clause or phrase is restrictive (essential to the meaning of the sentence):

> The thief who had entered through the window went straight to the safe.

5. Sets off words or phrases in apposition to a noun or noun phrase:

> Plato, the famous Greek philosopher, was a pupil of Socrates.
> The composer of *Tristan und Isolde,* Richard Wagner, was a leading exponent of German romanticism.

The comma should not be used if such words or phrases further specify the noun that precedes:

> The Greek philosopher Plato was a pupil of Socrates.
> The composer Richard Wagner was a leading exponent of German romanticism.
> The Dostoyevsky novel *Crime and Punishment* was required reading.

6. Sets off transitional words and short expressions that require a pause in reading:

> Unfortunately, Mrs. Lattimer hadn't read many Russian novels.
> Did he, after all, look American?
> Peterson lives with his family, of course.
> Indeed, the sight of him gave me quite a jolt.

7. Sets off words used to introduce a sentence:

> No, I haven't seen Rowbotham.
> Well, why don't you do as I ask?

8. Sets off a subordinate clause or a long phrase that precedes the principal clause:

> By the time they finally found the restaurant, they were no longer hungry.
> After the army surrendered, the general was taken prisoner.
> Of all the illustrations in the book, the most striking are those that show the beauty of the mosaics.

9. Sets off short quotations, sayings, and the like:

> Jo told him, "Come tomorrow for dinner."
> The candidate said, "Actions speak louder than words."
> "I don't know if I can," he said, "but maybe I will."

10. Indicates the omission of a word or words:

> To err is human; to forgive, divine.

11. Sets off the year from the month in dates:

> September 6, 1976, was Labor Day.
> Louis XVI of France was guillotined on January 21, 1793.

12. Sets off the state from the city in geographical names:

> Boston, Massachusetts, is the largest city in New England.

13. Separates series of four or more figures into thousands, millions, etc.:

> 57,395   12,364,903

The comma is not used in dates or page numbers:

14. Sets off words used in direct address:

> Mr. Wadsworth, please submit your report as soon as possible.
> Thank you, Emma, for your help.
> The forum is open to questions, ladies and gentlemen.

15. Separates a phrase that transforms a statement into a question:

> You did say you had the book, didn't you?
> Beethoven's "Eroica" is on the program, isn't it?

16. Sets off any sentence elements that might be misread if the comma were not used:

> Some time after, the actual date was set.
> To Mary, Anne was just a nuisance.
> Whenever possible, friends provide moral support.

17. Follows the salutation and complimentary close of informal letters and the complimentary close of formal letters:

> Dear Patsy,   Sincerely,

Dash

1. Indicates a sudden break or abrupt change in continuity:

> Well, you see—I—I've—I'm just not sure.
> He seemed very upset about—I never knew what.
> And then the problem—if it is a problem—can be solved.

2. Sets apart an explanatory or defining phrase:

> Foods high in protein—meats, fish, eggs, and

cheese—should be a part of the daily diet.

He suddenly realized what the glittering gems were
—emeralds.

3. Sets apart material that is parenthetical in nature:

He stares soulfully heavenward—to the great delight of the audience—while he plays Chopin.

Allen—who had a lean face, a long nose, and cold
blue eyes—was a stern, authoritarian man.

4. Marks an unfinished sentence:

Well, then, I'll simply tell her that—

"But if the plane is late—" he began.

5. Sets off a summarizing phrase or clause:

Noam Chomsky, Morris Halle, Roman Jakobson
—these are among America's most prominent lin-
guists.

6. Sets off the name of an author or a source, as at
the end of a quotation:

There never was a good war, or a bad peace.
—Benjamin Franklin

Ellipses

1. Indicate the omission of words or sentences in
quoted material:

This ended the power of the council ... and the
former regents were put on trial.

Because the treaty has not been approved by the
Senate ... it is not embodied in law.

Nor have we been wanting in Attentions to our
British Brethren.... They too have been deaf to
the Voice of Justice....

2. Indicate a pause in speech or an unfinished sentence:

"Y.... I mean ... what ..." she stammered.
I thought I had better not ...

3. Indicate the omission of a line or lines of poetry:

> Come away, O human child!
> . . . .
> For the world's more full of weeping than you
> can understand.
>
> —William Butler Yeats

Exclamation point

Indicates a command, an expression of strong emotion,
or an emphatic phrase or sentence:

Scram!	You can't be serious!
Go home immediately!	Bravo!
What a ball game that was!	

Hyphen

1. At the end of a line, indicates that part of a word
of more than one syllable has been carried over to
the following line:

> Anatole France's actual name was Jacques Ana-
> tole Thibault.

2. Joins the elements of some compounds:

> great-grandfather
> cure-all
> ne'er-do-well

3. Joins the elements of compound modifiers preceding a noun:

> a well-dressed woman
> built-in bookcases
> a happy-go-lucky fellow
> a fire-and-brimstone sermon

a four-hour seminar
ten high-school students
a two-thirds share

4. Indicates that two or more compounds share a single base:

   three- and four-volume sets
   six- and seven-year-olds

5. Separates the prefix and root in some combinations:

   anti-Semite, pro-American (prefix + proper noun or adjective)
   re-election, co-author (prefix ending with a vowel, root beginning with a vowel)
   re-form, reform (to distinguish between similar words of different meanings)
   re-creation, recreation

6. Substitutes for the word *to* between two figures or words:

   pages 6-20
   the years 1920-29
   the Boston-New York shuttle

Parentheses

1. Enclose material that is not an essential part of the sentence and that if not included would not alter its meaning:

   In an hour's time (some say less) the firemen had extinguished the flames.
   It was a dream (although a hazy one) of an ideal state, one in which poverty did not exist.
   Marion doesn't feel (and why should she?) that she should pay a higher rent.

2. Often enclose letters or numerals to indicate subdivisions of a series:

   > A movement in sonata form consists of the fol-
   > lowing sections: (a) the exposition; (b) the devel-
   > opment; and (c) the recapitulation, which is often
   > followed by a coda.

Period

1. Indicates the end of a complete declarative or mild
   imperative sentence:

   > The carved ornaments on the façade date back to
   > the fourteenth century.
   > Come home when you can.

2. Follows the abbreviation of a word or words:

Jan.	Ave.
Mr.	pp.
Ms.	Co.
Rev.	Inc.
St.	c.c.

Question mark

1. Indicates the end of a direct question:

   > What kind of work would you like to do?
   > Who was that odd-looking stranger?

   > *but*

   > I wonder who said "Speak softly and carry a big
   > stick."
   > He asked when Harold would leave.

2. Indicates uncertainty:

   > Ferdinand Magellan (1480?–1521)

Quotation marks
Double Quotation Marks

1. Enclose direct quotations:

> "What was Berlin like during the war?" she asked.
>
> "Gentlemen," the store manager said to the salesmen, "our first customer has arrived."
>
> Will Rogers said: "Things in our country run in spite of government. Not by aid of it."
>
> According to one critic, the conductor was "readier to persuade than to dictate."

2. Enclose words or phrases to clarify their meaning or use, or to indicate that they are being used in a special way:

> "Dey" is a title that was formerly given to governors of Algiers.
>
> By "brace" we mean the bracket and line joining two or more staves of music.
>
> "The Big Apple," a name for New York City, is a phrase that was originated by jazz musicians.
>
> Supervisors are urged to "prioritize" their responsibilities.

3. Set off the translation of a foreign word or phrase:

> *Hakenkreuz,* "hooked cross," "swastika"
>
> *déjà vu,* "already seen"
>
> The Latin word *reclāmāre* means "to exclaim against."

4. Set off the titles of series of books; of articles or chapters in publications; of essays; of short poems; of individual radio and television programs; of songs and short musical pieces:

"The Horizon Concise History" series
"Some Notes on Case Grammar in English"
Chapter 9, "Four in Freedom"
Shelley's "Ode to the West Wind"
"The Lucille Ball Special"
Schubert's "Death and the Maiden"

Single Quotation Marks

Enclose quoted material within a quotation:

> "To me, the key word for the American Indian is 'paradox,' " Hunter said. "The Indian's loyalty is to his heritage, but his problem is how to function in the dominant society."

Use With Other Punctuation Marks

Put commas and periods inside closing quotation marks; put semicolons and colons outside. Other punctuation (question marks and exclamation points) should be put inside the closing quotation marks only when it is actually part of the matter being quoted.

Semicolon

1. Separates the clauses of a compound sentence having no coordinating conjunction:

   > The questions are provided by the analyst; the answers come from the data.
   >
   > Many industries were paralyzed by the strike; factory owners left the district, taking their money with them.

2. Separates the clauses of a compound sentence in which the clauses contain internal punctuation, even when the clauses are joined by a conjunction:

   > Picnic baskets in hand, we walked to the beach, chose a sunny spot, and spread out the blankets;

and the rest of the group followed us in a station wagon.

3. Separates elements of a series in which items already contain commas:

Among the guests were Katherine Ericson; her daughter, Alice; Henry Faulkner, formerly of the Redding Institute; and two couples whom I could not identify.

4. Separates clauses of a compound sentence joined by a conjunctive adverb (*nonetheless, therefore, hence,* etc.):

The cities that had been bombed were in ruins; indeed, they looked like extinct craters.

We demanded a refund; otherwise we would get in touch with the Better Business Bureau.

Virgule (also called *slant, slash,* and *solidus*)

1. Separates the numerator of a fraction from the denominator:

c/d

2. Represents the word *per*:

miles/hour

3. Means "or" between the words *and* and *or*:

articles of linguistic and/or sociological importance.

Take skates and/or skis.

4. Separates two or more lines of poetry quoted in text:

The actor had a memory lapse when he came to the lines "Why? all delights are vain, but that most vain / Which, with pain purchas'd, doth inherit pain," and had to improvise.

Capitalization

The following should be capitalized:

1. The first word of a sentence:

   > Some diseases are acute; others are chronic.
   > Aren't you my new neighbor?
   > Great! Let's go!

2. The first word of each line in a poem:

   > Poets that lasting marble seek
   > Must carve in Latin or in Greek.
   >
   > —Edmund Waller

3. The first word of a direct quotation unless it is closely woven into the sentence:

   > Helen asked, "Do you think Satie was a serious composer?"
   > "For me," I answered, "he was simply amusing."
   > G. B. Shaw said that "assassination is the extreme form of censorship."

4. The first word of the salutation and of the complimentary close of a letter:

   > My dear Joyce   Sincerely yours
   > Dear Mr. Atkins   Very cordially

5. All words except articles, prepositions, and conjunctions in the titles of books, articles, poems, plays, etc.:

   > *All Quiet on the Western Front*
   > "The Finiteness of Natural Language"
   > "When the Lamp Is Shattered"
   > *Cat on a Hot Tin Roof*

6. Proper nouns and adjectives:

Billie Jean King	China, Chinese
Bruno Walter	Bohemia, Bohemian
Clare Boothe Luce	Morocco, Moroccan
Albert Einstein	Hegel, Hegelian

Do not capitalize words derived from proper nouns and adjectives and having distinct special meanings:

china plates
chinese red
a bohemian lifestyle
moroccan leather

7. The standard names of geographic divisions, districts, regions, and localities:

Arctic Circle	Mountain States
Western Hemisphere	Gulf Coast
South Pole	the North
Torrid Zone	the South
Continental Divide	the East
Old World	the West
Middle East	the Midwest
Far West	the Southwest

Do not capitalize words designating points of the compass unless they refer to specific regions:

Holyoke, Massachusetts, is eight miles north of Springfield. Turn east on Route 495.

8. The popular names of districts, regions, and localities:

the Barbary Coast	the Windy City
the Promised Land	the Loop
the Bible Belt	the East Side

43

9. The names of rivers, lakes, mountains, oceans, etc.:

Connecticut River Mount Shasta
Lake Maracaibo Long Island Sound
Rocky Mountains Pacific Ocean

10. Names for the Deity, for a supreme being, and for the Bible and other sacred books:

God Allah
the Almighty Jehovah
the Savior the Messiah
the Holy Spirit the Bible
the Virgin Mary the Koran
the Blessed Mother the Talmud

11. The names of religious denominations:

Catholicism
Judaism
Protestantism
Buddhism
the Roman Catholic Church
the Protestant Episcopal Church
the Society of Friends
the Church of Jesus Christ of Latter-day Saints

12. The names of historical periods, events, documents, etc.:

the Middle Ages
the Reformation
the American Revolution
World War II
the Battle of Shiloh
the Declaration of Independence
the Magna Carta
the Constitution

13. The names of political entities, divisions, parties, etc.:

   the Byzantine Empire
   the Holy Roman Empire
   the French Republic
   the Populist Party
   the Democratic Party
   the Republican Party
   Democrat
   Republican

14. The names of legislative and judicial bodies:

   Congress   Parliament
   the Senate   Diet
   the House of Representatives   Knesset
   the United States Supreme Court
   the Permanent Court of International Justice

15. The names of departments, bureaus, etc., of the federal government:

   the Department of Agriculture
   United States Department of State
   Central Intelligence Agency
   Tennessee Valley Authority

16. The names of treaties, acts, laws, etc.:

   the Versailles Treaty
   the Clayton-Bulwer Treaty
   the Volstead Act
   the Sherman Antitrust Law

17. Titles—civil, military, noble, honorary, etc.— when they precede a name:

   Justice Frankfurter

General MacArthur
Mayor White
Queen Elizabeth II
Pope John XXIII
Professor Kittredge

But all references to the President and Vice President of the United States should be capitalized:

President Truman   the President
Vice President Wallace   the Vice President

18. Epithets used as a substitute for a name:

Eric the Red   the Great Emancipator
Ivan the Terrible   the Iron Chancellor

19. The names of peoples, races, tribes, etc.:

Maori   Bantu
Caucasian   Ute

20. The names of languages and of periods in the history of languages:

German   English
Old High German   Middle English

21. The names of geological eras, periods, etc.:

the Paleozoic era
the Precambrian period
the Bronze Age

22. The names of the constellations, planets, and stars:

the Milky Way   Mars
the Southern Crown   Venus
Jupiter   Polaris

23. Genus—but not species—names in binomial nomenclature:

> *Chrysanthemum leucanthemum*
> *Macaca mulatta*
> *Rana pipiens*

24. The names of holidays, holy days, months of the year, and days of the month:

Independence Day	Passover
Labor Day	Yom Kippur
Thanksgiving	Ramadan
Christmas	January
Easter	Monday

25. Personifications:

> I met Murder in the way— / He had a mask like Castlereagh.
>
> > —Percy Bysshe Shelley

26. Trademarks:

Coca-Cola	Polaroid
Formica	Pyrex
Kleenex	Xerox

27. The names of buildings, streets, parks, organizations, etc.:

> the State House
> Symphony Hall
> Fort Tryon Park
> Logan Airport
> Tremont Street
> Route 91
> the Free and Accepted Masons
> Veterans of Foreign Wars
> the New York Yankees

Italics

1. Indicate titles of books, plays, and poems of book length:

   > *For Whom the Bell Tolls*
   > *The Little Foxes*
   > *Paradise Lost*

2. Indicate words, letters, or numbers used as such:

   > The word *buzz* is onomatopoeic; that is, it sounds like what it stands for.
   > *Can't* often means *won't*.
   > She formed her *n*'s like *u*'s.
   > A *6* looks like an upside-down *9*.

3. Emphasize a word or phrase. This device should be used sparingly:

   > Whenever Jack made a fool of himself, he was his *mother's* son.

4. Indicate foreign words and phrases that have not been assimilated into English:

   > editors, machinists, *pâtissiers,* barbers, and hoboes
   > his *Sturm und Drang* period

5. Indicate the names of the plaintiff and defendant in legal citations:

   > *Marbury* v. *Madison*

6. Indicate the titles of long musical compositions:

   > *The Messiah*
   > *Die Götterdämmerung*
   > Bartok's *Concerto for Orchestra*
   > Elgar's *Enigma Variations*

7. Indicate the titles of magazines and newspapers:

> *American Heritage* magazine
> *The New Yorker*
> the New York *Daily News*
> *The New York Times*

8. Set off the titles of motion pictures and television series:

> *The Sting*
> *All the President's Men*
> *Masterpiece Theater*
> *Upstairs, Downstairs*

9. Distinguish the names of genera and species in scientific names:

> *Homo sapiens*
> *Sciurus carolinensis*

10. Set off the names of ships, planes, trains, and spacecraft:

> *Queen Elizabeth II*
> *The Spirit of St. Louis*
> *The Wolverine*
> *Viking 1*

11. Set off the names of paintings and sculpture:

> *Mona Lisa*
> *Guernica*
> *Pietà*
> *The Burghers of Calais*

Basic rules of standard English grammar

What is grammar?

Grammar is a system of basic rules by which the words in a language are structured and arranged in sentences. Grammar deals with rules for word order, verb forms, plural and singular noun forms, and parts of speech, among other topics.

Virtually everybody who has heard English spoken from birth has learned *basic* English grammar. But not everybody has learned *standard* English grammar: the set of rules that govern what is generally considered to be "good" or "correct" grammar.

Some specific points of grammar present problems for many people whose native language is English. This section deals in particular with those points. Areas of difficulty are examined, and the reasons for difficulty are cited.

Traditional and new grammar

The second half of the twentieth century has witnessed a change in the way grammarians discuss grammar. Grammarians have begun to use new terms for certain classes of words. At the same time, other people have retained the traditional terms for these classes of words. The difference in classifying words does not make a difference in the way words are actually used.

The ways words operate in sentences have not substantially changed.

Verbs

English verb forms are fairly simple when you compare them with verb forms in many other languages.

The *present tense* of most verbs has only two forms, as illustrated by the verb "walk":

	Singular	Plural
first person	I walk	we walk
second person	you walk	you walk
third person	he, she, it walks	they walk

The two forms are *walk* and *walks*. The form *walks* is used only for the third-person singular. *He, she,* or *it* may be replaced by the name of one person, one thing, one place, or one idea.

> John walks.
> The cat walks.
> The puppet walks.
> Happiness walks the earth.

One basic rule of English grammar is:

A verb must agree with its subject in person and number.

That means that a first-person singular verb is used with "I," a third-person singular verb is used with any singular noun or third-person singular pronoun, and so on.

Some reasons people have problems when trying to apply this rule are:

1. They fail to recognize that *and* makes more than one.

   John and Jane walk out on the boardwalk. (John + Jane = third-person *plural*.)

   Jane and I walk out on the boardwalk. (Jane + I = we = first-person *plural*.)

2. They fail to recognize that *or* does not create a plural.

   Either John or Jane gets a paper each day. (Only one of the two of them gets the paper—sometimes one, sometimes the other.)

3. They fail to recognize the true subject.

   A deck of cards sits on the shelf. (The verb is third-person singular because *deck* is the subject, not *cards*.)

The *past tense* for most verbs has only one form.

I walked	we walked
you walked	you walked
he, she, it walked	they walked

Regular past tenses are formed by adding an *-ed* to the verb. Sometimes a final *e* is dropped before adding the *-ed* (save, saved), sometimes a final *y* is

changed to *i* before the *-ed* is added (worry, worried), sometimes a final consonant is doubled before adding the *-ed* (nap, napped). Most of these past tenses do not offer too much difficulty.

Many past tenses, however, are irregular. Irregular past tenses must be learned one by one. Most of these are learned during childhood. When in doubt, one can learn the past tense of a verb by consulting a dictionary.

Difficulties with past tenses arise when a person:

1. does not realize that a verb has an irregular past tense.
2. knows that a verb has an irregular past tense, but does not know what it is.
3. confuses the past tense with the past participle.

The *past participle* is the form of the verb that follows *have, has, had,* or another auxiliary verb.

I have walked	we have walked
you have walked	you have walked
he, she, it has walked	they have walked

Notice that for *walk* the past participle, *walked,* is the same as the past tense. This is true for all regular verbs. It is even true for some irregular verbs. But it is not true for *all* verbs.

Past tenses and past participles for irregular verbs have to be learned verb by verb. Although there are

some patterns that are followed in several verbs, mistakes are sometimes made because the pattern does not hold for all verbs that *appear* to fit a pattern. For example, "sing, sang, sung" has a pattern that is followed in "ring, rang, rung." But it is *not* followed in "bring, brought, brought." Mistakes are made because some people try to carry out a pattern in the wrong places.

Because past tenses and past participles present so many problems, it is worth noting some general patterns.

1. Some irregular verbs have the same irregular form for past tense and past participle:

hold	held	held
bring	brought	brought
feel	felt	felt
sit	sat	sat
make	made	made

2. Some irregular verbs have the same form for the present tense, the past tense, and the past participle.

hit	hit	hit
burst	burst	burst
put	put	put
spread	spread	spread
thrust	thrust	thrust

3. Some irregular verbs change their form for the past tense and again for the past participle.

give	gave	given
do	did	done
grow	grew	grown
go	went	gone
see	saw	seen

4. A few verbs change the form for the past tense, but have the same form as the present tense for the past participle.

come	came	come
run	ran	run

The English language has about two hundred irregular verbs. The faulty use of the forms of these verbs creates a great deal of the trouble people have with English grammar. The time spent looking them up in a dictionary until the irregular forms are mastered is valuably spent.

The differences between the past tense and past participle should also be mastered. Standard English grammar requires that the distinction be maintained when there is a distinction. For example,

nonstandard:	*should be corrected to:*
I done it.	I did it. *or* I have done it.
I seen it.	I saw it. *or* I have seen it.
I should have went.	I should have gone.
They have came.	They have come. *or* They came.

The *infinitive* form of the verb is the form that begins with *to* (to walk, to hit, to bring, to give). Most verbs

have an infinitive form. The infinitive form has several uses.

It follows another verb.

> I want *to go*.
> He tried *to walk*.
> She likes *to laugh*.

The infinitive may serve as a subject of a sentence.

> *To travel* requires money.

Split infinitives are subjects of much grammatical discussion. An infinitive is said to be split when a word or a group of words is placed between "to" and the rest of the verb. Although many grammarians do not object to splitting an infinitive, a few do.

> He had *to* hastily *wrap* the package.

may be changed to:

> He had *to wrap* the package hastily.

But an infinitive split by one adverb (as in the example above) is not universally considered objectionable.

Even people who do not usually object to splitting infinitives do object to splitting the infinitive with a long string of words:

> We had *to* carefully and slowly, picking out weeds as we went, *make* our way through the woods.

That example is generally considered to be poor grammar, or at least poor style. It can easily be changed to:

> We had *to make* our way through the woods slowly and carefully, picking out weeds as we went.

Defective verbs are verbs that do not have a full range of tenses and participles. Some examples of defective verbs are:

can	shall
could	may
will	must
would	ought
should	might

Note that the defective verbs do not have a separate third-person singular form:

I can	we can
you can	you can
he, she, it can	they can

Most of them do not have a past tense. *Could* is considered to be the past tense of *can,* and *would* the past tense of *will.* They do not have past participles or present participles. They have no future tense.

Different verbs must replace defective verbs for the sense of the missing tenses. The verb *to be* is a special case. Some grammarians do not consider it a verb at

all. It is unlike other verbs in the number of forms it has and in the ways it is used.

The present tense of *to be* has a separate form for the first-person singular as well as for the third-person singular:

I am	we are
you are	you are
he, she, it is	they are

It has two forms, not one, for the past tense. Note that the first-person singular and the third-person singular use the same past tense.

I was	we were
you are	you were
he, she, it was	they were

The misuse of forms of the past tense of *to be* is a common grammatical error. "You was" and "they was" are simply incorrect.

Greater confusion exists because there are correct uses of "I were" and "he, she, it were." These forms may be used in the *subjunctive* (or *conditional*) mood. For example, the word "if," or anything that suggests "if," in the present or future may be followed correctly by "I were" or "he, she, it were."

> If I were President
> Suppose it were true.

The past participle for *to be* is *been*. Little difficulty arises out of the use of *been*. The most frequent grammatical lapse is the omission of the auxiliary verb.

incorrect:	*correct:*
I been gone.	I have been gone.
He been thinking.	He has been thinking.

A common error made with the forms of *to be* is to omit it entirely.

incorrect:	*correct:*
I cold.	I am cold. I was cold.
He big.	He is big.
They strong.	They are strong.

Forms of *to be* may be followed by an adjective.

> I am cold.
> You are calm.
> It is weak.
> We were frightened.
> The rabbit was furry.

There are a few other verbs that may be followed by an adjective. The verbs that may be are sometimes called *linking verbs*. The adjective modifies the noun or pronoun. Some linking verbs are: *appear, seem, feel, look.*

I seem cold.
You appear calm.
We looked frightened.

Verbs may be *transitive* or *intransitive*. A transitive verb has to have an object. An intransitive verb does not have an object. Some verbs are only transitive, some are only intransitive, some are both.

Examples of transitive verbs:

He stole a pig.
She meets me every Saturday.
They towed the boat.

Examples of intransitive verbs:

He steals for a living.
Let us meet soon.
The baby teethed.

Nouns

Nouns are either *proper* or *common*. Proper nouns are usually capitalized. In general, proper nouns are names of people, places, or certain categories of things. Trademarks are also capitalized. Common nouns are usually preceded by a definite article and represent one or all members of a class.

In English the form of the noun is the same whether it is the subject or the object of a verb.

subject	*verb*	*object*
The dog	bit	John.
John	bit	the dog.

Noun plurals are usually formed by adding -*s* (book, books) or -*es* (dish, dishes) to the singular or by dropping a -*y* and adding -*ies* (spy, spies). Nouns that form their plurals in these ways are considered to be regular.

But many nouns have irregular plurals. Some plurals are irregular because they are the same as the singular (sheep, sheep). Some are irregular because they have distinctly different forms that go back to Old English (mouse, mice). Some are irregular because they form their plurals as in the languages from which they come (locus, loci). Many foreign words in the plural are now acceptable following the English rules. For example, both *cortices* and *cortexes* are now considered to be acceptable English for the plurals of *cortex*.

Irregular plurals do not necessarily follow logical patterns. We have mouse/mice, louse/lice, but house/houses. Irregular plurals must be learned individually.

Whether the plural is regular or irregular, it takes the plural form of the verb. And the form is the same whether the noun is the object or subject of a verb.

> The boys hit the girls.
> The girls hit the boys.

Collective nouns and *nouns that are plural in construction* often confuse people. Which form of the verb is used with "the committee," "clothes," "clothing," "army," etc.?

To some extent, the logic of the meaning has to be considered. For collective nouns like *committee, army, flock,* or *congress,* one must consider whether the members are behaving as a single unit or as a set of individual units.

> Congress votes today.
> The committee argue frequently about their opinions.
> The cattle run off in different directions.
> The jury is sequestered in the hotel.
> The jury are fighting about their verdict.

Some nouns are constructed so that the form is by nature singular or plural.

> The clothing is on the bed where I left it.
> The clothes are on the bed where I left them

It is not only necessary to have agreement with the verb; it is also necessary for any pronouns to agree in number with the noun.

Possessive forms of the noun are generally formed by adding *'s* to the singular and *'* to plurals that end in *s.* If the plural is irregular and does not end in *s,* then *'s* is added to the plural form.

singular	plural
the dog's bones	the dogs' bones
the lady's clothes	the ladies' clothes
the man's ties	the men's ties

The same possessive forms are used when the possessives are in the predicate position:

> These are the dog's.
> These are the dogs'.
> These are the lady's.
> These are the ladies'.
> These are the man's.
> These are the men's.

Pronouns

Personal pronouns present some of the greatest grammatical problems for speakers and writers of English. Unlike nouns, pronouns have different forms when they are used as subjects and objects. They also have two possessive forms and a reflexive form.

As *subjects* of verbs, the pronouns are:

singular	*plural*
I	we
you	you
he, she, it	they

Notice that "you" is both singular and plural; the same form is used whether one is addressing one person or several.

Most people tend to choose the correct form of the pronoun when there is only one pronoun required. (I went, he went, we went, they went.) Some people have problems when there is more than one pronoun.

incorrect	correct
Him and me went.	He and I went.
Us and them went.	We and they went.

A good rule is to try each pronoun separately and see if it sounds correct. That will help you select the correct form in combinations.

incorrect	correct
Him went.	He went.
Us went.	We went.

As *objects* of verbs or prepositions, the pronouns are:

singular	plural
me	us
you	you
him, her, it	them

Examples:

John hit him.

Mary fired her.

Sally kissed us.

James tried them.

Phil looked at you.

Henry gave the book to me.

Sue sent for it.

Once again, people tend to choose the correct form of the pronoun when there is only one object. Some people have problems when there is more than one object.

incorrect	*correct*
John hit him and I.	John hit him and me.
Sue sent for her and they.	Sue sent for her and them.

When in doubt, try each pronoun alone. You will probably select the correct form.

Possessive pronouns that occur before the noun are sometimes termed *determiners* or *determinatives*. Whatever grammarians call them, they have these forms:

singular	*plural*
my	our
your	your
his, her, its	their

Notice that there is no apostrophe in *its*.

These pronouns are generally placed before any adjectives that precede the noun:

my dog   my big dog   my big, red, ugly dog

Possessive pronouns in predicate position or in absolute form are:

singular	*plural*
mine	ours
yours	yours
his, hers, its	theirs

Examples of the use of these pronouns:

65

The book is mine.
Mine is the glory.
One room is ours, the other theirs.
Yours is not to reason why.
Is it his or hers?

In modern usage, these pronouns do not precede the noun. "Mine eyes have seen wonders" is archaic usage.

Reflexive pronouns end in *self* or *selves*.

myself	ourselves
yourself	yourselves
himself, herself, itself	themselves

They are used for emphasis or as an object (direct or indirect) of a verb or pronoun.

I hurt myself.
I did it myself.
Feed yourself.
You yourselves are to blame.
He talks to himself.
She gives herself airs.
It grew by itself.
They themselves saw it.

Notice that the reflexive pronouns have different forms for the second person singular and plural: yourself and yourselves.

There are other pronouns as well. For example,

either	each	all
few	somebody	anything
anyone	nobody	one
neither	both	some
something	someone	anybody
nothing	no one	many

People often have difficulty matching a pronoun to an antecedent. The pronoun must agree with its antecedent in person and number. But sometimes it is not clear what that person or number is.

> John lost his hat.
> One of the boys lost his hat.
> Somebody lost his hat.

The last example is acceptable if the hat was clearly a man's hat. For many years, *his* would have been acceptable whether the somebody were male or female— as long as it was not clear whether male or female. Grammatically, "somebody lost his hat" is still acceptable. But social forces have overtaken grammatical neatness on this issue.

Until recently, *his* was the correct pronoun to use if it were unclear whether the antecedent was male or female. But with greater insistence on women's equality, people are beginning to recognize a male bias in the universal use of *his* in such situations. A good alternative has not yet been discovered.

What are the possible solutions? Substitute "his or her" for "his." Rewrite the sentence entirely. Use the

grammatically improper "their."

> Each is entitled to his own opinion.
> Each is entitled to his or her own opinion.
> Each is entitled to their own opinion.
> One is entitled to one's own opinion.
> People are entitled to their own opinions.

None of the solutions satisfies all the objections. But "his or her," although awkward, is gaining wide use. The sentences that avoid "each" may solve the problem, but such solutions may drive out the use of the word "each." And the meaning of the sentences are subtly altered. For the present, "his or her" may be the best of several unsatisfactory solutions.

Unclear antecedents occur when more than one noun or pronoun can logically be the antecedent.

> Marie told Lucy that she had won a prize.

Who won the prize, Marie or Lucy? The word "she" could refer to either. Technically, "she" is supposed to refer to the nearest antecedent, but in practice that rule does not work well. Sentences of this kind cannot be corrected by a simple repositioning of words. The sentences must be rewritten.

> Marie had won a prize, and she told Lucy about it.
> Lucy had won a prize, and Marie told her about it.

Adjectives

Adjectives modify nouns. They normally are placed before the noun. Several may be grouped together.

> the *blue* sky
> the *clear blue* sky
> the *clear, blue, cloudless* sky

Adjectives may also be placed after the verb *to be* or a linking verb.

> The sky is blue.
> The sky looks blue and clear.
> The sky appears blue, clear, and cloudless.

Adjectives may be grouped together, or some may be placed before the noun and others after *to be*.

> The blue sky is clear.
> The clear blue sky is sunny and cloudless.

Most adjectives may have a comparative or superlative form.

> blue, bluer, bluest
> clear, clearer, clearest

Those that do not may form comparatives or superlatives by adding *more* and *most*.

> beautiful, more beautiful, most beautiful

Adverbs

Adverbs modify verbs, adjectives, or the predicate parts of sentences. Many adverbs end in *-ly,* but many do not. And not all words that end in *-ly* are adverbs.

An adverb may be placed in various parts of a sentence. Sometimes the placement of an adverb affects the emphasis. If there is a customary location for an adverb, it is at the end of a sentence or clause.

The moon rose *slowly.*
Slowly the moon rose.
The moon *slowly* rose.

Trouble occurs when people confuse adjectives and adverbs. Adverbs are used to modify verbs or adjectives. Adjectives modify nouns and pronouns.

incorrect	*correct*
She sings good.	She sings well. (*Well* modifies *sings.*)
He is real handsome.	He is really handsome. (*Really* modifies *handsome*)
The tie does not look well on you.	The tie does not look good on you. (*Look* is a linking verb and requires an adjective.)

Prepositions

Prepositions are words that show relationships, often between verbs and nouns or nouns and nouns.

70

Let's go *to* the movies.
the window *over* the door
I'll wait *for* you.

Prepositions take objects. That means that pronouns that follow prepositions should be in the objective form:

wait for *him*
talk to *her*
rule over *us*
write on *them*

The selection of the correct preposition is often a matter of custom. For example, you wait *for* somebody, if you are expecting him or her. You wait *on* somebody if you are a waiter or waitress. Many people say *wait on* when they mean *wait for*.

An old rule of grammar stated that a sentence should never end with a preposition. This rule is rarely observed. Often a sentence is made more stiff or awkward when a correction is made to avoid a preposition at the end.

Some words that are prepositions are also adverbs. The distinction between the two sometimes escapes people. Fortunately, there are few situations in which people must discern the difference. Unfortunately, some people who try to eliminate prepositions at the ends of sentences occasionally eliminate adverbs as well.

Conjunctions

Conjunctions are words that connect other words, phrases, or clauses.

Coordinating conjunctions connect equally constructed grammatical elements. These elements may be individual words, phrases, or independent clauses. For example, *and, or,* and *but* are coordinating conjunctions in the following:

> I like vanilla *and* chocolate.
> I do not like going to school *or* staying at home.
> Father works at home; *but* mother goes to an office.

The main concern when using coordinating conjunctions is to make sure the elements are equally constructed.

Correlative conjunctions come in pairs: *neither . . . nor, either . . . or, not only . . . but also.*

> He has *neither* the time *nor* the money for that scheme.
> We can *either* go to the zoo *or* visit grandma.
> *Not only* do I have to clean the mess, *but* I *also* have to pay damages.

Subordinating conjunctions introduce dependent clauses.

> We heard *that* you were sick.
> The man *who* came to dinner is my uncle.

Words into sentences

What is a sentence?

A sentence is a separate grammatical unit that conveys an idea. A sentence usually has at least one subject and one verb. A written sentence ends in a period, question mark, or exclamation point.

Declarative sentences

Most sentences end in periods. They are declarative sentences. The simplest standard sentence has a noun or pronoun and a verb.

subject	verb
I	sleep.
He	eats.
Kittens	play.
We	tried.
You	fell.
Henry	swam.

These simple two-word expressions are complete sentences. Each has a subject and a verb; each ends in a period. In actual speech and writing, very few sentences follow this simple sentence pattern. Details are added to each part. A written passage that contained nothing but two-word sentences would be choppy, dull, and immature. But such simple sentences are useful as starting points from which to examine form and structure in longer sentences. In a long and complicated

sentence it is often important to be able to pick out the subject and the verb.

> Whenever I have an exam the following morning, I *sleep* fitfully all night.
>
> subject → I *sleep* verb
>
> subject
>
> Despite heavy rains and rough weather, *Henry swam,* across the lake to rescue the children.
>
> verb — subject — verb
>
> Our pet *kittens,* those fluffy delights, *play* incessantly with balls of yarn.

Direct object

A simple *subject* + *verb* sentence, such as any of the preceding, must have an *intransitive verb,* a verb that does not take an object. If the verb is *transitive,* it must take a direct object.

The basic sentence pattern for a transitive verb is:

subject	verb	direct object
I	like	you.
He	eats	strawberries.
We	played	checkers.
Henry	hit	Charlie.
You	saw	something.

The verb, the object, and any words that modify the verb and object all belong to the *predicate* part of a sentence. A sentence has two parts: a *subject* and a *predicate*.

The direct object is part of the predicate of a sentence. Notice that in most cases the word order indi-

cates which is the subject and which is the object. The form of the word does not change. Only the position changes.

subject	verb	direct object
Henry	hit	Charlie.
Charlie	hit	Henry.
Lisa	likes	someone.
Someone	likes	Lisa.

But for certain pronouns, there is a different form whether the pronoun is the subject or the object.

subject	verb	direct object
I	greeted	him.
He	greeted	me.
She	likes	us.
We	like	her.

It is important to remember to use the correct form for subject and object when dealing with these pronouns.

Even these sentences are unusually short. There are various ways to lengthen sentences. In general sentences are made longer by adding details. Each detail makes a sentence more specific. Both the subject and the predicate of a sentence can be modified by adding details.

Modifying the subject

The subject of a sentence is usually modified by adding articles, pronouns, demonstrative pronouns (all

of which are sometimes called determiners), adjectives, and noun-modifiers. Adjectives can themselves be modified by adverbs.

Notice the way the subject of the simple sentence "The cat eats fish" can be given greater detail.

subject	predicate
The cat	eats fish.
The *striped tawny* cat	eats fish.
My striped tawny alley cat	eats fish.
That horribly fat alley cat	eats fish.

Modifying the predicate

The predicate of a sentence can also be modified. The verb may be modified or the direct object may be modified. Articles, pronouns, and adjectives may modify the direct object. Adverbs may modify the verb itself. Adverbs may also modify the adjectives that modify direct objects. In the simple sentence "The cat eats fish" the predicate can be also given greater detail.

subject	predicate
The cat	eats *raw* fish.
The cat	eats *raw smelly* fish.
The cat	eats *that* fish *quickly*.
The cat	eats *horribly smelly* fish.
The cat	eats *the raw, horribly smelly* fish *quickly*.

Notice the different functions of the adverbs, "horribly" and "quickly." The adverb "horribly" modifies

"smelly"—an adjective. The adverb "quickly" modifies "eats"—the verb.

Indirect object

The predicate may be enlarged further with an indirect object. The indirect object is usually—but not always—preceded by a preposition. When no preposition is shown, one is implied. The indirect object is *not* the object of the verb. It is the object of the preposition. Because it is not the object of a verb, the indirect object can follow an intransitive verb.

subject	verb	indirect object
He	looked	at her.
Tommy	went	to school.
Sarah	looked	for books.
Jenny	told	him.

The words "her," "school," "books," and "him" are the indirect objects.

A sentence with a transitive verb may have both a direct object and an indirect object. The indirect objects are in italics to help identify them.

subject	verb	objects
Jenny	told	*him* the news.
Jenny	told	the news to *him*.
He	gave	*me* a hand.
He	bought	*her* a present.
He	bought	a present for *her*.

An indirect object may be placed before or after a direct object. When the indirect object precedes the direct object, no preposition is used.

"To be" and other linking verbs

A few verbs do not take any objects. These verbs are called *linking verbs* and form the predicate by linking the subject to a following noun or adjective. The most common linking verb is the verb "to be" and all its forms. Certain other verbs such as "appear," "seem," "look," "taste," or "smell" may follow the same pattern when they function as linking verbs.

The chief point to note is that *the adjective* that occurs in the predicate part of the sentence *modifies the subject.*

subject	verb	predicate adjective
Joan	is	*pretty.*
John	appears	*tall.*
The cat	seems	*frightened.*
The dress	looks	*good.*
The soup	tastes	*delicious.*
The rose	smells	*sweet.*

The words in italics are all adjectives that modify the subjects of the sentences. They are known as *predicate adjectives* or *predicate complements.* It is important to recognize this group. Failure to recognize a linking verb causes some people mistakenly to use an adverb instead of an adjective.

Sometimes the verb "to be" links two nouns. Then "to be" or any of its forms acts almost like an equal sign. The noun that follows "to be" is not an object. It is known as a *predicate nominative*.

subject	verb	predicate nominative
I	am	*a person.* (I = a person.)
Eddie	was	*a giant.*
Claudia	is	*a soprano.*
The sign	had been	*a beacon.*
They	were	*the leaders.*
Allan	was	*chairman.*

The predicate nominative in each sentence has been italicized to help identify it.

Sentences beginning with "there"

Many sentences begin with "There."

There are ten *people* in the room.
There is *hope*.
There are no *ghosts*.
There does not seem to be any *chance*.
There may be *some* left.
There was *one* left.

In such sentences, "There" is *not* the subject. The verb must agree with the noun or pronoun that follows it. When "There" begins a sentence, it usually signals that the verb comes before the subject.

There + verb + subject.

Because this is not normal English word order, writers often fall into the trap of failing to make the verb agree with the subject. In the examples above, the subject has been italicized.

Passive voice sentences

All the sentences so far have been in the *active voice*. In the active voice, the subject acts on the verb and the verb acts on the direct object, when there is one.

In the *passive voice,* the subject of the sentence *is acted upon by the verb.* What would have been the direct object in an active voice sentence becomes the subject of a passive voice sentence. To illustrate the difference:

active

subject	verb	direct object
Amy	found	the treasure.
Paul	hears	the bells.

passive

subject	verb	
The treasure	was found	by Amy.
The bells	are heard	by Paul.

Notice that the verb agrees with the subject. Notice also that an auxiliary verb is needed in the passive.

subject	+ auxiliary verb	
Phil	*was*	*seen* leaving the building.
Strawberries	*are*	*eaten* in early summer.

Unkind rumors	*have been*	*spread* about Gail.
The soldiers	*were*	*killed* instantly.
The fish	*was*	*eaten* quickly.
Linda	*was*	*interviewed* at home.

The use of the passive places the emphasis on the receiver of the action. That kind of emphasis is important in many kinds of writing. It is useful when the agents performing the action are unknown, unimportant, or unidentified. The passive voice is very important in scientific and technical writing; in fact, the passive is often the preferred style. The passive voice is often important in news reporting when sources may not be named. It is also important when the writer wants to focus attention on the object of the verb's action.

Although many composition books warn people against excessive use of the passive, writers should not avoid it completely. Instead its use should be applied wisely. Even in writing about movement, the passive has its place:

The ball *was caught* as Slugger slid home.

If instead, the writer said:

Lefty caught the ball as Slugger slid home.

the attention would be shifted to Lefty. That is not what the writer intended to do.

Interrogative sentences

An interrogative sentence is a sentence that asks a question. A spoken question is generally signaled by a raised tone at the end of the sentence. A written question is signaled by a *question mark* at the end of the sentence.

There are a limited number of words that can begin a question. Some questions begin with auxiliary verbs such as *is, do, are, can, may, have,* or *has.* The auxiliary comes before the subject. Often this means splitting the verb, with the auxiliary before and the rest of the verb after the subject.

auxiliary	subject	remaining verb
Did	he	*give* her the book?
Will	John	*go* home?
Is	she	*singing* tonight?
Has	the mail	*arrived?*
Were	the dogs	*barking?*
May	Jason	*visit* us?

Occasionally *have* or *is* may be used without a second verb to form a question. The verb comes before the subject in these sentences.

Are they at home?
Is she a singer?
Have you any wool?
Has he a home?

Questions may also begin with one of a small group of words that are used to begin questions: *who, what, where, when, how, why, which, whose.*

Who is coming to dinner?   *How* did they learn of it?
What did he do?   *Why* hasn't John written?
Where are my socks?   *Which* house is yours?
When will you leave?   *Whose* mess is that?

A question may be a single word. One-word questions begin with capitals. When a single word does form the entire question, a previous question or statement is understood.

(Somebody told the secret.)   Who?
(Will he announce the winner?)   When?
(I discovered the treasure.)   How? Where?
(He is not going.)   Why?

Occasionally a question may be phrased in the word order that normally is reserved for declarative sentences. Such questions end with a question mark in written matter. Questions in this form often indicate surprise.

He went to the ball game?
They have been invited to dinner?
She discovered the treasure?

Indirect questions

Indirect questions are not interrogative sentences. They are declarative sentences and they end in periods. An indirect question is a sentence that mentions or suggests a question. To understand the difference, look below.

direct questions
Where do they live?
How much does it cost?
Where did he find it?

indirect questions
Ask them where they live.
Find out how much it costs.
She wondered where he found it.

An indirect question should not be worded the same way as a direct question. For example, "Ask them where do they live" is not good wording for an indirect question.

Exclamations

Exclamations are punctuated with exclamation points. An exclamation may express surprise, anger, or other strong emotion. Some words—interjections—are used chiefly in exclamations.

Wow!   Stop!
Phooey!   You rat!
You did it!   How good you are!
Don't hit me!   What a change!

Note that exclamations need not have subjects and verbs. The word order may be the same as or different from that of a declarative sentence.

Commands

Commands are always addressed to "you." In a command the word "you" is generally left out. It is usually understood without being said. A command is considered a full sentence even though the subject ("you") is not indicated.

Bring me the book.	Tell me a story.
Go to sleep.	Count to ten.

Sentence fragments

Sentence fragments are groups of words that *do not make a grammatical sentence*. Often they do not have a subject and a verb. They are incomplete.

There are many acceptable uses for sentence fragments. Sentence fragments are acceptable as exclamations:

What fun!
How lovely!

Sentence fragments are acceptable as questions, provided that a previous statement or question establishes the nature of the question:

fragment

"Mr. Smith is away on vacation."	"For how long?"
"He will be back soon."	"When?"

85

Sentence fragments are also acceptable as answers to questions.

question	fragment answer
Where did he go?	Upstairs to his room.
Do you like him?	No.
When will he return?	Next week.

Many good writers may use sentence fragments effectively to accomplish a purpose, to establish a certain pace, or to suggest a disjointed quality.

Into the alley he went. Up the fire escape. Over the wall. Around a corner. Into a bar.

Except for the first sentence, the passage above contains only sentence fragments. Such a passage may or may not work well in a given context.

The chief danger of using sentence fragments lies in not knowing that they are fragments, but thinking they are sentences. The writer of the following passage may or may not have known that the last two "sentences" are fragments:

Strolling the ancient city's streets, I seemed to hear the ghosts of history telling of its founding centuries ago. *Of its trade with the Scythians and with tribes up and down the Danube. Telling of Alexander the Great.*

Why is neither a sentence? Let us examine them:

> Of its trade with the Scythians, and with the tribes up and down the Danube.

The sentence has no verb. None of the nouns (trade, Scythians, tribes, or Danube) is the subject of the sentence. All are objects of prepositions.

> Telling of Alexander the Great.

The only suggestion of a verb is *telling* — the present participle of *tell*. And the only noun is *Alexander the Great,* and that is not the subject of the sentence.

How could this paragraph be corrected to turn all the fragments into sentences? There are several ways. The entire paragraph can be rewritten as one sentence.

> Strolling the ancient city's streets, I seemed to hear the ghosts of history telling of its founding centuries ago, of its trade with the Scythians and with tribes up and down the Danube, and also of Alexander the Great.

Or it can be rewritten by adding a subject to the two fragment sentences.

> Strolling the ancient city's streets, I seemed to hear the ghosts of history telling of its founding centuries ago. The ghosts seemed to tell of trade with the Scythians and with tribes up and down the Danube. The ghosts also told of Alexander The Great.

Sentence fragments may be long or short. But unless they are recognized, they cannot be avoided when avoidance is desired. People who are just beginning to master the elements of grammar and composition should try to avoid sentence fragments.

Sentence structures and patterns

Most of the sentences examined so far were fairly simple in structure. Each had a subject and verb. Some had a direct object and an indirect object. The subject, verb, or object may have been modified. But in each example there was generally only one subject, one verb, and one of each kind of object. It was fairly easy to identify the subject, verb, and objects in each.

Sentences can grow far more complicated than the examples we have seen. A sentence may have several subjects, verbs, or objects. Some sentences may have many *phrases* and *clauses*. The more complicated a sentence becomes, the more difficult it may be to identify the subject and predicate.

Coordinate elements

One of the simplest ways to enlarge a simple sentence is to use more than one subject, verb, or object. When there are multiple elements, it is important to keep them parallel in form. The multiple elements may be subjects.

multiple subjects:

Dogs and cats run wild in the street.

Men and women played tennis.

Wisdom and learning are not the same.

Sheep, horses, and pigs live on the farm.

Avoid such ill-matched combinations as "Wisdom, learning, and to know are not the same." "To know" is an infinitive and does not fit the pattern established by "wisdom, learning . . .". "Wisdom, learning, and knowledge . . ." would be better.

The multiple subject may be a series of phrases instead of individual words.

subjects

Going to school, keeping house, and *maintaining a job* complicate her life.

subjects

Antique tapestries from France, handwoven Navaho blankets, and *Early American samplers* cover the walls.

There should be no comma between the last subject and the verb. And, of course, the verb must agree with the subject.

Sometimes one preposition will work for all elements of a series: Dreams *of* wealth, fame, and happiness kept her going.

It is acceptable either to repeat the preposition or to allow the one preposition to govern the various elements: Dreams *of* wealth, *of* fame, and *of* happiness kept her going. (Wealth, fame, and happiness are all understood to be objects of the preposition "of.") It is not good style to repeat it once and not again. For

example, "Dreams of wealth, fame, and of happiness kept her going."

The same preposition may not work for all the elements in a series. It is then necessary to give the appropriate preposition for each element.

The multiple elements may be verbs:

multiple verbs:

    verbs

He *cut, fit, and sewed* the clothes in one day.

    verbs

She *tried, failed, and tried* again.

    verbs

The children *dried* their tears and *began* to sing.

Note that two or more verbs may accompany a single subject. Sometimes the verbs are simple. Sometimes, as in the third example, the entire predicate may be multiple.

It is possible to have more than one verb, each with its objects or modifiers. A comma should not separate the subject from either verb.

We *ate* our sandwiches and *drank* our milk.

Jimmy *waved* goodbye to his friends and *drove* home slowly.

When using auxiliaries with verbs, it is important to make sure that the tenses are maintained correctly. It is easy to forget that the auxiliary verb governs all the verbs in the series.

He has *come* and *gone*. "Gone" is correct, not "went" because "has" governs both past participles.

The time machine *has not been,* perhaps never *will be,* invented.

Two different auxiliaries are needed: "has been" for the present perfect tense and "will be" for the future. The past participle goes with both.

The multiple elements may be objects:

multiple objects:

(direct objects):

We ate *fish* and *chips.*

Felicia bought *books, clothes,* and *records.*

I enjoy *going to movies, riding a bicycle,* and *building bird-houses.*

(indirect objects):

Give the tickets to *Tom, Dick,* and *Harry.*

Did you throw the ball to *him* or at *him?*

In all the examples given so far there has been either one subject and several verbs, one verb and several subjects, or one verb and several objects. The verbs, the subjects and the objects may be multiple.

a. Dick and Jane ran and skipped all the way.

Note that both subjects govern both verbs.

b. The cat and the kitten sniffed and ate the fish and chicken.

Both subjects may govern both verbs, *and* both
verbs may govern both objects.

two subjects ── | 1st verb | 1st object | 2nd verb |

c.   The cat and the kitten ate the fish and drank

2nd object

the milk.

Example **c** differs from example **b**. In **c**, both subjects govern both verbs. But each verb has its own
direct object.

Clauses

A clause is a group of words that has a subject and
predicate. A clause may be *independent* or it may be
subordinate.

An *independent clause* can be a sentence in itself.
It can also be the main clause of a larger sentence.
The main clause is sometimes called the "basic
sentence."

A *subordinate clause* has a subject and a predicate,
too. But it cannot stand by itself as a complete sentence. It depends on the main clause. The subordinate
clause is sometimes called a "dependent clause."

subordinate clause ──── | Independent clause

If it rains, we'll go home.

"We'll go home" can be a separate sentence. It is
an independent clause.

"If it rains" cannot stand alone as a separate sentence. It is a subordinate clause.

Compound sentences

Compound sentences are made up of two or more *coordinate* independent clauses. *Coordinate* in this sense means of equal importance. A compound sentence is made up of clauses that could each be separate sentences if the writer wanted to write them as separate sentences.

> We tried and we failed.
>
> I tried to buy sugar, but the store was out of it.
>
> He will pick up the package tomorrow, or you will have to mail it.
>
> We climbed up the trail, and the snow nearly trapped us.
>
> John didn't win the trophy; he didn't even try.
>
> Henry will prepare the dessert, Molly will make the salad, and I'll cook the main course.
>
> People are born, people die, but the earth spins on.

Notice that the last two examples have more than two independent clauses. They are said to be in series. A series of three or more independent clauses may eliminate the coordinating conjunction after the comma in all but the last of the series.

Each of the above sentences can be rewritten as two or more separate sentences.

> We tried. And we failed.
>
> I tried to buy sugar. But the store was out of it.

He will pick up the package tomorrow. Or you will have to mail it.

We climbed up the trail. And the snow nearly trapped us.

John didn't win the trophy. He didn't even try.

Henry will prepare the dessert. Molly will make the salad. And I'll cook the main course.

People are born. People die. But the earth spins on.

The independent clauses of a compound sentence may be separated by:

- a comma and a coordinate conjunction *(and, and so, but, or, nor, for, yet, so): I tried to buy sugar, but the store was out of it.*
- a semicolon if there is no coordinate conjunction: *John didn't win the trophy; he didn't even try.*
- a coordinating conjunction alone only if the two clauses are very short: *We tried and we failed.*
- a comma may replace a semicolon only in very short sentences: *Sometimes you win, sometimes you lose.*

The subjects of the independent clauses in a sentence may be identical, or they may be different. But the subject must be stated in each clause. If it is not, the sentence is not a compound sentence.

Notice the difference between these two sentences.

> He ran, and he jumped.
> He ran and jumped.

The first sentence is a compound sentence. It can be separated into two sentences: *He ran. And he jumped.* The second sentence is not a compound sentence. Its subject is stated only once, and it is a simple sentence with coordinate verbs.

It is important to recognize the difference between the two kinds of sentences. The second sentence should not have a comma before "and." The first sentence should have a comma before "and."

Because independent clauses can be combined into a single sentence, some people have a tendency to overdo the combining or to punctuate incorrectly. Some common errors that arise from this tendency are:

Run-on sentences

Run-on sentences are sentences in which too many independent clauses have been combined. They are difficult to read. Run-on sentences can usually be corrected by separating the clauses into individual sentences. The conjunctions that connect the clauses of run-on sentences can then be eliminated.

run-on sentence	corrected to
The wicked witch cast a spell *so* the prince fell	The wicked witch cast a spell. The prince fell

asleep, *and* the princess didn't know what to do, *but* the king sent the knight to fight the dragon, *then* the prince awoke.

asleep, and the princess didn't know what to do. The king sent the knight to fight the dragon. Then the prince awoke.

Comma splice

A comma splice occurs when a comma without a coordinating conjunction separates the main clauses of a compound sentence. A comma splice can easily be repaired in one of four ways.

- insert a coordinating conjunction
- replace the comma with a semicolon
- rewrite the clauses to make separate sentences
- turn one clause into a subordinate clause

comma splice

The moon hid behind a cloud, all the world turned dark.

corrected to

The moon hid behind a cloud, and all the world turned dark.

or

The moon hid behind a cloud; all the world turned dark.

or

The moon hid behind a cloud. All the world turned dark.

or

Because the moon hid behind a cloud, all the world turned dark.

Fused sentences

Fused sentences are two or more sentences joined without punctuation. Often the writer is under the mistaken notion that a compound sentence has been created. Fused sentences can be separated into individual sentences.

fused sentence	corrected to
He didn't ask me he just did it.	He didn't ask me. He just did it.
John said he was going to enter the big race then his mother said that she would not allow it.	John said he was going to enter the big race. Then his mother said that she would not allow it.

Complex sentences

A complex sentence has an independent clause and a subordinate clause. The subordinate clause is usually introduced by a subordinate conjunction (*if, because, although, when, as soon as, whenever, even though, before, since, unless, until,* etc.).

The subordinate clause may come before or after the main clause. When it comes before the main clause, a comma usually separates the clauses. (The subordinate clauses are in italics.)

I'll go to the dance *if mother lets me.*

┌─ subordinate clause ─┐

If mother lets me, I'll go to the dance.

┌─ subordinate clause ─┐

Because I laughed, the teacher asked me to leave the room.

The teacher asked me to leave the room *because I laughed.*

When the rains fall, the river overflows.

He will return *as soon as he has train fare.*

Do you know the man *who sat next to you?*

We enjoyed the party *that you gave.*

Because the subordinate clause of a complex sentence has a subject and a verb, some people make the mistake of trying to set it up as a separate sentence. This results in sentence fragments. In this case, these sentence fragments can be corrected in two ways.

- The fragment can be woven into the main sentence.
- The subordinating conjunction can be eliminated, and the subordinate clause can become a main clause.

fragment	**corrected to**
He left the scene very quickly. Because the police were pursuing him for the theft.	He left the scene very quickly because the police were pursuing him for the theft.

or

> He left the scene very quickly. The police were pursuing him for the theft.

Compound-complex sentences

Compound-complex sentences are sentences that have two or more independent clauses and at least one subordinate clause.

┌─── subordinate clause ───┐ ┌─── independent clause ───┐
After the war ended, prices continued to rise,

┌─── independent clause ───┐
and the black market thrived.

┌─── independent clause ───┐ ┌─── independent clause ───┐
Everybody stopped speaking, and the ticking
                                        sub‑
───┐
clock was all that could be heard when the
ordinate clause
─────┘
maharishi took the stage.

┌─── independent clause ───┐ ┌─ subordinate
The children filed out of the school as soon as
── clause ──┐ ┌─── independent clause ───┐
the bell rang, and the janitors checked the class-
────┘ ┌─── subordinate clause ───┐
rooms because they wanted to clean them.

Subordinate clauses as subjects, objects, modifiers

When subordinate clauses occur in sentences, they often fill the job of a particular part of speech. The

entire clause may serve as a noun, an adjective, or an adverb.

When a subordinate clause fills the role of a noun, it may serve as a subject or an object.

as subject:

How the pyramids were built [— subject —] remains a mystery.

That she is an impostor [— subject —] cannot be proven.

What he found out [— subject —] is a secret.

as object of a verb:

The architect discovered *how the pyramids were built* [— object —].

Can you prove *that she is an impostor* [— object —]?

We know *that he found the secret* [— object —].

as object of a preposition:

John learned about *what had been said* [— object —].

She will go to *whatever school she chooses* [— object —].

as a predicate nominative:

The story is *that he disappeared* [— predicate nominative —].

It seems *that he did run away* [— predicate nominative —].

When a subordinate clause fills the role of an adverb, it modifies a verb, adjective, or another adverb.

modifying a verb:

He will *return* [verb] *as soon as he has train fare* [subordinate clause].

Sally will *dance* [verb] *if you ask her* [subordinate clause].

modifying an adjective:

The movie was *funnier* [adjective] *than I expected* [subordinate clause].

Simon is as *tall* [adjective] *as I am* [subordinate clause].

modifying an adverb:

She ran quickly *as a gazelle might*.
    adverb ⌐

    ⌐ adverb
He gossiped more indiscreetly *than I imagined possible*.

When a subordinate clause fills the role of an adjective, it generally modifies a noun.

modifying a noun:

    noun ⌐
I like the dress *that you bought*.

    ⌐ noun
I find myself on the street *where you live*.

    noun ⌐
The man *who is wise* avoids trouble.

To summarize: A *noun clause* is a clause that functions as a noun in a sentence. An *adverbial clause* functions as an adverb in a sentence. An *adjectival clause* functions as an adjective in a sentence.

A noun clause *is not* a clause that begins with a noun. An adverbial clause *is not* a clause that begins with an adverb. An adjectival clause *is not* a clause that begins with an adjective.

Each of the clauses is so labeled because of its function in a sentence.

Periodic sentences

A periodic sentence is one in which the main clause comes at the end. Two or more clauses or phrases — often parallel in construction — lead up to the main clause. A periodic sentence can be very dramatic in effect if it is used well and infrequently. In a periodic sentence, it is important that the main clause justify the lead-up.

periodic sentence with subordinate clauses:

Because he had burned their villages, because he had ignored

their pleas for mercy, because his cruelty increased with his

┌─ **main clause** ─┐

successes, *they attacked him* with unexpected savagery.

periodic sentence with phrases:

In winter, in summer, in good times and bad, in health and

┌─ **main clause** ──────────┐

sickness, *he always had time for others*.

Working long hours, saving every penny she could, denying

herself luxuries, using every resource she had, *she man-*

──── **main clause** ────┘

aged to save enough for an education.

By the light of the moon, in out-of-the-way places, unseen

┌─ **main clause** ─┐

by mortals, *the wee folk gather*.

Phrases and verb forms

A phrase is a group of words that together have some meaning. A phrase does not have to have a subject and a verb, but it may. A clause or a short sentence may be called a phrase, but most phrases would not be called clauses. Clauses must have subjects and verbs.

Phrases may be used to modify nouns, adjectives, verbs, and even complete sentences. The phrases may be used in the same way that single words may be used in a sentence.

Apposition

A noun or pronoun may have a noun or a phrase in *apposition*. That is, a noun or phrase may stand next to the noun or pronoun and extend its meaning.

Miss Grimsby, *our teacher,* is very strict.

We, *the committee,* are responsible for the decision.

My sister *Rosalie* has red hair.

You, *the organizer of the event,* deserve our thanks.

The girl *over there* is shy.

The book *under the counter* is rare.

The man *drinking coffee* is the spy.

We thanked our teacher, *Miss Grimsby.*

He winked at my sister *Rosalie.*

Notice that either the subject or the object may have a word or phrase in apposition. It is the first noun or pronoun—not the one in apposition—that determines the form of the verb. (We, the committee, *are,* not *is;* You—deserve, not "the organizer . . . deserves", etc.)

Object complement

Some verbs seem to have two objects. The second object is not really in apposition to the first. The second is an *object complement.*

The council elected John *president.*

We appointed Sara *leader.*

They named him *king of the jungle.*

An adjective can also be an object complement.

The heat made the plant *brown*.
Opposition turned the deal *sour*.

Verb forms in noun positions

The subject of a sentence need not be a noun. It may be a clause. It may also be an infinitive of a verb.

To travel requires money.
To speak honestly is difficult.

Even though the infinitive *(to speak)* may take the place of a noun, its verbal nature is maintained. It is modified by an adverb *(honestly)* as a verb would be modified. A noun would be modified by an adjective.

The infinitive can also serve as an object.

He likes *to sit*.
He wants *to play* hockey.

The object *(to play)* is still basically a verb. It has its own object *(hockey)*.

A *gerund* is the *-ing* form of a verb when used as a noun while conveying the meaning of a verb. A gerund may serve as a subject or an object. Many gerunds have become nouns in their own right.

Traveling requires money.
His *going* relieves us of a problem.
We enjoy *singing*.
Good *singing* gives us pleasure.
Singing well gives us pleasure.

Note that a gerund *(singing)* may be modified by an adjective *(good)* or an adverb *(well)*. When the gerund has more of a noun sense, an adjective modifies it; when it has more of a verbal sense, an adverb modifies it.

Gerunds have more nounlike functions than infinitives. Gerunds may be used in apposition, as object complements, and as objects of prepositions.

Participles and other modifiers

A modifier may modify a word, a phrase, a clause, or a whole sentence. A modifier may be a word, a phrase, a clause, or a whole sentence.

As you know, a clause or a phrase may function as an adjective, an adverb, or a noun. The phrase or clause that modifies must be placed in the correct relationship to the word it modifies.

> *Having seen the house,* she left.
> *Though sick,* he went to work.

These examples are grammatically acceptable. The sentences could also be rewritten.

> She left *having seen the house.*
> He went to work *though sick.*

They still make sense. That is because the modifying phrase logically belongs with the pronouns *(she* and *he).*

Dangling modifiers

These occur when a modifier does not modify the subject of the main clause. Dangling modifiers usually occur at the beginnings of sentences.

Sentences have to be rewritten to correct the dangling modifier.

dangling modifier

| *Though sick,* I saw him at work. | *After running the race,* we saw him faint. |

corrected to

| Though he was sick, I saw him at work. | We saw him faint after running the race. |

Notice that the problem with the dangling modifier occurs because it has no subject of its own. The subject of the main clause is usually taken to be the subject of the modifier. That creates some ridiculous images. Once a writer learns to recognize the silliness of what was said unintentionally, that writer will make fewer and fewer such errors.

> dangling modifier
>
> *On returning home,* the door slammed shut. (The door was not returning home.)
> *Falling from the tree,* the girl caught the apple. (In this case, the apple was falling from the tree, not the girl.)

Absolute construction

To complicate matters, there are some modifiers that modify the whole sentence. This kind of modifier

is said to be an absolute construction.

┌────── absolute construction ──────┐
The moment having arrived, we went inside the church. **absolute construction**

┌─── absolute construction ───┐
The cause lost, we abandoned our headquarters.

┌─
Apparently, the city was blacked out.
absolute construction

Such clauses, phrases, and individual words are acceptable English. They should not be confused with dangling modifiers. Sentence modifiers modify the whole sentence. Dangling modifiers unintentionally modify the wrong elements in a sentence.

Parenthetical remarks

Occasionally a writer wants to insert a comment or explanation within a sentence. That comment or explanation may not be a part of the actual sentence construction. The insertions are known as *parenthetical remarks*.

There are several kinds of parenthetical remarks and several different ways of punctuating them:

    with commas;
    with parentheses;
    with brackets;
    with dashes.

Commas are used only when the parenthetical remark is very short and flows well within the sentence.

My friend, *the one who moved to Chicago,* just got married.

John, *old and infirm though he is,* walked all the way home.

Commas are used in these sentences only for *nonrestrictive* phrases or clauses.

nonrestrictive	**restrictive**
My son, *the doctor,* sent me a letter. (The writer has one son who happens to be a doctor.)	My son *the doctor* sent me a letter. (The writer has more than one son. The one who is a doctor sent her the letter.)

Parentheses are used for longer material, further explanation, and side comments.

> The whole group (except for those who had resigned) agreed to settle the debt.

> The warriors had not really left town (as their letter seemed to indicate) but were waiting in ambush.

> The article on cryogenics (see page 38) suggests that the future may hold great appeal for some sufferers.

> He said he woodn't (*sic*) go. (*Sic* means that the word was originally written that way.)

Note that parentheses may be used for whole sentences as well as words or phrases.

Brackets are usually reserved for more formal situations than parentheses. But they may be used also in place of parentheses.

> . . . life, liberty, and the *pursuit* [italics added] of happiness.

> The women live in purdah [veils as required by religion and custom] and few men ever see their faces.

Dashes are used in the same way as parentheses are, to set off a parenthetical remark.

> The medium spoke of spirits—poltergeists, ghosts, ghouls—as if she thought we all believed in them.

> A two-week camping trip—whenever the weather allows us to leave—is the high point of our planned vacation.

Whether a writer uses parentheses, brackets, or dashes is often a matter of personal choice. Some writers tend to use parentheses; others use dashes. The important point is to be sure that the sentence that goes around the parenthetical remark makes sense in its own right. If you remove the parenthetical remark, the sentence should be grammatically correct.

Sentences into paragraphs

Almost everything we write—letters, essays, stories, memoranda, term papers—is divided into paragraphs. Why do we make the divisions? How do we know what goes into a paragraph and when to stop and begin the next one?

A paragraph is a unit of thought. A writer tries to organize each paragraph around one theme or idea, and groups sentences that deal with each theme in one paragraph. Then the next theme is explored in the next paragraph. The theme may be highly structured with a main idea and subdivisions of that main idea. Or the theme may be loose enough so that the only organizing theme is the writer's perception of connected thoughts.

Often a theme is stated in the paragraph's topic sentence. The remaining sentences in the paragraph expand on the topic sentence by giving specifics. Often, but not always, the topic sentence is the first sentence of the paragraph.

Within a paragraph, the ideas should move easily from one sentence to the next. There should be a logic in the progression from sentence to sentence. The logic should be clear to the reader as well as to the writer.

What is true for each paragraph is also true for groups of paragraphs. There should be a clear logic in the progression from paragraph to paragraph. Often

the progression of ideas can be seen just by reading the topic sentences in each paragraph.

These are some general rules for developing paragraphs:

1. Each paragraph should present a *unit*. It must be a grouping of sentences that are related to each other and to the main thought.
2. Each paragraph should present a complete thought and expand on it fully before ending the paragraph and beginning the next.
3. Within the paragraph, there should be a logic of movement: from general statement to specifics; from specific statements to general ones; from the beginning of an action to the end of the action; from a statement to a refutation to a re-examination of the original statement. The possibilities are numerous.
4. There should be a good balance of kinds of sentences. At times it is very effective to repeat the same structure in sentence after sentence within a paragraph. But this stylistic device can be overused. It is more effective to vary the rhythm, length, and construction of sentences.
5. It is important to maintain the same person throughout a paragraph. Switching from "you" to "one" to "they" can be very disconcerting to a reader.
6. It is important to maintain the same tense for the

same subject within a paragraph. Events in the past should not be described in the present and also in the past. At times, some of the events in a paragraph may have taken place in the far past, others over a period of time. The sequence of tenses should make the time relationship clear.

7. The introduction of a new topic requires the beginning of a new paragraph.

Some paragraphs require special attention. They have special places within a written work and serve special functions.

The opening paragraph

The opening paragraph is the first paragraph of a written work. A major function of the opening paragraph is to engage the reader's attention. There are several customary ways of doing this.

1. Ask a question. The question should go to the heart of the material you deal with. The question may be asked as a direct question ("Are sharks monogamous?") or as an indirect question ("We wanted to know if sharks are monogamous").
2. Make a statement. The statement should be clearly worded. No qualifying phrases should offset the force of the statement. The statement may be the basic theme of the work or it may be the reason for writing the work. ("There is no good published material on the breeding life of the shark.")

3. Begin with a quotation. You may then proceed to agree or disagree with the quotation. In either case, the quotation should be directly related to the theme of the work.
4. Present a short anecdote. The anecdote may be directly or obliquely related to the rest of the piece.
5. Cite an opinion by an authority, or offer a common view with which you agree or disagree.

Transitional paragraphs

In a sense, every paragraph makes a transition from the paragraph before to the paragraph after. Some paragraphs, however, must make a major transition from one block of ideas to another block of ideas. There are several devices that make transitions flow more smoothly.

1. Summarize what has gone before, and lead in to the next theme with a transitional word or phrase such as "on the other hand," "but," "however," etc.
2. Find a link for the ideas before and the ideas after, and lead from one to the other.
3. Use a short paragraph that picks up a word or phrase from the preceding paragraph. Then introduce a main idea for what will follow.

Concluding paragraphs

A concluding paragraph is the finishing touch to a piece of writing. When a reader encounters a good

concluding paragraph, there is no temptation to turn the page to see what comes next. How is this accomplished?

1. By summarizing the ideas that have gone before. This technique is effective only with long pieces of writing.
2. By drawing conclusions about what has been said.
3. By stating further questions to be explored at another time.

Correct Word Usage

Diction—The choice of words

Your purpose in writing is to communicate what you want to say. If you choose words carefully, you will achieve this purpose.

Good diction will help you make your points quickly, clearly, and memorably. Good writers expend words carefully, knowing exactly what they mean and imply. Poor writers cannot manage words; they fail to use—or misuse—words that could express their thoughts. To write well, *you* must be in control.

Diction is not judged on the basis of its "refinement," but on the basis of its appropriateness. There are different levels of diction, and they are appropriate in different settings. You might refer to the same male acquaintance as a *gentleman* in a letter of introduction, a *man* in a letter to a friend, a *guy* in informal conversation, or in certain situations, as a *dude*. As a general rule, write as you would speak in easy conversation with an educated person. Excessive formality will make your writing sound pretentious and stiff. Slang will make it sound careless. Avoid both.

Use general terms only for general statements, abstract concepts, summaries, and conclusions:

> *Children need attention.*
> *Power corrupts.*
> *Figures show that unemployment is rising.*

In other contexts, general vocabulary sounds watery

and vague. Capture specific objects or situations through precise observation and specific words. When you can, name names:

> *Frances and Mark spent the whole day at the Louvre.*
> (not: *My friends went to a museum.*)

> *The solitary grandee at the round table dined on spaghetti and black mushrooms.*
> (not: *The man had a meal.*)

> *The daffodils withered before the lilacs bloomed.*
> (not: *Some flowers bloomed earlier than others.*)

Do not distract the reader with trivial and fussy details.

Be thrifty with words, but not stingy. Say what you have to say in as few words as possible, but do not sacrifice meaning to brevity. Use the words you need; cut any that do not contribute. In writing, economy is elegance.

Never use words to show off. Choose them when you know exactly what they mean, and they express exactly what you mean. Fancy vocabulary, misused, is unimpressive. Even when used correctly, it generally lacks the force of well-chosen simple words.

Denotation and connotation

A word carries more than one meaning. It has sharply defined meanings as listed in the dictionary;

and it has a cluster of associated meanings that arise either through general usage or within a specific context. The *denotation* of a word is its narrow dictionary meaning. Its *connotations* are its implied meanings or associations.

To use a word well, you need to be conscious of the full range of its denotative and connotative meanings. Among several words with similar denotations, choose the one whose connotations most closely fit your meaning. Many words denote rapid movement. You can run, hasten, skitter, dart, flit, or skip, but if your house catches fire, you *flee* (rapid movement to escape danger). If you are late for your train, you *rush* (rapid movement to beat the clock). If you tear through the streets at 100 miles per hour, the police will stop you for *speeding*. You *hurry* to get somewhere, but *scurry* away.

If you ignore the connotations of the words you use, a reader may wonder what you are trying to imply and may not understand you at all. If, for example, you say that a band of musicians performed for a week and then skipped town, your reader will want to know if they did it to avoid paying their hotel bill. If you say they bustled off to their next gig, your reader will gather that they were operating on a tight schedule. Choosing words that say what you want them to in the first place will save you the chore of many later explanations.

Imagery

Images and likenesses make language striking. Sometimes they stress an individual point of a piece of writing; sometimes they form elaborate patterns that run through an entire piece and bind it together. The various means by which writers introduce images and likenesses are collectively known as *imagery*.

Imagery, like diction, is successful to the degree that it is appropriate. (Note: In writing, the term "image" does not necessarily suggest something visual. Sounds, feelings, scents, ideas, actions—all these, and more, can furnish images in language.) Any image that helps your reader grasp your meaning is good. Ingenious and remarkable images that confuse the reader are clutter —throw them out.

Like words, images have connotations. Likening a person's imagination to a landscape, you might call it a desert (if nothing flourishes there), a garden (if it brings forth new, attractive concepts), or a jungle (if it is teeming and unpredictable). Or you might call it a swamp. Choose images that reinforce the meaning you want to put across.

When you say that one thing is *like* another, you are using a *simile*. Similes are common in everyday use. Fresh ones can suggest a great deal in a little space.

> *Jennifer ran off like Cinderella at midnight.*
> *James greeted the tureen of mother's chicken soup like the Holy Grail.*

> *Mrs. Danvers glowered like the Czar of All the Russias.*

Similes are easy enough to concoct, but it is not always easy to avoid the trite:

> *Morris cried like a baby.*
> *Estelle's teeth were as white as pearls.*
> *Joey staggered in drunk as a skunk.*
> *Joan's heart is as big as all outdoors.*

the vague:

> *Signora Petti sang like a nightingale.*
> *Mr. Worthington behaved like a prince.*
> *Zelda was as pretty as a flower.*

or the far-fetched:

> *Maxine teetered on her spiked heels like a barrel on the edge of Niagara.*
> *Otto hopped like a coyote on peyote.*

Make sure the meaning of your reference is apparent. Do *not* leave it to the imagination of the reader. If you want to praise a pianist and write that he plays like Liberace, you will communicate nothing at all to people who have no opinion about the way Liberace plays, and something you don't mean to those who know how he plays and hate it.

Use similes sparingly. Readers tire of hearing that everything is like something else. If your subject is interesting only for the things it reminds you of, why aren't you writing about *them?*

The simile compares one thing with another; the *metaphor* identifies them with each other. Metaphors can be explicit and direct:

> *Mr. Novak's life was a dark night of confusion.*

or implied:

> *The death of his wife dimmed his reason.*

They can be very simple:

> *Mrs. Novak was his sunshine.*

or elaborately extended:

> *When they laid her in the grave, he knew no new dawn would ever scatter the gloom that was gathering around him.*

A well-chosen metaphor strengthens your writing by linking your subject to an image that makes it more immediate and vivid.

Metaphors, like similes, work through connotations. On the old-time radio serial *The Shadow,* an unidentified speaker announced:

> *The weed of crime bears bitter fruit.*

and went on:

> *Crime does not pay.*

This explanation adds nothing to the clear and striking image of the weed and its bitter fruit. If the unnamed speaker had wanted to suggest that crime was rewarding, he would have said something like:

> *The field of crime bears a rich harvest.*

If your metaphor contains a value judgment, let the image convey it without further explanation.

Good metaphors conjure up a sustained image. Be on guard against *mixed metaphors,* which violate consistency.

> *The ship of the hero's destiny is flying over the sands of time into the hornet's nest of war. The impostor dropped the cloak of her disguise as it melted under the chilly blast of the true princess's scorn.*

Jumbled images, piled on top of each other, create a rubbish heap of nonsense!

Metaphors are called *dead* when their images have lost their force through age or long use. There is nothing wrong with such phrases as *the face of the earth,* or *the hands of a clock.* But do not expect them to convey an image. The connotations that made them metaphorical when they were first coined will go unnoticed.

The same guidelines for similes apply to metaphors. Use them with caution. Try to find fresh images and make sure their connotations enhance your meaning. Do not try too hard to be "interesting." Writers who do are jitterbugging on a floor littered with banana peels.

An *analogy* presents a comparison. Its purpose is to show that the things compared conform, in some significant way, to the same principles. Analogies try

to justify, but strictly speaking they can never *prove* anything. Their success depends on convincing the reader that the comparison makes sense.

> *The human body is like a car. It burns fuel to release energy and produces waste.*

Analogies are never perfect. A human being deprived of "fuel" (food and air) will die; a car with an empty tank will start up again as soon as it gets gas; cars cannot have babies; humans do not have windshield wipers. But as a simple illustration of the fact that the human body consumes energy, the analogy with a car holds, and that is all it sets out to show. Good analogies may be short or long and account for few or many details; but above all, they must be valid as far as they go.

Personification gives inanimate objects and animals such animal or human attributes as names, action, behavior, and speech. It is used very commonly, as in the expressions *Mother Earth, Father Time, the foot of the bed.*

Explicit personification often sounds forced, pompous, or trite:

> *Victory showered her treasures on the nation.*
> *Folly tempted me to punch my boss in the nose, but Reason told me to calm down.*

But implied personification, suggested by vigorous diction, can be very effective:

> *The sea lashed the island.*
> *The wind howled at the door.*
> *The lightning sent shadows leaping through the room like demons.*

As the examples show, personification edges into simile and metaphor.

Use imagery to help your reader catch your meaning and hold on to it. Do not say more than you need to. Choose words and images with tact, care, and sense.

Using language more effectively

Using language effectively is the sum of skills in several areas: grammar and meaning, spelling and pronunciation, and usage, to enumerate some of the main ones. Style in writing and speaking may be somewhat less basic to language considered only as a means of communication, but style is surely another major ingredient of effective writing and speech. In this section the reader will find some practical aids to problems principally associated with style.

Unlike usage, style is less susceptible to classification by means of labels. A writer or speaker may have mastered grammar and be fully aware of usage levels and the pitfalls in usage presented by certain words and phrases—and still use lackluster language. Even a command of the basic mechanics of the language is no guarantee of correct usage. Style is more than technique. It encompasses a wide range of *choice of words* and their effective combinations, even within the rules of grammar and usage. Largely because of that latitude, one can go wrong very easily and still be entirely "within the rules."

All that follows in this section deals with choosing the right word. Getting the right word or words is also more than a matter of precise lexicography; here, too, staying within prescribed boundaries provides no assurance of good results. A choice of words also

implies avoiding the empty and overworked ones, and especially those excessively used even though individually they are all sound choices, to judge from their presentation in a dictionary.

dividually they are all sound choices, to judge from their presentation in the main, strictly lexical, part of this book.

Overwriting and its equivalent in speech—the use of too many words, especially those that duplicate or overlap meaning—is a common stylistic fault. Another is circumlocution, or roundabout, prolix, or evasive expression. Less often writers and speakers, perhaps too mindful of the danger of wordiness, use too few words—and create other problems. A more common fault is indulgence in clichés, or trite expressions. Lists of common redundancies, circumlocutions, and clichés are presented as examples of what to avoid. Another listing guides the reader in the choice of idiomatic prepositions, a recurrent source of difficulty (and a sure measure of how at home one is in a language). Following this section is a glossary of usage, a subject that is closely related to style.

Redundant expressions

Wordiness, by any of its corresponding names, specific or nonspecific, is to be avoided. One of the more general terms for this fault of using too many words is *verbiage*. The writer or speaker who makes

it *excess verbiage* (and many do!) is guilty of a fault typified by expressions in the first of the lists. *Excess* is used to convey the idea *too much,* but *verbiage* has that sense built in. (*Excess verbiage* is, in addition, a cliché, but that is getting ahead of our presentation.) A desire for absolute clarity is understandable and commendable, but more often a lack of thought is behind the use of such unneeded modifiers. An encyclopedist who writes that "a center line divides the tennis court into two halves" is underestimating the average reader's intelligence.

All the following come under the general heading *redundancy,* the use of more words than necessary to express a single meaning. Many, like *excess verbiage,* are also examples of *tautology* and *pleonasm,* narrower terms for expression that repeats the same sense in different words.

The expressions are listed according to the part of speech of the principal component (nouns in one group, for example; verbs in another, and so on). Superfluous words are enclosed in parentheses.

(old or *ancient) adage*
(other) alternative, in examples that limit to two the number of choices or courses
(complete or *total) annihilation*
anthracite *(coal)*
(important or *major) breakthrough* (sense of *achievement)*
capitol or Capitol *(building)*
(familiar, overworked, or *stale)/cliché*

(fellow) colleague
(final) completion
consensus *(of opinion)*
(joint or *mutual) cooperation* or collaboration
courthouse *(building)*
(general, habitual, or *usual) custom*
doctorate *(degree)*
(complete or *total) destruction*

128

(*baffling, difficult*, or *puzzling*)
  dilemma
(*pointed, succinct*, or *terse*)
  epigram
(*complete* or *total*) eradication
(*explosive, sudden*, or *violent*)
  eruption
(*important, necessary, requisite*,
  or *vital*) essential
(*violent*) explosion
(*complete* or *total*) extinction
(*true*) facts
(*passing, popular*, or *temporary*)
  fad
(*odd, peculiar, strange*, or
  unusual) freak (sense of
  phenomenon)
(*basic* or *essential*) fundamentals
(*opening*) gambit
(*free*) gift
(*invited*) guest
(*past* or *previous*) history
(*perfect*) ideal
(*current* or *present*) incumbent
(*new*) innovation
knots (*per hour*)
lawyer (*by occupation*) (and like
  expressions)
(*complete*) master
(*practical*) maxim
(*twelve* or *twelve o'clock*)
  midnight or noon
(*complete*) monopoly
(*local*) native
1 a.m. (*in the morning*) (and
  like expressions)
(*final*) outcome
(*all-powerful* or *universal*) panacea
(*fellow*) partner
(*advance*) plan or *planning*
plumber (*by trade*) (and like
  expressions)

(*difficult* or *troublesome*)
  predicament
(*chief, leading*, or *main*)
  protagonist
(*original*) prototype
prototype (*model*)
(*old*) proverb
(*new*) recruit
(*temporary*) reprieve
(*essential, indispensable*, or
  necessary) requisite
(*local*) resident
(*end*) result
Sahara (*Desert*)
(*old*) saw (sense of *saying*)
(*by vocation a*) teacher (and like
  expressions)
(*local*) townsman, townswoman,
  or *townsfolk*
to all intents (*and purposes*)
(*complete, entire*, or *whole*)
  total
(*pair of*) twins
undergraduate (*student*)
(*advance*) warning
widow (*woman*)
widow of (*the late*) . . .
annihilate (*completely* or *totally*)
appoint (*to the position of*)
ascend (*up*)
assemble (*together*)
attach (*together*)
blend (*together*)
climb (*up*)
coalesce (*together*)
collaborate (*together*)
combine (*together*)
commute (*back and forth*)
congregate (*together*)
connect (*together* or *up*)
continue (*on* or *still*)
continue (*to remain* or *to stay*)

cooperate (jointly or together)
cover (over)
depreciate (in value or in worth)
descend (down)
eliminate (altogether, completely, entirely, or wholly)
eradicate (completely or totally)
follow (after)
founder (and sink)
fuse (together)
gather (together or up)
hoist (up)
join (together or up)
make . . . (out) of
may (possibly)
merge (together)
might (possibly)
mix (together)
name (as or to the position of)
penetrate (into)
(continue to) persist
pierce (into)
prejudge (beforehand or in advance)
(pre) plan
protrude (out)
recall (back)
recoil (back)
recur (again or over and over)
return (back)
revert (back)
shuttle (back and forth)
skirt (around)
spell out (details or in detail)
strangle (to death)
swoop (down)

adequate (enough)
big (in size)
(entirely or wholly) complete
contemporary (in time)
equally (as) (In some examples *equally* is redundant in combination with *as*)
(absolutely) essential
few (in number)
(completely) filled or full
(all, completely, entirely, or wholly) finished
first (of all)
large (in size or in stature)
last (of all)
never (at any time)
over (and done or with)
(more) preferable
(one and) the same
short (in size or in stature)
small (in size or in stature)
sufficient (enough)
(more) superior
tall (in stature)
(completely) unanimous
and/or (Unless there is real point in setting forth three distinct and exclusive possibilities, in the sense of *one or the other or both*, the expression *and/or* can usually be replaced by *and* or *or* used singly, with no loss of meaning)
if (and when) or when (and if)
unless (and until); unless (or until)
(as to) whether

Most of the phrases in the preceding list permit a choice of one of two elements which in combination is redundant when paired with *only*.

Both is redundant with *alike, as well as, equal,*

equally, and *together: They are (both) alike; appeared (both) in films as well as on the stage; amounts that are (both) equal; plans that are (both) equally good; father and son who (both) acted together.*

In the expression *any and all, any* is sufficient. In *each and every,* either *each* or *every* suffices.

The articles *a* and *an* are redundant in the following: *no greater (an) honor; no such (a) thing; this kind, or sort (or type) of (a) problem.*

Of is redundant with the following prepositions: *alongside (of) the pier; atop (of) the tree; inside (of) the house; stepped off (of* or *from) the platform; outside (of) the building; outside (of) my authority.*

Circumlocution

Excess language is again a characteristic of writing and speech marked by circumlocution, but the problem is not one of saying the same thing in different words. The fault consists of roundabout, indirect, or evasive expression. Often it is induced by the knowledge that one is treating a difficult subject or a matter of considerable delicacy. Even in those circumstances (or perhaps, especially in them), the best approach is direct: language that is clear, concise, and to the point. In its most extreme form, circumlocution produces the kind of cumbersome and confusing speech and writing that only formal training can rectify. But much of the problem is within the power of the average speaker or writer to remedy, and therefore within the scope of this short discussion.

Circumlocution is by no means limited to the barely literate. Often it stems from a desire for an elevated style or for a "proper" style thought to be appropriate to business correspondence. Instead of taking a direct route to set forth an idea with a few concrete words, writers and speakers may feel that indirect expression, including abstract terms, will lend both beauty and gravity to what they say. Or they may have become so accustomed to seeing certain stock phrases in place of a few simple words that they feel such formula expression is the "proper" way to speak or write. Evasiveness is probably best represented by euphemisms, which are discussed under a separate heading. Another variety of evasive expression is the form of double negative exemplified by *not unusual* and *not unfriendly*. These are acceptable grammatically, despite the two negatives, and when employed judiciously they express a valuable shade of meaning, weaker than the corresponding positive terms *usual* and *friendly*. Overuse of such expressions, however, is frequently cited as a stylistic fault. Like other forms of circumlocution, they are vulnerable to the charge that they are not only wordy, but affected or pretentious—if not pompous.

The list of examples that follows is sketchy; unlike clichés and the kinds of wordiness illustrated by the preceding lists, circumlocution can take many forms, but the reader will be alerted to the problem by inspecting the following expressions, which will

probably suggest many others equally undesirable. After each example is a shortened version that most trained writers, editors, and speakers would consider far preferable.

a large percentage (or proportion) of—many

a statement to the effect that—a statement that

as per your letter—in accordance with . . .

at the present time—at present, currently, or now

be in possession of—have

be of the opinion that—believe or think

by all manner of means—of course or surely

by no manner of means—in no way

call to a halt to—cease or stop

during the time that—when or while

for the purpose of—in order to or to

have occasion to be—have reason to be

hold to the view that—believe or think

in a manner of speaking—in a sense or in a way

in advance of—before

in many instances—frequently or often

in the neighborhood (or vicinity) of—about, nearly, or some

in the field of economics—in economics

in view of the fact that—in view of or since

keep (or retain) possession of—keep or retain

make (or put in) an appearance—appear

of a generous nature—generous

on the occasion of—at or during

Euphemisms and genteelisms

Euphemisms are bland, inoffensive words or phrases used in place of corresponding language that is considered offensively explicit. As a class, they are to be avoided, according to most writers on style, since euphemisms, much more than the circumlocutions cited in the preceding section, call attention to a writer's or speaker's evasiveness. A steady diet of

such language is very apt to strike the average reader or listener as evidence of prissiness. Beyond that general statement, however, sound advice in individual matters is not easy to formulate, since taste varies rather widely in this area.

Whether *casket* for *coffin,* and *perspire* for *sweat* are self-conscious evasions is a matter on which opinion is probably sharply divided. Very likely there would be more agreement about the dubiousness of *slumber room* for *chapel* (of a funeral parlor). The problem of giving general guidance is complicated further by the practice of some religious groups in specifying terms as preferred usage (for example, *pass away* for *die*).

Not surprisingly, such unwelcome subjects as death, old age, poverty, and various bodily functions have spurred the coinage of the most common euphemisms. Death is responsible for *enter into rest, go to one's reward,* and *pass on.* The expression *supreme sacrifice* is the equivalent of death in the service of one's country; *mortician* is in common use for *undertaker, interment* for *burial,* and *remains* for *corpse.* Substitutes for *toilet* include *bathroom, washroom, lavatory, rest room, powder room,* and *comfort station. Indisposed* is a common evasion of specifying a form of illness, usually a mild one; *social disease* was formerly used for any of the venereal diseases. Common substitutes for *pregnant* are *expecting* and *in a*

family way, and *love child* is still occasionally found in place of *illegitimate child* or *bastard.*

Among the more common euphemisms are *expectorate* (for *spit*), *intoxicated* (for *drunk*), and *unmentionables* (for *underwear*). Despite a general trend toward frank language, *disadvantaged* has come into wide use for *poor* and *underprivileged.*

Genteelisms are expressions that their users consider appropriate to refined, well-bred discourse but that are frequently condemned as examples of over-refinement, artificiality, or prudishness. An illustration is *wish* as a substitute for the verb *want: Do you wish tea or coffee?* Even commercial usage has its share of these. *Advise* (for *inform* or *notify*) is a common one; another is *appreciate* for *realize: I appreciate your difficulty.*

Faults of omission

Too little can be a fault, as well as too much, in use of language. But it is a somewhat less common fault; in addition, it is more a matter of usage distinguished from style. The journalistic goal of brevity is responsible for the undesirable omission of the articles, *a, an,* and *the* in much reportage. For example: *Many entries in our photography contest are still arriving. Deadline will be announced shortly* (preferably, *The deadline will be . . .*).

Failure to repeat prepositions in certain extended constructions is another common fault, a source of poor style and often of ambiguity. In the following typical examples, the prepositions in parentheses are needed but often omitted: *a source of poor style and often (of) ambiguity; a problem inherent not only in city government but (in) all human relations; a question both of technique and (of) taste; something of concern to the welfare agency and, ultimately, (to) the entire state administration.*

In the examples that follow, the words enclosed in parentheses are essential to acceptable usage but are often omitted: *a record as good (as) or better than yours; equal (to) or better than mine; the equal (of) or better than his; applicants who did not graduate (from) college; a decision that depends (on) whether funds are available; a setback for our type (of) government.*

Clichés

These are expressions that are worn out from long use. They have been overused to the point of now seeming commonplace, their freshness and their vitality long since vanished. Clichés are trite, and one archaic (literal) sense of that adjective is *frayed or worn by use.* Stylistically, clichés surely fit that definition. They are so smooth from wear that they slip off the tongue or pen with great ease, and that can be the undoing of an unwary writer or speaker. A

blanket indictment of clichés would very likely be unwise, but a warning against their frequent use is much in order.

This fault is clearly a matter of style, distinguished from what we call usage, since the construction of most clichés is above reproach, and usually not burdened with redundancy or circumlocution. If the reverse were true, undoubtedly the temptation to continue employing them would be much less. The temptation is great merely because many of the expressions in question are catchy (or once were), and to an untrained user of language their surface appeal and never-ending appearance may seem a recommendation in itself—a sign that they are models of good expression. Unfortunately, the catchiness has been nullified by overuse, and although content often still exists, the force of the content of these expressions has undergone great reduction. *At a loss for words* and *better late than never* undoubtedly express useful ideas, but in a way that is now self-defeating. And some of the expressions, as now employed, seem devoid of whatever meaning they once had: *at the drop of a hat* is an example. These survive largely as verbal bric-a-brac, a sort of ornamental bridgework for passages of speech and writing.

Since most clichés do still express rather clear meaning, the writer or speaker will have to determine whether it is a shade of meaning that is hard to convey by fresher wording. If the process of substitu-

tion is too difficult, use of some of the phrases that follow may be advisable; writing or speaking around the formula expression may produce something worse than hackneyed language, such as strained, wordy, or ambiguous discourse. *Play the devil's advocate, pull one's chestnuts out of the fire,* and *wash one's hands* (of something) express ideas that are not easily rendered in other ways, and perhaps the same may be said of being a *Jekyll and Hyde* or a *stuffed shirt*.

Few on the following list qualify as indispensable, however. It is dominated by sayings that date back many years, for the most part. A few are of more recent origin, or have undergone a revival of late; old age is not invariably a characteristic of a cliché. But *do one's thing, bite the bullet,* and *keep a low profile* suggest that such expressions seem to age very fast through relentless use.

acid test
add insult to injury
age before beauty
agonizing reappraisal
agree to disagree
albatross around one's neck
all in all
all in a day's work
all in the same boat
all over but the shouting
all things to all men
all work and no play
apple of one's eye
armed to the teeth

as a matter of fact
as luck would have it
at a loss for words (or *never at a loss . . .*)
at first blush
at long last
bag and baggage
ballots, not bullets
bark up the wrong tree
bated breath
beard the lion in his den
beat a dead horse
beat a hasty retreat
beat around the bush

beggar description
bend (or lean) over backward
best foot forward
best-laid plans
better half
between the devil and the deep blue sea
beyond the pale
bigger than all outdoors
bite off more than one can chew
blood is thicker than water
bloody but unbowed
bloom of youth
bolt from the blue
bone of contention
brave the elements
bright and early
bright as a button
bright-eyed and bushy-tailed
bring home the bacon
burn the midnight oil
busy as a bee
butter wouldn't melt in his (her) mouth
by leaps and bounds
by the same token
calm before the storm
can't see the forest for the trees
carry (or have) a chip on one's shoulder
carry coals to Newcastle
carry water on both shoulders
(a) case in point
case the joint
cat has nine lives
chip off the old block
cleanliness . . . next to godliness
clear as mud
(to) coin a phrase (or an expression)
cold as ice
conspicuous by one's absence
cool as a cucumber

(by a) country mile
cross (or pass) the Rubicon
(a) crying need
crystal-clear
cut off one's nose to spite one's face
dead as a doornail
defend to the death your right to . . .
depths of despair
diamond in the rough
die in harness
disagree without being disagreeable
distaff side
do it up brown
dog in the manger
doom is sealed
doomed to disappointment
down in the dumps
down in the mouth
drunk as a lord
early bird gets the worm
early to bed . . . to rise
ears were burning
easier said than done
eat one's words
every inch a lady
exception that proves the rule
face the music
(the) fair sex
fall between two (or both) stools
fall on deaf ears
far be it from me
(a) far cry
fat's in the fire
fate worse than death
feather in one's cap
feel one's oats
few and far between
fiddle while Rome burns
fill the bill
filthy lucre

first and foremost
fit as a fiddle
flash in the pan
flat as a pancake
fly off the handle
food for thought
foot in one's mouth
foot the bill
foregone conclusion
forewarned is forearmed
fresh as a daisy
from the sublime to the ridiculous
garden variety
Garrison finish
generous to a fault
gentle as a lamb
get (or have) a green light
get down to brass tacks
get one's back (or dander) up
get one's feet wet
gift of gab
gild the lily
go over the top
goose that laid the golden egg
green-eyed monster
grin like a Cheshire cat
grind to a halt
hale and hearty
hail fellow well met
hand that rocks the cradle
handsome is as handsome does
handwriting on the wall
happy as a lark
have a foot in the door
have a leg up
heart of gold
heave a sigh of relief
high and dry
high as a kite (higher than a kite)
hit the nail on the head
hit the spot
hook, line, and sinker
hook or crook

hope springs eternal
hot as a firecracker (or as a
pistol)
hue and cry
hungry as a bear (or as a lion)
if the truth be told
ignorance is bliss
in durance vile
in full swing
in no uncertain terms
in on the ground floor
in seventh heaven
in the final (or last) analysis
in the limelight
in the long run
in the nick of time
in this connection
in this day and age
iron out a difficulty
irreparable damage (or loss)
it goes without saying
it is interesting to note
it's an ill wind
it's six of one and half a dozen
of the other
it never rains but it pours
it stands to reason
it takes all kinds to make a world
it takes two to make a bargain
(or to tango)
jig is up
just deserts
keep a stiff upper lip
keep (or lose) one's cool
keep one's chin up
keep one's ear to the ground
keep small problems (or worries)
small
knock into a cocked hat
knock on wood
labor of love
land-office business
land of milk and honey

larger than life
last but not least
last straw
lean and hungry
leave in the lurch
leave no stone unturned
lend a helping hand
let one's hair down
let the cat out of the bag
let well enough alone
like a house afire (or on fire)
lock, stock, and barrel
long arm of coincidence
long arm of the law
look a gift horse in the mouth
(as) luck would have it
mad as a hatter
mad as a hornet (or as a wet hen)
mad as a March hare
make a clean breast of
make a long story short
make a virtue of necessity
make bricks without straw
make ends meet
make hay while the sun shines
make no bones about
man's home is his castle
matter of life and death
meek as Moses
meet one's Waterloo
method in one's madness
milk of human kindness
mince words
mind one's p's and q's
model boy (or girl)
moment of truth
money is the root of all evil
 (a Biblical misquotation)
month of Sundays
more honored in the breach than
 the observance
more in sorrow (or pity) than in
 anger

more sinned against than sinning
more than meets the eye
(the) more the merrier
motley crew
name is legion
needle in a haystack
needs no introduction
neither fish nor fowl
neither here nor there
neither hide nor hair
never a dull moment
never say die
nip in the bud
none the worse for wear
no sooner said than done
not a fit night out for man
 nor beast
not wisely but too well
nothing new under the sun
on cloud nine
once in a blue moon
one's own worst enemy
on one's uppers
on the ball
on the best (or unimpeachable)
 authority
on the bum (or on the Fritz)
on the lam
on the other hand
on the QT
on the wagon
open secret
other side of the coin
other things being equal
out of the frying pan into the fire
over a barrel
paint the town red
part and parcel
pay the piper (or fiddler)
penny for one's thoughts
penny wise, pound foolish
people who live in glass houses . . .
perfect gentleman

141

persona non grata
  (except in diplomatic usage)
pet peeve
pillar to post
pinch pennies
(a) plague on both your houses
play fast and loose
play it by ear
play second fiddle
plumb the depths
(at this) point in time
point with pride
(the) powers that be
pretty as a picture
pretty kettle of fish
pretty penny
pull the wool over one's eyes
put a bug in one's ear
put on the dog
quiet as a mouse
rain cats and dogs
raise Cain
raise the roof
read the riot act
(the) real McCoy (the McCoy)
red as a beet
red-letter day
ripe old age
Rome wasn't built in a day
rub one the wrong way
run a taut (or tight) ship
sadder but wiser
sail under false colors
save for a rainy day
seal one's fate (or doom)
second to none
sell like hot cakes
separate the men from the boys
separate the sheep from the goats
(a) shot in the arm
sick and tired
sight to behold
silver lining in the cloud

skeleton in one's closet
small world
smell a rat
sour grapes
sow one's wild oats
stagger the imagination
start (or get) the ball rolling
steal one's thunder
stem to stern
stick out like a sore thumb
stick to one's guns
(a) stitch in time
stormy petrel
strait and narrow
straw in the wind
straw that broke the camel's back
strong as an ox
stubborn as a mule
sweat of one's brow
sweet sixteen
sweet smell of success
take a dim view of
take a raincheck
take the bull by the horns
take up the cudgels
take with a grain of salt
talk through one's hat
that's for sure
throw a monkey wrench into
  the works
throw caution to the winds
throw in the towel (or sponge)
throw the book at one
time hangs heavy
time immemorial
time of one's life
time's a-wastin'
time waits for no man
tit for tat
too little, too late
to tell the truth (truth to tell)
to the manner born
trip the light fantastic

truth is stranger than fiction
turn over a new leaf
unaccustomed as one is
uncharted seas
understatement of the . . .
usually reliable sources
vale of tears
view with alarm
wax poetic
wear two hats
wee hours
what makes the world go round
what with one thing or another
when all is said and done
when you come down to it

wide-open spaces
wise as an owl
wish is father to the thought
without further ado
wolf in sheep's clothing
(a) woman scorned
words fail one
(a) word to the wise
wreathed in smiles
you can say that again
you can't take it with you
you win some, you lose some
you're damned if you do and
   damned if you don't
your guess is as good as . . .

Picking a preposition

The following list contains forms of verbs, adjectives, and nouns that regularly appear in combination with certain prepositions. Following each entry word are the prepositions which are idiomatically linked with that word.

Picking the right preposition is often a matter of idiom. Related verbs such as *acquiesce, agree,* and *concur* might be thought to agree in every detail in the choice of prepositions, but they do not. So consulting a list of idiomatic expressions is the only sure method of avoiding error. Even people who work with the language every day—such as professional writers and speakers—often consult such a list. The list is not intended to imply that the entry word must be followed or preceded by a preposition, but rather that in certain contexts it is often used with that preposition. Only usages that commonly give difficulty are treated.

The prepositions listed are the ones most often used with the words in question; where the choice is determined by a particular sense of the entry word, the sense is indicated and illustrated when an example of the particular combination is not likely to come to the reader's mind readily. No adverbial usage is included, nor are the countless combinations of entry words followed by infinitives. Phrasal verbs, such as *bottom out* and *carry forward,* are also omitted.

abashed at
abhorrence of
abhorrent to
ability at or *with*
  (*at mechanics; with tools*)
abound in or *with*
absolve of or *from*
accede to
access to
accessible to
accession of or *to*
  (*of property; to the throne*)
acclimate or *acclimatize to*
accommodate to or *with*
  (*to changing circumstances;
  with everything she requested*)
accompanied by or *with*
  (*by her husband; with every
  difficulty imaginable*)
accord (n.) *between, of,* or *with;*
  (v.) *to* or *with* (*accord every
  consideration to her; a statement that accords with the law*)
account (v.) *for* or *to*
  (*for things; to persons*)

accrue to
acquiesce in
acquit of
adapt for, from, or *to*
addicted to (plus noun, but not
  plus infinitive) : *addicted to
  heroin; to taking heroin;* not *to
  take heroin*
adept at or *in*
adequate for or *to* (*for a goal or
  purpose; to a need*)
adjacent to
admit to, into, or *of* (*admit one
  to* or *into a club; a passage
  admitting to the lobby; a matter
  that admits of several views*)
adverse to
advocate (n.) *of;* (v.) *for*
affiliate (v.) *with* or *to*
affinity of, between, or *with*
akin to
alien (adj.) *to* or *from*
ally (v.) *to* or *with*
aloof from
amenable to

amused by or *at*

analogous in, to, or *with (in qualities; to* or *with each other)*

analogy of, between, to, or *with*

angry at, with, or *about*

antidote to, for, or *against*

antipathy to, toward, or *against*

anxious for or *about*

apprehensive of or *for (of danger; for one's welfare)*

apprise of

apropos of

arrogate to or *for*

aspiration toward or *after*

aspire to, toward, or *after*

assent to

attempt (n.) at or *on (at realizing an achievement; on a person's life)*

attended by or *with (by persons; by* or *with conditions or circumstances)*

attest to

attune to

augment by or *with*

averse to

aversion for, to, or *toward*

basis for, in, or *of (for a rumor; in fact* or *in law; of a medicinal compound; of* or *for an official's authority)*

bid (v.) for or *on (for nomination; on property)*

blame (v.) for or *on (blame her for the delay; blame the delay on him)*

blink (v.) at (sense of connive; without preposition, sense of *ignore* or *overlook)*

boast (n., v.) of or *about*

boggle at

capacity of or *for (of four quarts; for growth)*

capitalize at or *on (at $4 million; on an opponent's mistakes)*

careless about, in, or *of (about her attendance; in her speech; of* or *about the children's welfare)*

caution (v.) about or *against*

center (v.) on, upon, in, or *at (but not around)*

charge (v.) for or *with (for services; with manslaughter; with a duty; with strong emotion)*

clear (adj.) of; (v.) of or *from*

climb up (though usually redundant), down

coincide with

common (adj.) to

comparable to or *with*

compare with or *to (like things that are strictly comparable, with each other; unlike things to each other in sense of likken; things with each other in sense of be worthy of comparison)*

compatible with

complementary to

compliment (n., v.) on

concern (n., v.) about, in, or *with*

concur in or *with (in a plan or policy; with a person or view)*

conducive to

confide in or *to*

conform or *conformity to* or *with*

connive at or *with (at a fraud; with an accomplice)*

consequent (adj.) or *consequential to, on,* or *upon*

consist of or *in (an alloy consisting chiefly of nickel; treason, which consists in aiding the enemies of one's country)*

consistent with

contemporaneous with
contemporary with
contemptuous of
contend with, against, about, or over (with or against rivals, enemies, or unfavorable circumstances; about or over disputed matters)
contiguous to
contingent on or upon
contrast (n.) between, to, or with (between things; in contrast to or with); (v.) with
conversant with
convict (v.) of
correspond to or with (a statement not corresponding to or with his earlier account; a part that corresponds to the bore of a musket; when I corresponded with her)
culminate in
cure (v.) of
decide on, upon, for, or against (on or upon a matter or issue; for or against a principal in a legal action)
deficient in
deprive of
derive from
desire (n.) for
desirous of
desist from
despair (v.) of
destined for (for an end, use, or purpose; for a locality)
destitute of
destructive to or of
deviate (v.) from
devoid of
devolve from, on, to or upon
differ from, on, over, or with (from another person in out-

look; on or over issues; with a second party to an argument)
different from or than (a job different from his; an outcome different from what we expected; how different things seem now than yesterday). Different from is the preferred form when it works readily—when from is followed by a single word or short clause. Different than is most acceptable when it aids conciseness—when from could not be used except ponderously and when than is followed by a condensed clause.
differentiate between, among, or from
diminution of
disappointed by, in, or with (by or in a person; in or with a thing)
discourage from
disdain (n.) for
disengage from
disgusted with, at, or by (with a person or an action; at an action or behavior; by a personal quality, action, or behavior)
dislike of
dispossess of or from
disqualify for or from
dissent (n., v.) from
dissimilar to
dissociate from
dissuade from
distaste for
distinguish from, between, or among (distinguish one species from another; distinguish between or among shades of meaning)
distrustful of

divest of
dote on
emanate from
embellish with
emigrate from
empty (adj.) *of*
enamored of or *with*
encroach on or *upon*
end (v.) *with* or *in* (*with a light dessert* or *with a benediction; in divorce*)
endow with
entrust to or *with* (*entrust a mission to a confidant; entrust a friend with a mission*)
envelop in
envious of
essential (adj.) *to* or *for;* (n.) *of*
estrange from
exclusive of
excuse (v.) *for* or *from* (*for a fault; from an obligation* or *duty*)
exonerate of or *from*
expect from or *of* (*expect an apology from a mistaken person; expect integrity of a partner*)
experience (n.) *in* or *of*
expert (adj., n.) *in, at,* or *with* (*in* or *at weaving; with a loom*)
expressive of
exude from
favorable to, toward, or *for*
fear (n.) *of* or *for* (*of death; for my safety*)
fond of
fondness for
foreign to
free (adj., v.) *of* or *from*
freedom of or *from*
friend of or *to*
frightened at or *by*
fugitive (n., adj.) *from*

grateful to or *for* (*to a person; for a benefit*)
grieve for, after, or *at*
habitual with
hanker after
heal by or *of*
hinder from
hindrance to
hint (v.) *at*
honor (v.) *by, for,* or *with* (*by* or *with a citation for bravery; for his bravery; with one's presence*)
hope (n.) *for* or *of;* (v.) *for*
identical with or *to*
identify (*oneself*) *with* (*with the hero of a play*)
immigrate to
impatient at or *with* (*at a condition of affairs; with a person*)
impervious to
implicit in
impressed by or *with*
improve on or *upon*
inaccessible to
incentive (n.) *to* or *for*
incidental to
incongruous to
inconsistent with
incorporate in, into, or *with*
independent (adj.) *of*
infer from
inferior to
infested with
influence (n.) *on, upon, over,* or *of*
infuse with
inimical to or *toward*
initiate into
innocent of
inquire about, after, or *into*
inroad into
insight into
inspire by or *with*

instruct in

intention of

intercede with, for, or *(on behalf of)*

intrude on, upon, into

inundated with

invest in or *with (in bonds; with the rank and duties of an office)*

involve in

isolate from

jealous of or *for (of his power; for her rights and welfare)*

justified in

lack (v.) *in (lacking in support);* or transitive usage *(lack support),*

laden with

lament (n., v.) *for* or *over*

laugh (n.) *at* or *over;* (v.) *at*

level (v.) *at* or *with (level a gun or a charge at a person; level wood with a plane; with a person—that is, be honest in dealing)*

liable for or *to (for an act; for or to a duty or service; to a superior)*

liken to

martyr (n.) *to;* (v.) *for*

mastery of or *over (of a subject; of or over an adversary or obstacle)*

means of, for, or *to*

meddle in or *with*

mediate between or *among*

meditate on or *upon*

militate against or *(rarely) for*

mindful of

mistrustful of

mock at

monopoly of

muse on, upon, or *over*

necessary (adj., n.) *for* or *to*

necessity for, to, or *of*

need (n.) *for* or *of*

neglectful of

negligent in or *of*

oblivious of or *to*

observant of

obtrude on or *upon*

occasion for or *of (for rejoicing; of my visit)*

occupied by or *with*

offend against

opportunity of or *for*

opposite (adj.) *to* or *from;* (n.) *of*

opt for or *against*

original (adj.) *with*

originate in or *with*

overwhelm by or *with*

parallel (adj.) *to;* (n.) *between* or *with*

partake in or *of*

patient (adj.) *with* or *of*

peculiar to

permeate into or *through*

permeated by

permit (v.) *of (a rule that permits of two interpretations)*

persevere in or *against*

persist in

persuaded by, of, or *into*

pertinent to

pervert (v.) *from*

possessed of, by, or *with (of great wealth; of a keen wit; by or with an urge to kill)*

possibility of or *for*

precedence of or *over*

precedent (adj. *to;* (n.) *for* or *of (for a ruling; of seating members according to rank)*

preclude from

prefer to (prefer concerts to opera)

pregnant by or *with* (*by a person; with significance*)

prejudicial to

preoccupied by or *with*

preparatory to

prerequisite (adj.) *to;* (n.) *of*

preside at or *over*

presume on or *upon*

prevail over, against, on, upon, or *with* (*over* or *against an adversary; on, upon,* or *with a person to provide a service*)

prodigal (adj.) *of*

productive of

proficient in or *at*

profit (v.) *by* or *from*

prohibit from

prone to

provide for, against, or *with* (*for* or *against an emergency; for a dependent child; for annual elections, by law; with food and medicine*)

pursuant to

qualify for or *as*

receptive to

reconcile to or *with* (*to hard times; one's belief with another's*)

redolent of

regard (n.) *for* or *to* (*for a person; in* or *with regard to a matter*)

repent of

replete with

respect (n.) *for, to,* or *of* (*for a person; with* or *in respect to; in respect of*)

responsibility for

restrain from

revel in

rich in

rob of

satiate with

saturate with

scared at or *by*

secure (adj.) *in*

similar to

slave (n.) *to* or *of*

solicitous of, about, or *for*

subject (adj.) *to*

suffer from

suitable for; to

superior (adj.) *to*

sympathetic to or *toward*

sympathy for, toward, or *with* (*for* or *toward a person or cause; in sympathy with a cause*)

tendency to or *toward*

thrill (v.) *to, at,* or *with* (*to* or *at a source of delight; with delight*)

tolerance for, toward, or *of* (*for, toward, of persons* or *causes; of pain; of a scientific instrument*)

treat (v.) *as, to, of,* or *with* (*as a friend; to a meal; of a subject* or *topic; with another person in negotiations*)

vary from

vest (v.) *in* or *with* (*authority vested in an official; an official vested with authority*)

vie with

void (adj.) *of*

vulnerable to

wait (v.) *for* or *on* (*for one who was delayed; on a customer* or *patient*)

want (n.) *of;* (v.) *for* (*did not want for money*)

wanting (adj.) *in*

wary of

yearn for, after, or *over*

zeal for or *in*

Usage glossary

The material in this section, arranged alphabetically by topics, attempts to provide guidance in problems that are basic and therefore recurrent, especially in usage of the written word with its more exacting standards. The guidance in turn is based on usage notes in *The American Heritage Dictionary of the English Language,* which were prepared with the assistance of a Usage Panel of more than a hundred professional writers, editors, speakers, teachers, and others with demonstrated skill in use of the language.

This glossary has also striven for wide-ranging coverage in concise form with a minimum of technical terms. *Formal usage,* as employed here, refers to that which conforms to established educated usage. *Informal* (colloquial) is applied to that which belongs to the usage of natural spoken language but which is considered usually inappropriate to careful writing, especially in certain cultural contexts, as in the standard written prose of ceremonial and official communications.

a, an   Use *an* before words beginning with vowels (*a, e, i, o,* and *u*) and before words beginning with an unpronounced *h*. For example: *an athlete; an enormous cake; an umbrella; an heir; an honor.* Use *a* before all other words—those beginning with a consonant sound: *a doctor; a good decision.*

A is used before words beginning with *u* or *e* whose sound rhymes with *you: a union; a university; a usage glossary; a European.*

Both *a* and *an* are possible before words beginning with *h* in an unaccented syllable: *historic, historical, historian, hotel,* and *hypothesis,* for example. In modern usage, *a* is preferred in such examples, but *an* is also acceptable, especially in combinations such as *an historic occasion* and *an historical novel.*

When numbers are used in a sentence, treat them as corresponding words and make your choice of *a* or *an* according to the rules above: *a 40-hour week* (*a* before *forty*); *an 8-hour day* (*an* before *eight*).

able   This adjective is often followed by an infinitive in the active voice (*able to see*), but not in the passive (not *able to be seen*).

(not) about to   This construction, or variant also in the negative, is used to emphasize intention or express determination by means of understatement: *troops not about to surrender.* Though based on a legitimate meaning of *about* (ready or prepared), the expression is informal, often found in regional speech and writing reproducing that.

above   With reference to something stated earlier in a piece of writing, *above* is better used as an adjective or adverb: *the above* (aforementioned) *statement; the material quoted above.* The noun usage is undesirable outside legal or commercial writing: *consult the above*

(preferably *the above material, the figures cited above,* or the like).

accept, except Of these verbs, only *accept* means to receive or admit, to regard as right or true, or to bear up under. *Except,* often misused in the preceding senses because of similar pronunciation, means to leave out, exclude, or excuse.

acceptance, acceptation To denote the act of accepting or state of being accepted, use *acceptance. Acceptation* is employed, much less often, to denote the usual or accepted meaning of a word or expression.

act, action As nouns these are sometimes interchangeable. But *act* is usually applied to a specific brief deed of a person, and *action* to a performance complex or long-range. *Act* stresses what is done rather than the process of doing; *action* emphasizes such process or function: *an act of mercy; one's actions* (acts considered collectively or as a chain of events); *the action of a drug.*

A.D. This abbreviation precedes the date, which is always a specific year rather than a century: *died A.D. 405* (not *in the fifth century A.D.*).

adapt, adopt Both refer to taking something or someone. *Adapt* adds the idea of changing or adjusting to a different use, need, or situation; *adopt* does not imply such change: *adapt machinery; a novel adapted for stage presentation; adapt to new surroundings;*

adopt a child; adopted the costume and customs of her new homeland.

admission, admittance   Use *admittance* for physical entry to a specific place: *no admittance to the jury room.* Use *admission* for figurative entry (*admission of evidence*) or, when physical entry is involved, in the further sense of right or privilege of participation: *admission to a society; the price of admission to a theater.*

admit   When it means to confess or acknowledge, *admit* is followed by a direct object, not by *to: admit a mistake; admit having made an error.* See the section headed "Picking a Preposition" for correct use of prepositions with *admit.*

adopt   See **adapt, adopt.**

adopted, adoptive   In a foster home, one refers to *adopted* children and *adoptive* parents.

advance, advanced, advancement   The noun *advance* is applied to both actual forward movement and figurative progress; *advancement,* to figurative progress: *advances in science; the advancement of science; an advancement in rank.* The adjective *advance* implies actual precedence in position (*advance guard*) or time (*advance word*); *advanced* implies figuratively forward position with respect to a norm: *advanced mathematics; advanced thought.*

adverse, averse Both words express opposition, but from different points of view. Something *adverse* to a person or thing reflects opposition contrary to the subject's interest or will: *adverse decisions*. To be *averse* to something indicates opposition on the subject's part: *a perfectionist averse to overlooking any shortcoming*.

advice, advise The noun *advice* is the equivalent of counsel or guidance. The verb *advise* means to offer such guidance.

affect, effect Each is a verb and a noun. In practice, however, *affect* is almost always a verb and *effect* most often a noun. As verbs, *affect* is used principally in senses relating to influencing or causing a change in, and to simulating or imitating so as to make a desired impression (*drugs that affect the nervous system; affected poor health to gain sympathy*); *effect* means to bring about or make: *layoffs designed to effect savings*. As nouns, *affect* is now confined to psychology as a technical term; *effect* is used chiefly in the senses of result or influence: *a plea to no effect; the effect of drugs on the nervous system*.

afterward, afterwards Both are acceptable, but *afterward* is preferred in American written usage.

agenda Though plural in form, this noun is used with a singular verb: *The agenda is complete*. It is

construed in a collective sense: a list of things to be done, especially the program for a meeting. *Agendum* (singular) is an item on an agenda. *Agenda* has developed its own plural: *agendas*.

aggravate Strictly, the verb means to make worse or more of a burden: *Smoking aggravates a sore throat.* Only informally does *aggravate* mean to annoy, provoke, irritate, or vex.

ago Use *ago* alone or followed by *that* or *when: I saw her last a week ago. It was a week ago that* (or *when*) *I saw her last. Ago* is redundant in combination with *since,* which stands alone: *It has been a week since I saw her last.*

ain't This contraction of *am not* is appropriate only to deliberately informal usage, chiefly to record uneducated speech, or as a device for providing humor, shock, or other special effect. Like all such devices, this one leaves the writer open to the risk of having his or her intention misunderstood. The interrogative form *ain't I?* has the virtue of agreement between pronoun and verb (unlike *ain't* used with other pronouns such as *it, he,* or *they,* or with nouns); but even this form has only slightly more acceptance than the others.

alibi In formal usage, employ *alibi* only as a noun: a form of defense whereby a defendant seeks to prove

he or she was elsewhere when a crime was committed. When it means, in effect, an excuse, the noun is used informally. The verb (to make excuses) is used only for informal writing or speech.

all When *all* is the equivalent of *everything, the whole,* it takes a singular verb: *All is not in vain.* When the meaning is *each one of a group,* a plural verb follows: *All are now accounted for.* When a noun follows the expression *all but one,* it is singular and so is a verb after the noun: *All but one ship is accounted for. All of* invariably precedes a pronoun: *all of us;* it can precede a noun, but *all* is sufficient: *all (of) the buildings.* An informal usage couples *all* (adverb) with *that* in negative and interrogative sentences implying comparison: *She's not all that good. Is she all that good?*

all-around, all-round The second form, *all-round,* is preferable. Both forms are hyphenated, and each is used only as an adjective before a noun: *all-round* (comprehensive) *capability; an all-round* (versatile) *athlete.* These should not be confused with *all round* (or *all around*), written without hyphens and used adverbially (*a plan better all round*) and prepositionally: *went all round the town.*

all ready, already *All ready* expresses complete readiness; *already* expresses time adverbially: *He was now all ready, but the carriage had already departed.*

all right, alright   The form *alright* is a misspelling. These forms differ not in meaning but in acceptability. Use *all right*.

all together, altogether   *All together* is always applied collectively in the sense of closeness or unity, physical or figurative: *cattle huddled all together; democracies standing all together*. *Altogether* has the collective sense of *in all; all told: four choices altogether*. Or it can mean *entirely* (*altogether satisfactory*) or *on the whole: Altogether, I'm satisfied*.

allude, elude   They resemble each other in sound and appearance but not in meaning. To *allude* is to make an indirect reference to something. To *elude* someone or something is to avoid, evade, or escape from the person or thing.

allusion, illusion   These unrelated nouns are confused because they look and sound alike. An *allusion* is an indirect mention or reference. (Both *allude* and *allusion* are sometimes misused when a direct, explicit reference is indicated.) An *illusion* is an erroneous perception or impression. See also **delusion.**

alongside   See "Redundant Expressions."

along with   When these words introduce an addition, following the subject of a sentence or clause, the addition does not alter the number of the verb, which is governed by the subject: *The prime minister, along*

157

with the secretary, is expected in an hour. The rule also applies to phrases introduced by *as well as, besides, in addition to, like, together with,* and *with*.

also This is an adverb, not a connective. It cannot replace *and* in an example such as *fumes that pollute the air also damage building exteriors*. Make it: *and also damage*.

alternative As noun and adjective, the word can denote or describe the second of two courses or choices: *annihilation, the alternative to surrender*. Or it can be used acceptably for more than two: *four alternative economic plans*.

although, though These are often interchangeable. *Although* is most often the first word of a concessive clause: *Although she was tired, she accepted*. *Though* does not always come first: *Tired though she was, she accepted*. *Though* is the more common in linking single words or phrases: *wiser though poorer*.

alumnus This is the masculine form for a graduate or former student; the plural is *alumni*. The feminine terms are *alumna* and *alumnae*. The plural *alumni* is often used to denote all graduates or former students of co-educational schools.

ambivalent This very special word is increasingly used, and misused. It describes the simultaneous existence of conflicting emotions or ideas (love and hate,

for example) about a single person or thing. It is misused when the prevailing sense is that of *ambiguous* (unclear and thus open to several interpretations) or *equivocal* (evasive).

amend, emend Both verbs refer to improving by revising or editing. *Emend* is limited to that sense; *amend* most often refers to changing a document, such as a constitution, by formal addition.

among See **between, among.**

an See **a, an.**

anachorism, anachronism The first of these nouns denotes something out of place geographically (unsuited to its location), and the second something out of its proper time.

and etc. Make this just *etc*. The word *and* is part of et cetera (abbreviated etc.), which means *and other unspecified things of the same class*.

and/or See "Redundant Expressions."

anticipate In constructions in the passive voice, *anticipate,* unlike *expect,* is not followed by an infinitive: *Trouble is expected* (or *expected to occur*). *Trouble is anticipated* (but not *anticipated to occur*). *A severe storm was anticipated* (but not *The storm was anticipated to be severe*).

anxious, eager   These terms overlap to some extent when *anxious* has the sense of eagerly or earnestly desirous. In such instances, however, *anxious* should be used only when anxiety is present in some degree. Otherwise, *eager* is usually a much better choice: *anxious to hear that you arrived safely; anxious to see the new quarters* (where there is ground for concern); *eager to see your new apartment, your new car,* or the like.

any   The pronoun *any* takes either a singular or plural verb, depending on how *any* is construed: *Any of these gifts* (any one among three or more) *is appropriate. Are any* (some; more than one) *of them within our means?*

In comparisons of like things, *any other* is preferable to *any* in an example such as: *The house seemed finer than any other he had known.*

An even less desirable use of *any* (adjective) with a singular noun is illustrated by *the most famous of any Spanish composer.* Make it *most famous Spanish composer; most famous of Spanish composers,* or *of all Spanish composers.*

Any (adverb) is chiefly appropriate to informal usage in interrogative and negative constructions such as: *Did the new part help any? At least it didn't hurt any.* See also "Redundant Expressions."

anymore, any more   *Anymore* is an adverb of time, used in negative and interrogative constructions: *He doesn't go anymore* (at present). *Will they be away anymore* (from now on)? The two-word form is used in referring to a given thing, specified or understood: *The lamps were reasonable, but we don't need any more.*

anyone   Especially in written usage, *anyone* should not be used in a construction such as *the most conscientious person of anyone I know.* Delete *of anyone* or make it *of all I know.*

anyone, any one   *Anyone* is equivalent to *anybody;* it refers only to persons (indefinitely to any person whatsoever), and stresses *any.* In contrast, *any one* refers to any person or thing of a specified group and stresses *one: Anyone could foresee what might happen. There are five candidates; select any one. She recognized five possible courses, any one of which would present difficulty.*

anyone (anybody)   These are singular terms that are used with singular verbs. Accompanying pronouns and pronominal adjectives within such constructions are also singular, especially in formal writing: *In such circumstances anyone is liable to lose his* (or *her* or *his or her,* but not *their*) *head occasionally.*

anyplace, any place   *Anyplace* is an adverb equivalent to *anywhere.* In formal writing *anywhere* is the

better choice. Only *any place,* the two-word form consisting of adjective and noun, is possible in an example such as *free to take any place that is not occupied.*

anyway, any way   These are interchangeable only in the sense of *in any manner whatever: Handle it anyway,* or *in any way you choose.* When the sense is *nevertheless; at any rate; anyhow,* only *anyway* is possible: *The cost was exorbitant but we proceeded anyway.* When the sense is *any course or direction,* only *any way* is possible: *Try any way that seems appropriate. Any way they turned, danger was present. Anyways,* for *anyway,* is not acceptable on any level of usage.

anywhere   The spelling as indicated is the only acceptable one. *Anywheres* is characteristic of uneducated speech.

apt, liable, likely   Each of these is employed with an infinitive to express likelihood or probability. *Likely* is always appropriate when mere probability is involved: *It is likely to snow. Apt* implies probability based on a natural or known tendency: *storms apt to occur during the rainy season; apt to stammer when she becomes excited.* The idea of the possibility or probability of risk or disadvantage is inherent in *liable,* in careful usage: *liable to injure himself by scratching the wound.* In many examples, more than one of these adjectives is possible, but *liable* is misused in

expressing only probability: *liable* (preferably *likely*) *to leave tomorrow*.

aren't I? As a variant of *ain't I?*, this phrase has more acceptance than *ain't I?* especially in speech. In American usage, contrasted with British, however, *aren't I?* is often considered a self-conscious evasion, a genteelism, or an affectation.

as When *as* is a preposition, meaning in the role, capacity, or function of, it is always followed by a noun or pronoun in the objective case. Otherwise the case of pronouns following *as,* or *as to,* may be nominative or objective, depending on the function of the pronouns and the desired sense: *You need her as much as I* (that is, *as much as I need her*). *You need her as much as me* (that is, *as much as you need me*).

When *as* is a conjunction equivalent to since or because, ambiguity sometimes results; *as* may be misconstrued as a reference to time: *She did not hear the bell as she was on the terrace.* Use of *since* or *because* makes the desired sense clearer. Omissions occur in the clauses introduced by the phrases: *As far as money, we haven't a great deal. There is no problem so far as time.* In both examples an addition is needed to complete the reference, such as: *as far as money is concerned; so far as time is involved.*

The conjunctive use of *as* for *that, whether,* or *if* is informal only: *I don't know as I can.*

Another conjunctive sense of *as* is *though: Strong as he was, he was unable to make headway.* Note that in such an example, *strong* (or another adjective) is not preceded by another *as*.

as if, as though   These are both acceptable and generally interchangeable: *It seemed as if* (or *as though*) *the day would never end.*

as . . . as, so . . . as   In positive comparisons, *as . . . as* is the construction employed: *as strong as an ox.* In negative comparisons, either *as . . . as* or *so . . . as* may be used: *not as* (or, *so*) *bright as his sister.*

In positive comparisons, a common error is omission of the first *as* of a pair: *The sound was clear as a bell.* Make it *as clear as.*

For a discussion of the omission of *as* in examples such as *as good* (*as*) *or better than,* see "Faults of Omission."

as far as, so far as   Errors of omission are common in sentences employing either of these phrases.

assume, presume   Both verbs indicate an act of taking something for granted. *Assume* is more appropriate to setting forth a hypothesis; *presume* is stronger in implying belief in the truth of the matter involved, in the absence of proof to the contrary. *Presume* may also imply an unwarranted conclusion. In senses not directly related to these, *presume* means to act over-

confidently or to take unwarranted advantage of something.

assure, ensure, insure All mean to make secure or certain, and all may be applied to the act of making something certain: *Success is assured* (or *ensured* or *insured*). Only *assure* means to make secure in the sense of setting a person's mind at rest: *assured her of our interest*. *Ensure* and *insure* also mean to make secure from harm: *ensure* (or *insure*) *a country against invasion*. In American usage, only *insure* is now in wide use in the sense of guaranteeing life or property against risk.

as well as See **along with.**

at The word is not expressed in indicating a location or position of rest in sentences such as *Where is he now? This is where he is.* In neither example is *at* used, following *he* (in the first) or *is* (in the second).

atop See "Redundant Expressions."

author Its use as a transitive verb (*authored two books on astronomy*) has the sanction of earlier practice and of present-day definitions of the word. But many writers and editors now regard this usage as an unnecessarily graceless and pretentious device for expressing a simple idea.

avenge, revenge *Avenge* is only a verb; *revenge* is both noun and verb, though more common as a noun.

Here they are compared as verbs. *Avenge* generally connotes the achieving of justice, whereas *revenge* stresses retaliation. *Avenge* usually has for its subject someone other than the person wronged; the latter, or the wrong itself, often serves as the direct object: *Hamlet avenged his father* (or *his father's murder*). *Revenge* usually has for its subject the person wronged, and is often used reflexively: *He revenged himself* (*of the wrong done him*).

averse See **adverse, averse.**

avert, avoid To *avert* something is to ward off or prevent it. *Avoid* is often loosely used for *avert* in that sense, but properly refers to staying clear of something. An organization such as the United Nations seeks to *avert* (not *avoid*) wars, to keep them from coming about. One *avoids* something in existence; a nation desiring to maintain neutrality tries to *avoid* a war in progress.

awake, awaken, wake, waken Though alike in meaning, these verbs are differentiated in usage. Each can be employed transitively and intransitively (that is, with a direct object and without one). But *awake* is principally intransitive (*awoke early*) and *waken* is transitive (*avoided wakening them*). In the passive voice, *awaken* and *waken* are the more common: *They were awakened* (or *wakened*) *by the sound of gunfire*. In figurative usage (distinguished from actual rousing

from sleep), *awake* and *awaken* are the more prevalent: *awoke to the peril; when her fears were awakened.* Only *wake* is used with a preposition (*up*). The preferred past participle of *wake* is *waked*, not *woke* or *woken: after she had waked him.* The preferred past participle of *awake* is *awaked*, not *awoke: He had awaked once earlier during the storm.*

awhile, a while *Awhile* is an adverb and modifies a verb: *rest awhile.* In the combination *a while, while* is a noun. *Awhile* is not preceded by *for*, whereas *while* can be. All the following are acceptable ways of expressing the same idea: *Stay awhile. Stay for a while. Stay a while.* But *stay for awhile* is a common misuse of *awhile.*

back of, in back of These equivalents of *behind* are found on all levels, including formal: *a mile back of* (or *in back of*) *the front lines.* The principal objections to them are stylistic—that they are wordy and unattractive.

backward, backwards Only *backward* is an adjective: *a backward glance; backward nations* (behind others in development). The corresponding adverb may be spelled either *backward* or *backwards,* and the forms are applicable interchangeably in all examples: *directed a glance backward; a mirror facing backward; going steadily backwards* (toward a worse condition).

bad, badly In formal writing, the adjective *bad* is the only acceptable word of these two following linking verbs such as *feel* and *look: She felt bad* (ill). *He felt very bad* (regretful) *about his part in the unfortunate affair.* The adverb *bad* is informal (for *badly*); to qualify verbs such as act, dance, and write, *badly* is required, as it is in the example *His arm pained so badly* (or *severely*) *that he was unable to sleep.* In the corresponding sense of very much or greatly, *badly* is appropriate to all levels of usage in examples such as *badly in need of renovation.*

baited, bated The first of the two participles is often misused for the second in the expression *bated breath,* which is proper as given. Traps and fishhooks are *baited;* animals and persons are *baited* when lured, attacked, or tormented.

balance In bookkeeping this noun means remainder: the difference between the totals of the debit and credit sides of an account. By extension the same meaning (remainder or rest) is conveyed by *balance* in general usage: *The morning session runs until ten-thirty, and the balance of the time is your own.* In such examples *balance* is employed informally.

baleful, baneful Both adjectives describe what is harmful. *Baleful* is applied especially to what menaces, exerts evil influence, or foreshadows evil: *baleful surroundings; a baleful look. Baneful* is more often

used in the sense of being directly destructive: *baneful treatment; a baneful influence.*

barbarian, barbaric, barbarous The adjectives are applied to primitive peoples, usually with distinctions that follow. *Barbarian,* the most general, means rough and uncivilized: *a barbarian society; barbarian culture. Barbaric* stresses crudeness or wildness of taste or style: *barbaric modes of expression; barbaric splendor. Barbarous* describes what is savage, cruel, or coarse: *barbarous customs; barbarous treatment.*

barbarism, barbarity *Barbarism* is applied to an uncivilized condition in general, with special emphasis on crudity of expression. A *barbarism,* in one sense of the term, is a word or form of language considered incorrect or nonstandard. *Barbarity* primarily denotes harsh or cruel conduct or an act that exemplifies such conduct.

barracks This noun is plural in form, used with either a singular or a plural verb. It can denote a single building: *Our barracks is well maintained.* Or it can be applied to a group of military buildings: *The barracks are situated in the south part of the base.*

bated See **baited, bated.**

B.C. This abbreviation always follows the date (unlike A.D.), and may be applied to any specified period (year, century, or era): *95 B.C.; first century B.C.*

When neither A.D. nor B.C. appears, the time is assumed to be after Christ.

bear The past participle of this verb is always *borne* for all senses except that which applies to the act of giving birth: *They had borne the load for generations. He has borne up well. She had borne the scar since childhood. The soil has borne abundant crops.* In the sense related to giving birth, the past particle *borne* is the usual form for all active-voice constructions and for passive constructions when followed by *by*. The alternate past participle *born* is employed for all other passive constructions indicating the fact of birth: *She has borne three children. Three children were borne by her, one of whom was born deaf.*

because See **reason.**

befit The past tense is *befitted,* not *befit*. The past participle also is *befitted.*

behalf This word presents more than the usual problem involved in selecting a preposition. Two related but different senses are conveyed by *behalf* when preceded by *in* and *on*—but the distinction has become blurred by the widespread practice of using *on* with *behalf* to convey both senses. In careful usage, however, *in behalf of Smith* (or *in Smith's behalf*) means in the interest of or for the benefit of Smith. *On behalf of Smith* (or *on Smith's behalf*) means as the agent of or on the part of Smith. If you speak *in behalf of*

another, you may be acting quite independently and without the knowledge of the other person; if you speak *on behalf of another,* you are presumably the other person's agent or representative. In some examples either preposition might be defensible, for the two senses are not mutually exclusive.

being as, being as how   As variants of *since, because,* or *inasmuch as,* these expressions occur principally in the speech of certain regions and are not acceptable in written usage except in reproducing the speech as dialogue: *We proceeded leisurely, being as* (or *being as how*) *the bus was not due for another hour.* Make it *since, because,* or *inasmuch as the bus was not due.* The expression *seeing as how* is used in approximately the same sense, and it too is not appropriate outside dialogue.

beside, besides   In modern usage *beside* is usually a preposition: *a hut beside* (next to) *the road; a small contribution beside* (in comparison with) *yours. Besides* is also a preposition: *contributed a great deal besides* (in addition to) *that; had few friends besides* (except for) *us. Besides* is an adverb in these examples: *He wants to do this besides* (in addition; also). *I was tired; besides* (moreover; furthermore) *I had done my share. She cleaned her room but did very little besides* (otherwise; else). See also **along with.**

best, better   As adjectives and adverbs, these are the comparative (*better*) and superlative (*best*) forms of

good and *well*. *Better* is the proper word to indicate superiority of one with respect to another (where only two are present): *The house is better* (adjective) *than ours. She dances better* (adverb) *than Sue. Best* is used to indicate pre-eminence in a group of three or more: *the best house on the block; dances best of all the chorus members. Best* is sometimes used in the sense of foremost to indicate not necessarily the position of one person or thing but of those in the front rank: *the ten best films of the year.* A less acceptable usage is that of *better* adverbially in the sense of more: *a distance better than a mile; spoke for better than a half-hour.* This is not confined to informal, but is less appropriate than *more* to formal writing.

between, among   Of this pair of prepositions, *between* is always the choice when only two persons or things serve as objects: *distinguish between right and wrong. Among* precedes three or more when they are considered collectively and no close relationship is indicated: *distribute food among the poor; a custom among the rich; life among the lowly.* When more than two are involved, some authorities invariably prescribe *among,* but even more recommend the use of *between* in certain of such examples. *Between* is also the choice when the objects number more than two and when they are considered individually and in a close working relationship: *a treaty between four nations.* Thus *between* is appropriate to terms such as treaty, pact, agreement, and discussion.

between . . . and   When *between* is used with two objects to indicate choice, *and* is the proper connective of the objects: *choose between luxury and integrity* (not *luxury or integrity*).

between each, between every   A usage common in speech but better avoided in writing is that employing *between* before *each* or *every* and a singular noun: *a rest between each class; cheese with paper between every slice.* Make it *after each class;* or *between classes, between the slices;* or *between each class (slice) and the next.*

between you and me   In this construction, the second pronoun is invariably *me,* not *I.* Both pronouns must be in the objective case. *Between you and I* is a very common error, sometimes a genteelism resorted to by those who think that *I* is somehow a finer or "more correct" word than *me.* But *between you and I* is still an error, and the attempt at refinement is misguided.

biannual, biennial   *Biannual* is the equivalent of semiannual (happening twice each year). The three meanings of the adjective *biennial* are: lasting or living for two years; happening every second year; having a normal life cycle of two years.

bid   The noun is well established on all levels of usage in a sense popularized by journalism: an effort

or a striving. Thus, *a bid to restore harmony in a political party; a bid for the nomination.*

The following examples illustrate the past tense and past participle of the verb in various senses: (to direct; command) *bade him leave* and *had bidden,* or *bid, him leave;* (to utter) *bade her good-by* and *has bidden,* or *bid, her good-by;* (to summon) *bade him to the court* and *has bidden* or *bid him;* (card games) *bid four clubs* and *has bid four clubs;* (to offer) *bid $500 for the vase* and *had bid $500;* (to seek to win something; strive) *bid for the governorship* and *has bid for it.*

bimonthly The only acceptable sense is that signifying every two months—once every two months. *Semimonthly* describes what occurs or is issued twice a month.

bite The past participle of the verb is *bitten* or *bit,* but only *bitten* is now standard in the passive voice: *She was bitten* (not *bit*) *by a snake.*

biweekly The word describes what happens every two weeks. *Semiweekly* has the sense of twice a week.

biyearly This term is applied to something occurring or issued every two years. *Semiyearly:* happening twice a year.

blame for, blame on See "Picking a Preposition."

blanch, blench *Blanch* refers to whitening or becoming pale; *blench,* to drawing back or flinching.

blatant, flagrant Applied to what is offensive or evil, both adjectives stress conspicuousness. *Blatant* often implies loudness, bluster, or conduct that calls attention to itself through its force and crudity. Something *flagrant* calls attention to itself through its shocking violation of what is right and proper. *Blatant* stresses the mode of commission, and *flagrant* the nature or effect of the deed: *a blatant appeal to prejudice; blatant huckstering of a candidate; a flagrant miscarriage of justice.*

blink See "Picking a Preposition."

bloc, block The first of these nouns is limited to the political sense of a group or coalition united by a common purpose. *Block* less often expresses that sense and has many others as well.

blond, brunet As adjectives, these may be applied to both sexes. As nouns they are usually restricted to males. *Blonde* and *brunette,* as nouns and adjectives, are applied only to females.

boast The verb, in its transitive sense, to take pride in possessing, is well established but distasteful to some through its association with the primary sense of *boast:* *boasted one of the best-equipped laboratories.*

born, borne See **bear.**

both In all its usages, *both* is limited to two. In the following example it should be deleted: *famous in both America, Europe, and the Far East. Both* is loosely used for *each* in the following: *Both criticized the other. An image was projected on both halves of the screen* (make it *on each half* or *images on both halves*).

The phrase *the both* should be avoided. In the following, delete *the: congratulated* (*the*) *both of us*.

Possessive constructions with *both* are illustrated by *the parents of both* and *the fault of both* (preferable to *both their parents, both their fault,* or *both's fault*).

For combinations in which *both* is used redundantly, see "Redundant Expressions."

bourgeois, bourgeoise, bourgeoisie The last of these terms is the collective noun signifying the middle class. *Bourgeois* is applied to a single member of that class; it is also the adjective that describes someone or something considered typically middle-class. *Bourgeoise* is the noun denoting a female member of the middle class, and the corresponding adjective applied to females.

brief, short The adjective *brief* is generally restricted to time (duration), whereas *short* is applied to both time and extent (physical measurement): *a short,* or *brief, visit; short hair; short pants; a short,* or *brief, introduction.*

bring, take *Bring* indicates movement toward the writer or speaker or person named, or toward a place usually occupied by him or her. *Take* expresses movement away from the writer, speaker, or person named, or from such a place. *Bring* implies *come here with* (to my place); *take* implies *go there with* (to another's place): *Bring proof of identity when you come. I took checks to the bank and brought back cash. She brought a friend to her house for dinner, and later took the friend home.*

The past tense and past participle of *bring* is *brought* —never *brung*.

Britain, Briton *Britain* is the country, the island comprising England, Scotland, and Wales. A *Briton* is a native of Britain.

broad, wide *Broad* is the usual choice when the noun it modifies is a surface or expanse considered as such: *broad shoulders; broad river. Wide* is used when the desired sense stresses space (distance across a surface) considered specifically (*a table five feet wide*) or indefinitely but emphatically: *The river is wide here.* Often the terms are interchangeable. In more figurative senses, the choice is governed solely by established idiom: *broad smile; wide mouth.*

broadcast The past tense and past participle is either *broadcast* or *broadcasted.*

broke, broken *Broke* is acceptable only as the past tense of *break.* The past participle is *broken: She broke her toe yesterday. She has broken her toe. The bone is broken.*

brunet, brunette See **blond, brunet**

bug The noun meaning a device for electronic eavesdropping has established itself on all levels of usage. The same is true of the verb, to install such a device in (a room).

bureaucrat, bureaucratic Though the noun and adjective are usually defined in neutral terms, these words are generally employed derogatorily with the implication of excessive rigidity, self-importance, or pettiness.

burgle The word is the informal variant of the verb *burglarize.*

bus The verb meaning to transport (schoolchildren) in a bus has established itself on all levels. The past tense and past participle is usually *bused* and the present participle *busing.* The practice of such transporting of children is also expressed by *busing.*

but One of the senses of *but,* both as a preposition and as a conjunction, is except. When an inflected word such as a pronoun follows *but* in such usage, the choice of a pronoun depends on the part of speech

one assigns *but*. When *but* and the word that follows it occur at the end of a sentence, *but* is generally construed as a preposition, and the word that follows is in the objective case: *No one saw it but me.* In a typical variant of that example, *but* is construed as a conjunction, and the pronoun agrees in case with the word that precedes *but: No one* (subject) *but I* (nominative) *saw it.*

The adverb *but,* meaning *no more than* or *only,* should not be used in a sentence containing another related negative: *It will last but a week* (not *won't last but a week*).

For a list of words with which *but* is redundant, see "Redundant Expressions." See also **cannot but; help.**

but that, but what These expressions, containing a redundant *but* and meaning *that* (conjunction), are typified by *There is no doubt but that* (or *but what*) *they will try.* They usually occur in sentences that begin with a negative and follow with the words *doubt* or *question.* The example with *but that* is found on all levels of usage, including formal; the variant employing *but what* is not acceptable on any level. Even the *but that* construction is objected to by many writers and editors on the ground that it is unnecessarily wordy. *There is no doubt that they will try* expresses the identical meaning.

cacao, coco, cocoa *Cacao* is the tree whose seed, cacao bean, is the source of chocolate, cocoa (the

powder and beverage), and cocoa butter. *Coco* is the tree whose fruit is the coconut.

callous, callus Only *callus* is the noun denoting thickened skin (and the noun is one of the most frequently misspelled words in the language). *Callous* is an adjective describing hands and feet having calluses, and something showing emotional hardness and insensitivity. *Callous* (verb) means to make or become callous. *Callus* (verb) means to develop a callus. Thus *callous hands; hands calloused* (or *callused*) *by hard work; callous disregard for others' rights.*

can, may Although the distinction is not often observed in everyday speech, these auxiliary verbs have different functions, especially in formal writing. *Can* is used to indicate ability to do something; *may,* to ask, grant, or deny permission to do it.

cannot but Though it is a form of double negative, this expression is acceptable in examples such as *We cannot but regret this action.* The same sense is expressed by *can but regret, can only regret, must regret,* and *cannot help regretting.*

canvas, canvass The material associated with sails, tents, and paintings is *canvas*. *Canvass* (noun and verb) has reference to the acts of examining, soliciting sales orders or votes, and surveying public opinion by polling.

capital, capitol Congress and state legislatures meet in the building called *capitol*. The town or city that is the seat of a government is a *capital*. The latter term also is the noun used in finance and accounting and in architecture; it is the adjective meaning chief and first-rate. *Capital letter* and *capital punishment* are written thus.

careen The verb expresses two senses: that of moving rapidly in an uncontrolled manner, lurching or swerving; and that of leaning and tilting, in nautical usage. In the first sense, a synonym is *career* (to move or run at full speed; go headlong).

casual, causal The adjective describing chance occurrence and informal or relaxed dress or behavior is *casual*. The adjective referring to a cause is *causal*.

celebrant, celebrator The second of these nouns denotes a participant in any celebration, more often nonreligious festivities: *New Year's Eve celebrators*. *Celebrant* is now widely found in that general sense, but the usage is disputed by some who would confine the word to a priest or other person participating in a religious ceremony or rite.

center See "Picking a Preposition."

ceremonial, ceremonious The first of these adjectives is applied principally to things, and the second to persons and things. In addition, *ceremonial* is essen-

tially a general, categorizing term pertaining to ceremony: *ceremonial garb; ceremonial occasion*. *Ceremonious* stresses formality and display, often in the unfavorable sense of pompousness.

certain The word is frequently qualified by *more* and *most: Nothing could be more certain than that*. This despite the fact that in most of its senses, *certain* seems to be an absolute term, not capable of comparison. In short, in usage there are degrees of certainty.

certainty, certitude Both nouns imply the absence of doubt. *Certainty* is applied to a clearly established fact or to the condition of being certain when one's belief is based on careful examination of evidence. *Certitude* is complete assurance which may be based more on faith than on objective grounds.

chafe, chaff Chafe is principally a verb meaning to wear away or irritate by rubbing, or to annoy or become annoyed. As a noun, *chaff* denotes grain, hay or straw, and trivial or worthless matter. As a verb, *chaff* means to make fun of good-naturedly.

chain reaction Use this term in the sense of events each of which induces or otherwise influences a successor. A chain reaction is more than a series of similar occurrences which have no such relationship as described.

chair, chairman   The verb *chair* is well established in the sense of installing (a person) in office. In the sense of presiding over (a meeting), *chair* and *chairman* (verb) are widely used in journalism but are less well established in more formal writing. A recent noun coinage, *chairperson*, is applied to a presiding officer of either sex, as an alternative to *chairman*.

chaperon   The noun is also spelled *chaperone*. The principal verb forms are illustrated by: *She chaperons her niece. She chaperoned; has* or *had chaperoned; is chaperoning; used to chaperon*.

childish, childlike   When applied to adults, *childish* is almost invariably a derogatory term; applied to children, the word lacks that connotation. *Childlike* is generally favorable on all age levels, suggesting endearing traits characteristic of children.

Chinaman   This is considered an offensive term used in place of the preferred a *Chinese* or *a Chinese man*.

chord, cord   *Chord* is the noun used in music and geometry and to denote emotional response. *Cord* is the term for string, electric wire, a raised rib on fabric, and a unit of measure for cut wood. Common terms in anatomy are *spinal cord* (or *chord*) and *vocal cord*.

cite, quote   Both verbs apply to making reference to something. To *cite* is to make mention, not necessarily by reproducing exact wording, which is the sense inherent in *quote*.

claim The verb is established on all levels in the sense of asserting or maintaining, a usage once disputed: *The air force claims that the battleship is obsolete. Claim,* meaning to demand as one's due, has always been good usage.

classic, classical These adjectives are interchangeable in some senses, including those dealing with ancient Greek and Roman culture, though *classical* is more frequent in that respect. *Classic* is invariably the choice to indicate, in a general way, highest rank.

clean, cleanse These are distinguished in usage when employed as verbs. *Clean* is applied literally to express the action of removing dirt, stain, or the like. *Cleanse* can be employed in that way, but more often means to free from sin or guilt.

clench, clinch Both mean to secure or hold. Transitively (employing a direct object), either can be used to indicate the fastening of nails or the like (though *clinch* is the more common) and in nautical usage (to fasten by knotting). One *clenches* an object held, the fingers or fists, and the jaws or teeth. One *clinches* (secures) a bargain, argument, or verdict. *Clinch* is also used, intransitively, in boxing in referring to the act of holding an opponent.

climactic, climatic *Climactic:* pertaining to or constituting a climax. *Climatic:* pertaining to climate (meteorological conditions).

close, near   Both describe proximity in time or space, but *close* is the better choice when immediate proximity is meant.

clue   This is the preferred spelling for the noun that denotes an aid in the solution of a problem or mystery, and also for the corresponding verb. The variant form, *clew,* also has other senses that are not in as widespread use.

coco, cocoa   See **cacao.**

cohort   Only in informal usage does the word mean a companion or associate. The well-established senses are a division of a Roman legion, and a group united in a struggle. Note that both refer to collectives, not to an individual.

collide, collision   In their literal (physical) senses, the words often refer to the coming together of persons and things that are both in motion. But the words are also acceptably applied to situations in which one person or thing is in motion and the other stationary.

company   Use it with a singular verb when the word means any of the following: a business association, companionship or society (*company that is congenial*), a military or naval unit, a theatrical troupe. When *company* denotes any group or assemblage or a group of guests, it may take a singular verb, with reference to a unified body, or a plural one, when the members are considered individually.

compare See "Picking a Preposition."

compare, contrast To *compare* is to examine in order to note similarities or differences, or to liken. To *contrast* is to set in opposition in order to show or emphasize differences. Like or unlike things can be *compared;* only essentially unlike things are *contrasted.*

complacent, complaisant *Complacent* most often describes one who is self-satisfied. It can also be applied to one who shows a desire to please, but that sense is more often expressed by *complaisant.* The corresponding nouns are *complacency* (less often *complacence*) and *complaisance.*

complected In formal usage, make it *complexioned: dark-complexioned. Complected* is a regional term, one identified with a geographic area and having identifiable differences from the standard form of a language.

complement, compliment *Complement* is something that completes; *compliment,* an act of expressing praise or courtesy. *Compliments* is the term for a greeting or remembrance. *Complimentary* is the term that describes something given free: *a complimentary ticket.*

complete In certain of the adjective's senses (having all necessary or normal parts, and concluded or ended), *complete* is an absolute term and therefore not capable of qualification by the words *more* or *most.*

When *complete* refers to comprehensiveness of scope or thoroughness of treatment, however, the word is not considered absolute and is acceptably used in examples such as *the most complete book on American judo*.

compose, comprise   *Compose* means to make up the constituent parts of something, and therefore to constitute or form it. *Comprise* means to consist of or be composed of. The whole comprises the parts; the parts do not comprise the whole, nor is the whole comprised of its parts: *The Union comprises fifty states. Fifty states compose* (or *constitute*) *the Union. The Union is composed of fifty states.*

comprehensible, comprehensive   Something *comprehensible* is capable of being understood. Something *comprehensive* is large in scope or content. In a lesser-used sense, *comprehensive* refers to one capable of understanding or perceiving easily or well.

comprise   See **compose, comprise.**

condition   In the sense of disease or ailment, the noun is acceptable on all levels of general usage: *a heart condition*. It is not a scientific term, however, and is better avoided in scientific writing.

confidant, confidante, confident   A *confidant* is a male person to whom secrets or private matters are confided. *Confidante* is the corresponding feminine

term. *Confident* is an adjective describing one who has confidence, self-assurance, or lack of doubt in a more general sense.

congenial, congenital   These are wholly unrelated adjectives. *Congenial* describes a person having one's tastes, habits, or temperament. Or the term is applicable to something agreeable. *Congenital* means existing at birth but not hereditary (*congenital deformity*) or having a specified character as if by nature: *a congenital liar.*

consensus of opinion   See "Redundant Expressions."

consequential   In the sense of being important or significant (that is, having consequence), this adjective is disputed by some modern usage authorities. The word is still used to mean self-important, pompous, or conceited, and, in its primary sense, to mean resultant (following as an effect, result, or conclusion). In that last-named sense, the word is synonymous with the adjective *consequent*. *Consequent* is the more common term and is the choice when resultant is meant: *Theft was charged, and the consequent investigation led to his dismissal. Consequential* sometimes implies an indirect or secondary result.

consider   When the verb means *to regard as* or *think to be* or *to believe,* it is followed by a direct object without *as: She considered him a fool.* The construc-

tion *consider . . . as* is used when the verb means to study or examine: *The documentary considers him as statesman and as writer.*

considerable, considerably *Considerable* is principally an adjective meaning fairly large in amount, extent, or degree (*a man of considerable means*), or worthy of consideration. *Considerably* is the corresponding adverb, and only this word can qualify a verb, as in *aided him considerably* (to a fairly great extent). Only *considerably* can qualify an adjective, as in *acted considerably strange.*

consist of, consist in See "Picking a Preposition."

consul, council, councilor, counsel, counselor *Consul* denotes an officer in the foreign service of a country. *Council* and *councilor* refer principally to a deliberative assembly (a city council or student council, for example), its work, and its membership. *Counsel* and *counselor* pertain chiefly to advice and guidance in general and to a person who provides it (a lawyer or camp counselor, for example).

contact As a verb meaning to get in touch with, *contact* is informal. On the level of formal writing, preferable alternatives include more specific verbs: write, telephone, and call, for example. As a noun meaning an acquaintance (who might be of use) or connection, *contact* is better established and appropriate to all levels.

contemporary   As an adjective, the word sometimes causes confusion over the period meant. When it is used in a context having no other reference to time, it indicates the period of the writer or speaker. When it appears in a context with persons or things of the past, the logical assumption may be that it pertains to the same past period, though often the intended meaning is otherwise. As a result, *modern* may be a better choice in some examples: *a Restoration play in modern dress.* Such wording is more explicit than *a Restoration play in contemporary dress.*

contemptible, contemptuous   *Contemptible* is applied to what deserves contempt. *Contemptuous* describes someone who manifests or feels contempt or scorn for another person or for a thing.

continual, continuous   *Continual* can refer to uninterrupted action but is now largely restricted to what is intermittent or repeated at intervals: *the baby's continual crying. Continuous* implies either action without interruption in time or unbroken extent in space: *a continuous vigil; a continuous slope of terrain.*

continuance, continuation, continuity   In law, *continuance* refers to postponement or adjournment to a future date. In other senses of the word, it is sometimes interchangeable with *continuation.* But *continuance* is the choice when reference is being made to duration of a condition: *the governor's continuance in*

office; a machine's continuance in service. Continuation has special reference to prolongation or resumption of action and to physical extension: *the continuation of a welfare program; continuation of the hallway to the rear of the house. Continuity* has the more special sense of that which is uninterrupted: *the continuity of bipartisan foreign policy preceding a change of administrations.*

contrast See **compare, contrast.**

convince, persuade The verbs, though related, are not identical in meaning. *Convince* means to persuade one decisively of a truth or a necessity. *Persuade* suggests winning over by reasoning, argument, or inducement. The words differ also in structural application. *Convince* is followed by *of* or a clause introduced by *that,* but not by an infinitive with *to. Persuade* is used with all three constructions: *He convinced her* (or *she was convinced*) *of his sincerity. He convinced her* (or *she was convinced*) *that she should leave. He persuaded* (not *convinced*) *her to leave.* The use of an infinitive following *convince* is an especially common error.

cope In formal usage, the verb is used with *with* to indicate the act of contending or striving, especially on even terms or with success. The object of the preposition *with* specifies the person or thing contended against: *cope with unhealthy living conditions.* Re-

cently the verb has been used increasingly, on an informal level, without the preposition *with;* no adversary is stated, and the sense is the general one of getting along well by overcoming obstacles: *To survive in business, one must be able to cope.*

cord See **chord, cord.**

corespondent, correspondent *Corespondent* denotes the partner of the defendant in a divorce suit; *corespondent,* one who communicates by means of letters or who writes for newspapers or periodicals.

council, counsel See **consul.**

couple When the noun denotes a man and woman united, it may be used with either a singular or plural verb, but the plural construction is more common. Whatever the choice, it should be expressed consistently within the context: *The couple are changing their voting residence* (or *is changing its*).

In the sense of *a few* or *several,* the noun is employed, informally, with *of: a couple of years.*

credible, creditable, credulous Someone or something *credible* is believable or worthy of confidence. A *creditable* person or thing deserves commendation. A *credulous* person is given to believing too readily and is therefore gullible; or the term can describe something arising from or characterized by too ready belief, such as an act or manner.

criteria This is the most common plural form of the noun *criterion*. It may not be used in any of these expressions: *a criteria; one criteria; the only* (sole) *criteria*. Use *criterion* in all these.

czar This is the form commonly found in American usage to denote a king or emperor, a tyrant or autocrat, and (informally) a chief or leader: *the energy czar*. *Tsar,* considered a more accurate transliteration of the Russian, is found in scholarly writing in reference to one of the Russian emperors.

dare A peculiarity of this verb is that it has two forms in the third-person singular, present tense indicative. The regular form is inflected, *dares: He dares to disagree*. The other is uninflected, *dare,* which occurs mainly in interrogative and negative constructions employing an infinitive without *to* or an unstated but understood infinitive: *Dare he disagree* (or *Does he dare disagree*)? *He dare not.*

The form *dare say* (or *daresay*) is usually followed by a clause without an introductory conjunction: *I dare say she regretted it.*

dastardly The adjective stresses the idea of cowardice, and is loosely used when it is applied to any reprehensible act that is not cowardly.

data The noun is plural in form. The singular is *datum,* denoting a fact or proposition. In its most common meaning, the collective *data* refers to infor-

mation, especially that organized for analysis or used as the basis for decision-making. As a collective, *data* is capable of being construed as both a singular and a plural term; it is followed by both plural and singular verbs in modern usage: *These data are inconclusive. This data is inconclusive.* The example with a plural verb is more appropriate to a formal level.

deadly, deathly As adjectives, these are distinguished in usage. *Deadly* is now largely confined to what causes death or extreme distress: *a deadly disease; deadly boredom. Deathly* is applied to what resembles or suggests death: *deathly silence; deathly pallor.* As adverbs, *deadly* means to an extreme (*deadly earnest*) and *deathly* means extremely or very: *deathly afraid.* Idiom governs the choice in these related adverbial senses.

debut Use it as a noun only. The verb usage (*a company that debuts its new models; a television series that debuts tonight*) is not well established.

defective, deficient *Defective* describes that which has a discernible fault, and is therefore primarily concerned with quality. *Deficient*, followed by *in*, is applied to what has insufficiency or incompleteness, and is therefore a quantitative term associated with *deficit*.

definite, definitive Both refer to the condition of being defined precisely or set forth explicitly. *Definitive*, moreover, is applied to what is unalterably final, a sense that *definite* does not have. A *definite* decision

is precise and unequivocal; a *definitive* decision is, in addition, usually beyond change or appeal.

delusion, illusion   A *delusion* is a false belief, held without reservation, that comes from self-deception, the imposition of another person, or mental disorder. An *illusion* is a false impression that may result from faulty observation, wishful thinking, or false perception that one eventually recognizes as false—or that one knows all along is false, as in the case of a magician's tricks (also called *illusions*) or the images in a carnival fun-house mirror (*optical illusions*). *Illusion* suggests what is transitory; *delusion* more often portends disadvantage or harm.

depend   When the word indicates condition or contingency, it is always followed by *on* or *upon: The incumbent is the favorite, but it depends on how heavy the vote is.* Especially in written usage, *on* must not be omitted in such an example.

deprecate, depreciate   The primary sense of *deprecate* is to express disapproval of; to protest or plead against. In one sense, *depreciate* means to make (someone or something) seem less; to belittle. No doubt because the words look so much alike, they have been subject to confusion, and *deprecate* is now often found in examples expressing the approximate meaning of *depreciate,* often with reference to mild self-belittlement or self-effacement: *deprecated her own contribution; a self-deprecating* (or *self-depreca-*

tory) *manner.* Such use of *deprecate* is disputed, though common, and a safer course is to write *played down,* or *depreciated, her contribution; a self-effacing* or *self-depreciatory manner.*

dessert, desert *Dessert* has only the sense of last course of a meal. *Desert* denotes an arid region and that which is deserved, as in *just deserts.* As such, these are nouns. *Desert* is also a verb synonymous with forsake, leave, and abandon.

die In assigning a cause of death, the usual construction is *die of* or *as a result of: died of* (not *from*) *heart disease.*

different from, different than See "Picking a Preposition."

dilemma In careful usage the word should be applied only to a situation that permits choice between two equally balanced alternatives. Usually the choices are equally undesirable; less often *dilemma* refers to a hard choice between attractive courses. The word denotes a predicament that seemingly defies a satisfactory solution, not just any predicament or difficult problem.

direct, directly The two adverbs are interchangeable when they mean *in a straight line,* or *not deviating from a course* (*went direct,* or *directly, to my home*) and when the sense is that of *without anyone or any-*

thing intervening (direct, or *directly, from wholesaler to buyer).* When the meaning is either *exactly* or *at once,* only *directly* is possible.

discomfit, discomfiture   The verb and corresponding noun were originally confined to the senses of defeat and frustration. In modern usage they are more often applied to examples in which the prevailing sense is merely that of discomfort, disconcert, uneasiness, or confusion.

discover, invent   Something that is *discovered* was in existence before a person became the first to find or learn of it. Examples of discovered things are countries, bodies of water and other geographic features, deposits of precious metals, the elements studied in chemistry and physics, and scientific laws and truths. Something that is *invented,* like the typewriter and Braille system, did not have prior existence. *Invent,* therefore, may be equated with *create.*

disinterested, uninterested   *Disinterested* means lacking self-interest and bias: *approached the problem as a disinterested observer, desirous only of determining facts.* One who has no concern with a subject and is therefore indifferent to it is *uninterested,* not *disinterested.* The distinction, still valued by most usage authorities despite the blunting of it by common practice, is that between impartiality (*disinterested*) and indifference (*uninterested*).

dissociate, dissociation   These are the usual forms, used interchangeably with *disassociate* and *disassociation*.

distinct, distinctive   *Distinct* applies to what is clear-cut, and *distinctive* to what sets a person or thing apart from others. A *distinct* sound is readily heard, whereas a *distinctive* sound is both that and unlike others. *Distinct* speech is clear; *distinctive* speech calls attention to the style of delivery. *Distinct* organizations are separate from each other or one another; *distinctive* organizations have qualities that set each apart from all others.

dive   The past tense of the verb is either *dived* or *dove*. *Dived* is the more common in formal writing. The past participle is *dived*. Examples are: *They dived (or dove) into the water. After the contestants had dived from four platforms, their efforts were graded.*

done   As an adjective meaning finished, this word is often found in speech or informal writing, though not confined to that level. In formal writing, *finished* or *completed* is usually preferable. Sometimes this meaning of *done* is not made clear in a given sentence; the word is capable of being construed as a form of *do*, expressing action, and confusion results: *The work will be done next year.* The intended sense (completed or finished) may not come through, and the reader may assume that the work will begin, as well as end,

next year. *Finished* or *completed* is preferable in such examples.

don't   This contraction is not acceptable when used with a subject in the third-person singular. *Doesn't* is required: *It doesn't happen often. He* (or *she*) *doesn't really care. Smith doesn't know.*

doubt, doubtful   Clauses introduced by *that, whether,* and *if* often follow the verb and noun *doubt* and the adjective *doubtful: We doubt that the deadline will be met. It is doubtful whether the work will be completed on time.* In sentences having a negative sense or in the form of questions, what is expressed is not doubt but a denial of it; in such examples the clause almost invariably begins with *that: I have no doubt that he will succeed. Do you really doubt that he will succeed?* When the writer wants to express genuine doubt, *whether* and *if* are the better choices (and *whether* is usually considered better than *if* in formal writing): *It was considered doubtful whether the terms of the contract could be fulfilled.* In positive statements, such as the last example, use of *that* (for *whether* or *if*) conveys the sense of unbelief rather than genuine doubt. Reread the example, employing *that,* and note how the change of a single word seems to alter the sense—from uncertainty to unbelief. See also **but that, but what.**

doubtless, undoubtedly   *Doubtless* and *no doubt* are

rather weak terms for expressing certainty or assurance, since they can also express presumption or probability. *Undoubtedly* and *without doubt* are much stronger; they convey only certainty and conviction. Contrast these examples: *He will doubtless leave. He will undoubtedly leave. No doubt she will be tired after the trip. Without doubt she will be tired.*

dove   See **dive.**

dozen   In modern usage, *dozen* is generally not followed by *of,* except when reference is made to a quantity that is part of a larger, specified quantity: *a dozen eggs; a dozen of those eggs; a dozen of her closest associates.* When the plural *dozens* is employed in the sense of an indefinitely large quantity of something specified, it is followed by *of: He showed his bravery on dozens of occasions.*

drag   The past tense and past participle is *dragged,* not *drug.*

drunk, drunken   As adjectives, these have separate functions. *Drunk* is used predicatively after a form of the verb *be: She was always drunk.* In contrast, *drunken* is employed attributively (before a noun): *a drunken scoundrel; a drunken driver; drunken driving.* The combinations *drunk driver* and *drunk driving* have become stock expressions, especially in certain varieties of journalism, but they are not acceptable in serious writing on a formal level.

due to   This phrase has two related meanings; in expressing them, it has different functions, one of which is always acceptable and the other of which is disputed. When *due to* means attributable to or caused by, *due* is a predicate adjective that follows a form of *be* or another linking verb: *His concern for her safety was largely due to his own lack of confidence.* Such examples are always acceptable. When *due to* means *because of,* the phrase functions adverbially to set forth a reason for, or cause of, some action expressed by a nonlinking verb: *The machine broke down due to faulty maintenance.* Constructions of the latter kind are very common (*game called due to rain*), but this adverbial usage is better avoided in formal writing. Alternative ways of expressing the same sense include the substitution of *because of, on account of, owing to,* or *through.* For example: *The machine broke down because of faulty maintenance.* Or such examples can be rephrased by employing the adjectival construction: *The breakdown was due to faulty maintenance.*

On any level of usage, when *due to* means because of, the unnecessarily wordy expression *due to the fact that* should be avoided; *the fact that* adds nothing.

dye   The present participle is *dyeing: He is still dyeing his hair these days.*

each   When the pronoun is used as a subject, it takes a singular verb in formal usage: *Each is involved to*

some extent. The verb is also singular when *each* is followed by *of* and a plural noun or pronoun: *Each of the men was implicated.* When related pronouns or pronominal adjectives occur in such sentences, they are likewise singular in form: *Each of the four is liable for his own part in the shady transaction.* (Informally, especially in speech, such an example might be phrased *each . . . are liable for their own part.*)

When *each* occurs after a plural subject with which it is in apposition, the verb is generally plural: *They each need expert counsel. The company president and treasurer each have retained special legal staffs.* In examples having compound subjects, such as the second, a singular verb sometimes occurs: *each has retained a special legal staff.*

each and every   As is noted in the section headed "Redundant Expressions," *each and every* is a wasteful expression, and it is preferable to use either *each* or *every* singly. When *each and every* is employed in that form, however, it takes a singular verb and related modifying words: *Each and every girl is expected to do her part.* See also **between each, between every.**

each other, one another   In practice, these expressions are used interchangeably in most examples, and acceptably so. Some grammarians and usage authorities make a distinction, however. They recommend *each other* when the reference is to only two persons or things, and *one another* when more than two are

present: *The boxers pounded each other furiously for two rounds. Employees in such a large company regard one another impersonally.*

The possessive forms of the expressions are written as follows: *each other's* (not *others'*); *one another's.*

eager   See **anxious, eager.**

earthly, earthy   Both adjectives express relationship to the earth. *Earthly,* however, is most often a categorizing term used to distinguish something from what is heavenly or divine: *earthly considerations.* Or the term may mean conceivable or possible: *no earthly reason for such unreasonable delay* (that is, no reason on earth). *Earthy* distinguishes something from what is spiritual. It applies to what is down to earth in the more special sense of being concerned with the satisfaction of material wants and the more primitive human instincts: *earthy pleasures; earthy creature* (that is, uninhibited).

easily, easy   *Easily* is only an adverb, whereas *easy* is principally an adjective. As an adverb, *easy* occurs for the most part in the expression *easy come, easy go,* and informally in *go easy on, take it easy,* and *easier said than done.* Otherwise *easy* and the comparative form *easier* are not acceptable in examples such as: *The lock works easily. The matter can be settled easily. Your problem is more easily resolved than mine.*

economic, economical In usage, *economical* is largely restricted to the sense of not wasteful; prudent in management: *an economical way to recycle tin*. *Economic* is applied more generally to matters of economics (the science), finance, and to the necessities of life: *economic goals; an economic formula*.

effect See **affect, effect**.

egoism, egotism The two nouns are closely related, and in some examples either is possible. In their primary senses, however, they are not identical. *Egoism* is the tendency to think or act with only oneself and one's personal interests in mind. *Egotism* is the tendency to speak or write of oneself excessively and boastfully. *Egoism* is related to self-interest, as is the corresponding noun *egoist*. *Egotism* is related to conceit, as are the corresponding *egotist, egotistic,* and *egotistical*.

either Particularly in formal writing, the pronoun *either,* used as a subject, takes a singular verb and related pronouns or pronominal adjectives: *Either is capable of reversing its course automatically*. The rule applies when *either* is followed by *of* and a plural noun or pronoun: *Either of the unmanned space vehicles is capable of reversing its course*. The singular verb prevails also when the sentence has a negative sense or is in the form of a question: *We doubt that either of them is really practicable. Is either of them practicable?* In informal speech, examples such as the

last two often employ plural verbs.

As pronoun and adjective, *either* is preferably limited to constructions specifying two persons or things: *Take either* (one of two). *Either course* (of two) *presents difficulty*. Although *either* sometimes occurs in sentences involving more than two, *any* or *any one* (written as two words) is preferable to *either* in them. The conjunction *either,* used in combination with *or,* is likewise most appropriate to statements involving two alternative elements. The elements themselves may consist of more than one component, in which case the components, taken together, have the sense of one: *The consent of either the patient or a parent or guardian is required.*

either . . . or When the alternative elements within an *either . . . or* construction are both singular, the verb governed by the elements is singular: *Either coffee or tea is served.* When the elements are both plural, the verb is plural: *Either apples or oranges are suitable.* When the elements differ in point of number, the verb agrees in number with the element to which it is nearer, or with the final component of the nearer element: *Either coffee or soft drinks are available. Either soft drinks or beer is provided. Either the patient or the patient's parents or legal guardian is required to sign a statement of consent.* When the nearer element is a personal pronoun, the verb agrees with it. *Either Harry or I have the necessary authority.*

Either he or I am authorized to grant permission. Examples with personal pronouns, such as the last, often produce clumsy or unnatural-sounding phrasing, and a more desirable course is to rephrase by discarding the *either . . . or* formula: *He and I are both authorized to grant permission.*

When possessive pronouns or pronominal adjectives appear in *either . . . or* constructions, they agree in number with the verb: *I can provide the necessary money if either Frank or Jim has forgotten to bring his* (not *theirs*).

elder, eldest, older, oldest As forms of adjectives, *elder* and *eldest* refer only to persons; *older* and *oldest* can refer to both persons and things. *Elder* and *eldest* are now used only attributively (before a noun or proper noun), unlike *older* and *oldest: He is older than I. She is the oldest member. Elder* and *eldest* are further limited in usage to references to members of a specific family or business establishment, as indications of age or seniority: *the elder Harris; my eldest brother; the elder partner. Elder* is always the form used in the term *elder statesman.*

elegy, eulogy An *elegy* is a poem written to mourn one who is dead. A *eulogy* is a tribute to one recently deceased, and usually has the form of an oration.

elicit, illicit These merely sound alike. *Elicit* (verb) means to bring out or draw forth: *questions designed to elicit straightforward responses. Illicit* (adjective)

is applied to what is improper, in the sense of being not sanctioned by custom (*an illicit love affair*) or illegal (*illicit traffic in drugs*).

else The possessive forms of combinations with *else* are usually written: *anyone* (or *anybody*) *else's; everyone* (or *everybody*) *else's; no one* (or *nobody*) *else's; someone* (or *somebody*) *else's.* Both *who else's* (followed by a noun) and *whose else* are in use, but not *whose else's: Who else's work might it be? Whose else could it be?*

elude See **allude, elude.**

emend See **amend, emend.**

emigrate, immigrate, migrate Persons *emigrate from* a country or region when they leave it to settle in another. Persons *immigrate to* a country or region upon moving and settling there. Persons, and certain birds and animals, are said to *migrate from* one place, an old home, or to *migrate to* another, a new home. The corresponding nouns are *emigrant, immigrant,* and *migrant.*

eminent, imminent Someone or something *eminent* towers over others, either literally (*an eminent building*) or in the sense of achievement, rank, or talent (*an eminent physician; eminent discoveries*). Something that is *imminent* is about to occur: *the imminent arrival of fresh combat forces.*

enormity This noun denotes outrageousness or great wickedness, or an offense that reflects such qualities: *the enormity of an assassination plot.* Mere size or physical extent is not conveyed by *enormity* but by words such as *enormousness* or *hugeness.*

enquire, enquiry These are variant forms of *inquire* and *inquiry,* which are the more common spellings.

en route The term, meaning *on the route,* is written thus.

ensure See **assure, ensure, insure.**

enthuse This verb, a back-formation from *enthusiasm,* is for informal use only: *She enthused* (showed enthusiasm) *over the rise in membership. She was even more enthused* (made more enthusiastic) *by the caliber of the newcomers.* More acceptable wording is indicated within the parentheses.

envelop, envelope *Envelop* is the verb: *enemy forces enveloping the peninsula; mist that envelops the hilltops.* The noun is *envelope* with a plural form *envelopes.*

enviable, envious Someone or something *enviable* arouses envy through being highly desirable: *an enviable record.* Someone who is *envious* feels or shows envy: *envious friends plotting his downfall.*

envy, jealousy The nouns name qualities that are related but not identical. *Envy* is discontent and re-

sentiment arising over one's awareness of another's possessions, which one covets. *Jealousy,* which has wider range, may denote bitterness arising from rivalry, a fearful or suspicious attitude stemming from possible loss of position or affection, or close watchfulness that reflects overpossessive or oversolicitous tendencies.

epithet   In its primary sense, the noun means a term used to characterize a person or thing. The term may not be derogatory. President Kennedy, for example, spoke of "that seemingly unending war to which we have given the curious epithet 'cold.'" Increasingly, however, *epithet* is used, without elaboration or description, to convey a much narrower meaning: an abusive or contemptuous word or phrase employed to describe a person. This usage is still in dispute, though it is now common, and a surer way to express the narrower meaning is to say *shouted abuse,* or *words of contempt,* instead of *shouted epithets,* which actually tells nothing about the nature of what is being shouted.

equable, equitable   *Equable* can describe something, such as a climate, that is steady and unvarying, or something, such as a person's nature, that is tranquil. *Equitable* is applied to something, such as a settlement or arrangement, that is impartial and just.

equal   By definition, the adjective *equal* seemingly defies comparison, in the sense of being preceded by

the words *more* or *most*. To all appearances it is an absolute term. In usage, however, it is often qualified by *more* and *most,* and acceptably so: *a more equal distribution of the burden.* As used thus, *equal* is equated with *equitable* and *nearly equal.*

In a somewhat different form of comparison, *equal* sometimes creates other problems. See "Faults of Omission."

equally as　See "Redundant Expressions."

equitable　See **equable, equitable.**

errata　This plural noun, from Latin, is regularly employed in the collective sense of a list of errors. The word is nevertheless construed as plural in choice of a verb and when preceded by an adjective: *these errata are . . .*

escalate　For better or worse, the war in Vietnam established this verb, in both transitive and intransitive usages, in the sense related to increasing, enlarging, or intensifying: *Both sides in the conflict escalated the fighting. The war has escalated with each succeeding year.* The antonym (word having an opposite sense) is *de-escalate,* not *descalate.*

escape　When the verb means to break out of confinement, it is used with *from: He escaped from the prison* (not *escaped the prison*). In other senses, *escape* is used without *from: escaped harm; a clue that escaped him at the time; a sigh that escaped her lips.*

especial, especially, special, specially *Special* and *specially* are the more general of these pairs and therefore have wider use. They are always the choice when the desired sense is merely the opposite of ordinary or routine, without particular emphasis: *dress appropriate to special occasions; personnel specially trained for such emergencies. Especial* and *especially* are often preferred to indicate pre-eminence or exceptional degree: *an especial friend; especially bright children.* Here *special friend* would be somewhat weaker; *specially,* used with reference to *bright children,* would not be in accord with established idiom. *Specially* is used most often to modify a verb form, such as *trained,* rather than a word, such as *bright,* that is only an adjective. *Especial* and *especially* are the choice to express individuality or a particular circumstance: *This is for her especial benefit. Smith especially is at fault. Prudence is the best policy, especially now.* In these last examples, *special* could replace *especial* in modifying *benefit,* though the substitution would make the desired sense less strong; but *specially* could not replace *especially* in the two sentences that follow, or in like examples.

et al. The abbreviation meaning *and others* is written thus, with a period after the second element only. The term is very useful in bibliographies, and also is employed in some special areas, including legal writing. Otherwise it has rather little use in more general formal writing, and as a rule should not be used as a

substitute for the words *and others* (aside from listings such as bibliographies). Occasionally it is employed for humorous effect: *Mencken et al.* The abbreviation is applied only to persons, not to things.

etc. This abbreviation stands for *unspecified things of the same class*. It is not appropriate to formal writing in general but is found in technical reporting and business correspondence. When it is used anywhere, *etc.* should suggest a reasonably clear idea of what additional things the writer has in mind; it should never be a lazy way of finishing a thought whose meaning the reader can only guess. The abbreviation should be written once, not as *etc., etc.* or as *and etc.* (since *and* is inherent in the meaning).

ethical, moral Both describe proper human behavior, but from somewhat different points of view. *Ethical* implies a philosophical standpoint and stresses more objectively defined, though essentially idealistic, standards such as those applied to the conduct of doctors, lawyers, and people in business. *Moral* is applied especially to sexual conduct and suggests a rather subjective code of right and wrong.

eulogy See **elegy, eulogy.**

ever The word is usually hyphenated in combinations used attributively (before nouns): *ever-rising waters; ever-growing problems.* But no hyphen is used when such combinations come after verbs: *waters*

were ever rising; problems that are ever growing in scope. See also **rarely.**

ever so often, every so often   These expressions have different meanings and are therefore not interchangeable. *Ever so often* is the equivalent of frequently; repeatedly. *Every so often* means occasionally; now and then.

everybody, everyone, every one   When they are used as subjects, the pronouns *everybody* and *everyone* take singular verbs in formal writing, and accompanying personal pronouns and pronominal adjectives are correspondingly singular in form: *Everybody raised his* (or *her*) *hand in hearty approval. Everyone is entitled to sufficient time to make up his own* (or *her* or *his* or *her*) *mind.* Informally, especially in speech, *their hand* (or *hands*) and *their own mind* (or *minds*) appear in such examples, but formal writing requires a consistently singular construction. Objection is sometimes taken to the masculine *his* when it refers to a group including both sexes. *His* can be justified in examples such as these, both on the ground of long usage and on the ground that it is used indefinitely with reference to the indefinite pronouns *everybody* and *everyone.* Use of *his and her* is a possible solution to the problem of accounting for both sexes, though a rather cumbersome one. Where the writer has strong feeling against use of *his,* perhaps the best solution is to rephrase, abandoning *everybody, everyone,* and

such other problem words as *anyone* and *someone:*
*All hands were raised in hearty approval. One is en-
titled to sufficient time to make such a decision.*

Everyone and the two-word form *every one* are distinguished in usage. *Everyone* is the choice when
everybody can be substituted for it—when the sense
is that of every person considered indefinitely: *Everyone was aware of her presence. Every one* refers to
each person or thing of a specific group; it is typically
followed by *of*, or else *of* and an object are implied:
Every one of them is at fault (or *Every one is to
blame*). *There were four choices, every one of which
presented serious problems.*

everyplace, every place The adverb *everyplace*, written as a single word, is an informal term for *everywhere;* in formal usage, make it *everywhere. Every
place*, written as two words, has a different meaning—
that of every one of a group of places specified or
understood: *Every place was taken. We shall try to
visit every place that the book mentions.* The two-
word form is acceptable on all levels of usage.

every way Write it as shown, not as one word: *We
found something difficult about every way she mentioned.*

everywhere This is the only acceptable spelling—
not *everywheres.*

except When the word means with the exclusion of,

other than, or but, it is construed as a preposition. A pronoun following *except,* used in that meaning, is therefore in the objective case: *No one except me was affected. Every member of the committee was implicated except him.*

As a conjunction, *except* can mean *if it were not for the fact that.* In that sense, especially in formal writing, *except* is followed by *that: She would have accepted the invitation, except that the trip was very expensive.* See also **accept, except.**

except, excepting As prepositions, both words mean excluding. In theory, *excepting* can replace *except* in all examples expressing that meaning, including those in the preceding entry: *No one excepting me was affected. Every member was implicated excepting him.* In practice, in modern usage, *except* is almost always used in examples of that kind. But *excepting* is still employed in negative constructions to the exclusion of *except: All employees, not excepting part-time ones, must be familiar with the emergency procedures.*

exceptionable, exceptional These are often confused, and unfortunately so, since they have quite different meanings. That which is *exceptionable* is open or liable to objection: *He insisted that there was nothing exceptionable about the requirement he set.* That which is *exceptional* is uncommon (out of the ordinary): *The job calls for exceptional skills, but there was nothing exceptional in her performance.*

exodus In careful usage, the term applies only to a departure of a large number of people.

expect As a synonym for the verbs *presume* or *suppose*, *expect* is used informally: *We will hear from them soon, I expect.* This usage is characteristic of speech. It is related to, but different from, *expect* used in *We expect to hear from them soon.* The latter example, appropriate to all levels, including formal, employs *expect* in the primary sense of looking forward to the probable occurrence of (something).

eye The present participle of the verb is either *eyeing* or *eying: He is said to be eyeing* (or *eying*) *an ambassadorship as a possible reward.*

farther, farthest, further, furthest In examples dealing with literal (actual) distance, *farther* and *farthest* are the better choices, though *further* and *furthest* are also possible: *The arrow traveled farther* (adverb) *than we expected. The ride is farther* (adjective) *than I thought. This is the farthest* (adjective) *point from the center of the city.* Where figurative extent is involved (opposed to measurable distance), *further* and *furthest* are preferable and more common, though *farther* and *farthest* cannot be ruled out: *further from the truth; the furthest flight of the imagination. Further* is more common than *farther* when they are used as adjectives meaning additional: *no further reason for delay. Further* and *furthest,* as adverbs, express the

sense of *to a greater extent* or *more: went further in debt; carried the investigation furthest.* As adverbs, both *further* and *farther* may be employed with the meaning of in addition or furthermore, but *further* is much more common: *She disliked the idea in general and felt, further, that this example was especially ill-timed.* A major distinction between *farther* and *further* is that only *further* is a verb, meaning to help the progress of; to forward; advance: *discoveries that further the cause of preventive medicine.*

Note that the related word *furthermore,* meaning moreover or in addition, is always spelled thus, not *farthermore.*

fatal, fateful Although there is considerable overlapping of meaning between these adjectives, usage has given them rather well-differentiated roles. In the following examples, the word given is the more common one in that sense, though by definition the other could be substituted: *a fatal wound* (causing death; mortal); *something fatal to our hopes* (causing ruin; disastrous); *a fateful decision* (affecting one's destiny). *Fateful* is the choice when the sense is related clearly to the operation of fate: *no escaping a fateful conclusion* (seemingly controlled by fate; predetermined); *a fateful sign* (full of significance; in particular, foreboding or ominous).

fault Like *author,* this word is now widely employed

as a transitive verb after a lengthy period of disuse. As such, *fault* means to find a fault in (a person or something pertaining to the person); to criticize or blame. Like that of *author,* this usage is disliked by many writers and editors, though it has long had dictionary sanction.

feasible, possible *Possible* is the more general of these adjectives; it describes what is capable of happening or existing. *Feasible* is applied to that which is capable of being accomplished or brought about; in that sense the word implies practicability and applicability to need or purpose. *Feasible* also can describe what is capable of being utilized or dealt with successfully, in which case it implies suitability.

feel The verb is followed by an adjective when the sense relates to a person's perception of his or her condition of being: *I was ill last week but now I feel different; today I feel strong again.* The adjectives *different* and *strong* describe the subject; *feel* serves as a linking verb. When the sense relates to having strong emotional involvement through an opinion or conviction, an adverb often follows: *She has always felt strongly about women's rights. He once agreed with her position, but he feels differently now.* In these examples, *strongly* and *differently* qualify *feel* with respect to degree and condition. See also **bad, badly.**

feel like This phrase is for informal usage: *did not feel like going to work; felt like a round of golf in-*

stead. In formal writing, the corresponding meaning is expressed by one of these: want; be in the mood for; have a desire for.

fellow Terms such as *fellow citizen, fellow student,* and *fellow worker* are written thus, as two words without hyphens. *Fellow* is an adjective in such expressions. The same rule applies to *fellow feeling, fellow servant,* and *fellow traveler. Fellow man* is written thus or as one word (no hyphen).

female, feminine *Female,* like *male,* is largely limited to classifying by sex: *the female population; female* (biological) *characteristics; female birth,* or *death, rate; female diseases. Feminine* is less frequently used as such a categorizing word: *the feminine lead in a play or film.* It often precedes nouns naming things considered characteristic of women (and thus corresponds to *masculine*): *feminine charm; a feminine taste for finery.* In grammar, *feminine* is always the term that describes words or forms classified as *female: feminine nouns such as "confidante" and "protégée."*

fewer, less Use *fewer* when referring to numbers or units considered individually and therefore capable of being counted or enumerated. Use *less* in references to collective quantity and to something abstract. For example, *fewer jobs, less opportunity; fewer teachers, less individual instruction. Fewer* is seldom misused but *less* often is, and tends to take over the functions

of both words. In the following examples, *less* should not replace *fewer* (though it often does in the hands of unskilled writers): *fewer people in a period of declining birth rates; no fewer than ten applicants seeking information; fourteen fewer seats in Congress.* *Less* is generally the choice in sentences setting forth periods of time, sums of money, and measures of distance, weight, and the like; here the sense is collective, even though the nouns qualified by *less* name things that can be counted or enumerated: *less than two months; less than forty years of age; less than $1,000; weighing less than 100 pounds.*

figure As a verb bearing on mathematics, *figure* is used formally when it means to calculate or compute: *figure the distance between two planets.* In several related usages, the verb is for informal writing only. Among them are *figure out* for solve or decipher, and *figure on* for depend on or expect: *figure on her to be a big help; figure on having sufficient time to finish the job.* Also informal is *figure* for conclude, believe, or predict (*figure that they may leave*), and *figure* for interpret or see: *figured him for a coward.* Informal, at best, is the expression *it figures* as the equivalent of it is to be expected: *It figures that Congress won't pass such a tax bill in an election year.*

finalize The verb has widespread use, almost invariably in quite formal settings. It is so roundly disliked by many writers, editors, and students of language,

however, that its users take what amounts to a calculated risk. The dislike stems from the word's association with coinages that suggest bureaucracy and self-importance. The meaning of *finalize,* moreover, is readily expressed by *complete, conclude, make final, put in final form,* or the like, most of which are no less economical.

fine The adverb *fine* occurs principally in compounds such as *fine-wrought* and *fine-cut* to express the sense of discriminatingly or minutely. As the equivalent of *very well,* as in *doing fine,* the adverb is for informal use only.

first, last In modern usage, the adjectives *first* and *last* almost invariably precede the numeral in collective expressions such as *the first three pages* and *the last two chapters.* There is an alternative way of expressing the same ideas: *the three first pages* and *the two last chapters.* The alternative way is the older one; it is still acceptable usage when only low numbers are employed. Especially in formal writing, however, this older form is now less desirable, for it occurs rather infrequently and tends to puzzle some readers, who are liable to confuse a reference such as *two last chapters* with the idea of two versions of the last chapter—that is, with alternative modes of presenting the same unit.

fit The past tense and past participle of the verb is *fitted* or *fit. Fitted* is the more common form, but

idiom is also a determining factor in making a choice to express different senses. The following examples illustrate the various meanings of the verb: *The suit fit (or fitted) him very well. The punishment fit (or fitted) the crime. The equipment was fitted to their needs. The training fitted her for the ordeal. They fitted him out for the journey. She fitted it into the last part of the program. He fitted the washer in the valve. The explanation fitted (or fit) in with the rest of the account.*

flagrant See **blatant, flagrant.**

flail, flay To *flail* is to thresh, beat, or wave (the arms, in particular). To *flay* is to strip off the skin of, plunder, or criticize savagely.

flair, flare *Flair* denotes natural talent or instinctive discernment. *Flare* is the term for a blaze of light and for a device that produces the light. Only *flare* is a verb: *The torches flared. The suggestion that she was malingering caused her to flare up.*

flammable, inflammable These are alike in meaning and interchangeable when they describe something actually capable of burning. But only *inflammable* can refer to a nature quickly or easily aroused to strong emotion. The popularity of *flammable* in literal usage is due to the feeling that the word expresses a warning more clearly than *inflammable,* which is sometimes mistaken for nonflammable or noncombustible. *Flam-*

mable is therefore especially appropriate in technical writing and where it serves as a warning (as a label).

flare See **flair, flare.**

flaunt, flout To *flaunt* something is to exhibit it ostentatiously: *flaunt power; flaunted her diamonds.* To *flout* is to show contempt for (something), to scorn or scoff at it. In examples dealing with showing disregard for laws, rules, and regulations, especially in a contemptuous way, *flaunt* is often misused for *flout: repeatedly flaunted the no-parking ordinance.* Only *flout* is acceptable in such examples.

flay See **flail, flay.**

flier, flyer The second is a variant spelling of *flier.* Both forms are in widespread use in most senses of the noun.

flounder, founder *Flounder* is the verb expressing clumsy movement. *Founder* refers to becoming disabled, collapsing or giving way, and sinking below the surface of a body of water.

flout See **flaunt, flout.**

flyer See **flier, flyer.**

folk, folks *Folk* is the singular and plural form when the noun denotes a people (ethnic group or race) and people of a specified group or kind: *city folk* (collective plural). The plural *folks* is informal and is applied to

one's relatives and to people in general: *Folks are a pretty good lot, all told.*

(as) follows The established and unchanging form of the expression preceding a listing is *as follows,* not *as follow.* This is true regardless of the grammatical number of the noun that comes before: *The text is as follows. The components of the remedy are as follows.* In such examples the subject of *follows* (singular) is construed as *it* unexpressed: *as it follows.*

foot *foot* (singular) and its plural *feet,* as units of measure, are distinguished in usage according to the following typical examples: *a six-foot man; a man six feet tall* (or *six feet in height*); *a two-foot space; a gap two feet wide; a ledge six feet below; a crevice about a foot above him.*

forbear, forebear As nouns, both denote an ancestor. Only *forbear* is a verb meaning to refrain or desist from or to be tolerant: *Despite much provocation, the police forbore* (or *have forborne*) *retaliating* or *forbore from retaliation.*

forbid This verb is used with an infinitive or a gerund to express the same idea: *forbid her to leave; forbid her leaving.* The common misuse, with *from,* should be avoided: *forbid her from leaving.* The usual past tense is illustrated by *they forbade.* The usual past participle is *forbidden: they have* (or *had*) *forbidden.*

forceful, forcible   *Forceful* describes what is characterized by or full of force and therefore effective: *a forceful argument. Forcible* is applied to what is accomplished by force: *forcible entry; forcible ejection.*

forebear   See **forbear, forebear.**

forecast   Constructions in past time are illustrated by *forecast,* or *forecasted, trouble; has forecast,* or *forecasted, trouble; trouble was forecast,* or *forecasted.*

forego, forgo   *Forego,* spelled only as given, is the verb meaning to precede or go before in time or place. *Forgo,* less often spelled *forego,* is the verb meaning to relinquish or abstain from: *forgo* (or *forego*) *worldly pleasures.*

foregoing   This is the adjective meaning just past; preceding; previously mentioned: *the foregoing statement.*

foregone conclusion   The expression for an end or result regarded as inevitable is written thus.

foremost   This can be applied to one person or thing to indicate undisputed leadership. Or the adjective can describe a small group regarded as representing the front rank, which permits expressions such as *the foremost writers* and *one of the foremost writers of the time.*

foresee The verb meaning to see or know beforehand is written thus. The corresponding noun is *foresight*.

foreswear See **forswear**.

foreword The noun meaning preface or introductory note is spelled thus.

forgo See **forego, forgo**.

former As a term corresponding to *latter,* use *former* only with reference to the first of two: *Paderewski and Hess were noted pianists, and the former* (Paderewski) *was also famous outside music.* When three or more occur in an enumeration, reference to the first should be by means of *the first* or *first-named.* Often it is more desirable to repeat the name of the indicated person or thing in such constructions, as an aid to the reader; especially if the second reference to the given person or thing is far from the first, such repetition will spare the reader the pause otherwise necessary to determine who or what is meant by *former* or *first-named.*

forswear This is the preferred spelling of the verb meaning to renounce, disavow, or swear falsely. The alternative form is *foreswear.*

fortuitous, fortunate *Fortuitous* is used only to describe something happening by accident or chance and thus unplanned. It does not mean fortunate or lucky.

A *fortuitous* thing is sometimes fortunate and sometimes not. To employ *fortuitous* in examples in which there is no clear indication of chance or accident is loose usage. *Fortunate* means occurring by good fortune or favorable chance, or having unexpected good fortune (and therefore lucky).

forward, forwards The adjective is always written *forward,* in all senses: *a forward cabin; forward movement; a forward* (presumptuous; bold) *person; a forward* (progressive) *country. Forward* is the usual form of the adverb (when the word follows a verb that it qualifies). But either *forward* or *forwards* is possible when the meaning is toward the front, or frontward: *Drive forward* (or *forwards*) *a bit.* In other adverbial senses, the only form is *forward: look forward to seeing you* (that is, toward the future); *came forward from obscurity* (into view or prominence).

founder See **flounder, founder.**

free The word is both an adjective and an adverb. The comparative and superlative forms are *freer* and *freest;* the corresponding forms for the adverb *freely* are *more freely* and *most freely.* The expression *for free* is a slang, and wordy, variant of *free.*

froze, frozen Froze is the past tense of *freeze,* and *frozen* the past participle: *The storm froze the citrus crops,* or *has frozen them. The crops were frozen.*

fulsome   Especially in the expression *fulsome praise,* this adjective is often misused as a synonym of full and abundant. In modern usage *fulsome* combines the idea of fullness or abundance with that of excess or insincerity. *Fulsome praise* is therefore praise so lavish that it has a false ring. In a related sense *fulsome* means loathsome or disgusting.

fun   A newer use of the word, as an adjective, is informal: *Mayor Lindsay called New York a fun city.*

further, furthest   See **farther, farthest.**

gage   See **gauge.**

gamut   In its most familiar sense, the word means the complete range of anything. The expression *run the gamut* should not be confused with *run the gantlet* (or *gauntlet*).

gantlet, gauntlet   These words are found most often in several stock expressions, of which *run the gantlet,* or *gauntlet,* is the most familar. In earlier times, as punishment a person was sometimes forced to run between two lines of men facing each other and armed with sticks or other weapons. The two lines made up the *gantlet* (*gauntlet*). Though people are seldom subjected to such beatings at present, the word's figurative sense of a severe trial or ordeal survives, and so does the expression: *run the gantlet* (*gauntlet*) *of criticism; legislative sponsors who ran the gantlet* (*gauntlet*) *of*

economy-minded legislators. Both spellings of the noun are commonly used, and both are acceptable, though some usage authorities insist on or prefer *gantlet*. *Gauntlet* is the preferred spelling of the glove worn with medieval armor; that term survives in the expressions *fling* (or *throw*) *down the gauntlet* and *take up the gauntlet*—to issue a challenge and to accept such a challenge.

gauge *Gauge* is the first spelling, and *gage* an acceptable alternative, of the noun meaning a standard of measurement, an instrument for measuring or testing, the position of a vessel, the distance between two rails or between two wheels, the diameter of a shotgun barrel, thickness (of metal or wire), and fineness of knitted cloth. The corresponding verb meaning to measure or evaluate is spelled only *gauge*.

get The past tense is *got*, the past participle *got* or *gotten*. (In British English, *got* is virtually the sole form of the participle.) In usage, the constructions *has* (or *have*) *got* and *has* (or *have*) *gotten* are distinguished as follows: *got* indicates possession (*has got two cars*), without indication of time, and *gotten* usu-*ally* implies, besides possession, the idea of recent acquisition (*has gotten two cars*). Especially in writing, the idea of mere possession is better expressed without *got*—by *has* or *have* alone: *has* (or *have*) *two cars*.

gibe, jibe As verbs and nouns, both words express the sense of taunting or scoffing. Only *jibe* is used for the verb expressing agreement and for the lesser-known nautical (sailing) term.

gift The word's use as a transitive verb—to present (a person) with a gift—is informal. In such constructions, the recipient is the direct object: *gifted his niece on her confirmation.*

glamour This is the preferred spelling; the alternate is *glamor.* But the usual forms of the adjective and verb are *glamorous* and *glamorize.*

glassful The plural is *glassfuls.*

good In formal usage, as a descriptive word *good* is only an adjective, not an adverb. As an adjective it can qualify a noun attributively by preceding the noun (*a good aircraft*), or it can follow a linking verb such as *be, feel, seem, smell, sound,* and *taste: The soup smells good. The news sounds good.* In such examples *good* once more describes a noun, the subject of the sentence, though its position in the sequence of the wording is different. Adverbs, rather than adjectives, qualify nonlinking verbs, but *good* may be used as an adverb only in dialogue or other deliberately informal usage, as in *She speaks good.* On a formal level, *well* replaces *good* in such examples: *speaks well; sings well; dances well; a machine that runs well,* or *works*

well. The expression *good and,* preceding an adjective, is acceptable informally: *good and tired*.

got, gotten See **get**.

graceful, gracious *Graceful* is applied to persons, animals, or things that show beauty or charm of movement, form, or proportion. *Gracious* principally describes human demeanor that reflects a kind and compassionate nature or, less often, elegance of taste.

graduate The idea of successfully completing a course of study is expressed by either *graduated* or *was graduated: He graduated* (or *was graduated*) *from college.* Both constructions are acceptable on a formal level, and both require *from. He graduated college* is not acceptable on any level.

grisly, grizzly What is *grisly* is horrifying or gruesome. That which is *grizzly* is grayish or flecked with gray. *Grizzly* (noun) is also the term for the grayish form of the brown bear.

groom In all but the most formal contexts, this noun is an acceptable substitute for *bridegroom*.

ground, grounds An area of land set aside for a particular purpose is denoted by either the singular or plural form in many cases: *burial ground(s); fairground(s)*. In some, however, only the plural appears: *baseball grounds. Grounds* is always used to designate land surrounding or forming part of a build-

ing: *the rectory grounds*. Either form may be employed to denote the foundation for an argument, belief, or action, in the sense of basis or premise: *little ground for dispute; the grounds cited by Charles Darwin in expounding his theory of evolution*. The plural form is generally employed in the case of an underlying condition that prompts an action: *grounds for divorce; grounds for impeachment*.

group Like most collective nouns, *group* can be construed as singular or plural in determining the grammatical number of the verb that *group* governs. A singular verb is used when the persons or things forming the group are considered as one or as acting as one, or when they are related by membership in a class or category. A plural verb occurs when reference is made to persons thought of as acting individually. The grammatical number of related pronouns or pronominal adjectives agrees with that of the verb: *The group* (of persons), *though varied in many respects, is bound together by an all-powerful common interest in maintaining its secular form of education. This group* (of animals) *manifests many of its characteristics most clearly in second-generation offspring. The group* (of persons) *were divided in their sympathies.*

hail, hale *Hail* (noun and verb) is the term for precipitation, literal and figurative (*a hail of abuse; hailed curses at the enemy*); it is also the verb meaning salute, designate, and signal (*hailed the new president;*

hailed her queen of the tribe; hailed a cab). Hail from, meaning come from, is written thus. *Hale* has the narrower application: as an adjective describing good health and as a verb meaning compel to go (*haled them into court*).

half In written usage, *a half glass of water* is preferable to *half a glass*, though the latter form is acceptable (but not *a half a glass*). The expression *in half* means into halves. It is good usage, therefore, to write *cut a cake in half*. The construction is not only acceptable but more natural to most persons than *cut a cake in halves*.

handful The plural is *handfuls*.

hanged, hung When the verb *hang* refers to execution (capital punishment), the past tense and past participle is *hanged,* not *hung: The outlaw was hanged. The dictator's forces hanged many political prisoners.* In all other senses of the verb, the corresponding past tense and past participle is *hung: hung the clothes, the drapes, a flag, a scythe* (to its handle); *hung her head in shame; after the wallpaper was hung; a jury that was hung* (deadlocked); *an argument that hung* (depended) *on slim evidence; a listener who hung on every word as the verdict hung in the balance.*

happen, occur, take place Each of these refers to the coming about of something. *Happen* and *occur* are used when the action is spontaneous, accidental, or

unforeseen: *The accident happened an hour ago. It occurred a mile south of the bridge.* Action that is pre-arranged is preferably expressed by *take place: An inquiry into the cause of the accident will take place on Monday. Happen* and *occur* are often interchangeable, as in the preceding examples. But *happen* is especially applicable to what is accidental; *occur* also works in such examples and is the better choice when the action is traceable to a clear cause. In sentences in which *occur* could be misconstrued to mean come to mind, *happen* is mandatory: *Something like that might have happened to them.* When the desired sense is to be met with or appear, *happen* cannot express it; *occur* is the choice (and less often *take place,* in the case of prearrangement): *Violence frequently occurs* (or *takes place*) *in the later plays of Tennessee Williams. Widespread sickness of this kind seldom occurs* (not *takes place*) *now.*

hardly Since the word has a sense verging on the negative, it is not used with another negative in the same construction: *They could hardly hear* (not *couldn't hardly*). *She accepted the verdict with hardly a sign of emotion* (not *without hardly*). *Hardly* is followed by clauses introduced by *when* or, less often, *before,* but not by *than* or *until: They had hardly arrived when* (or *before*) *the call came.*

harebrained The adjective meaning giddy or flighty is spelled thus, not *hairbrained.*

head   When the verb is used transitively, meaning to be in charge of (something), *head* is preferable to *head up,* especially in formal writing: *head a committee; head an investigation.*

headquarter, headquarters   The noun *headquarters,* plural in form, is more often used with a plural verb (*headquarters are located*), though a singular one is also possible. As a verb, *headquarter* is informal in both intransitive and transitive senses: *The company will headquarter in Providence. It has headquartered the sales department in an outlying district.*

healthful, healthy   *Healthful* is applied to what promotes or encourages good health: *a healthful climate; healthful working conditions.* *Healthy* expresses the same meaning, and could be substituted in the preceding examples, but primarily it describes someone or something that possesses good health.

hectic   By extension of its medical meanings, this adjective has come to describe that which is characterized by feverish activity, confusion, or haste: *a hectic day.* The word is well established in that sense, on all levels of usage.

height   The word is spelled as given. *Heighth,* an earlier spelling, is now a misspelling.

help   The expression *cannot help but,* especially common in speech, is found in examples such as *We*

cannot help but regret it. In formal writing, preferable ways of expressing the same idea are *cannot help regretting it* and *can* (or *cannot*) *but regret it*.

here   The adverb meaning in this place follows the noun (never precedes it) in constructions introduced by the demonstrative *this: this house here* (not *this here house*). Constructions introduced by *here is* and *here are* are similar to those beginning *there is* and *there are* with respect to determination of the grammatical number of the verb. For an explanation of the procedure, see **there.**

hero   The plural is *heroes*.

hers   The possessive pronoun is written thus, without an apostrophe: *The money is hers*.

herself, himself   Like other *-self* pronouns, these have a variety of functions that are never disputed. As reflexives they form the direct or indirect object of a verb or the object of a preposition: *She cut herself. He wants it for himself*. They are used for emphasis: *She did it herself. He himself did the work*. They are also employed as an indication of real, normal, or healthy condition or identity: *He's more like himself again*. In written usage they are less appropriate than *her* or *him* as elements of compound objects: *Mary expressed the hope that they would give Frank and her* (preferable to *herself*) *enough time*. The *-self* words are even less acceptable as parts of compound

subjects: *If the tests prove negative, Mrs. Ford and he* (not *himself*) *will leave the hospital tomorrow.*

historic, historical   Use *historic* when the thing it describes is important in or contributes to history: *the historic* (history-making) *moon landing in 1969. Historical* refers more broadly to what is concerned with history: *historical novel.*

homogeneous, homogenous   The general senses related to likeness in nature or kind and to uniformity in structure or composition can be expressed by either word. *Homogenous* is the term used in biology to indicate homogeny (correspondence between organs and parts).

hopefully   When the adverb means with hope or in a hopeful manner (*looked forward to the meeting hopefully*), it is always used acceptably. A much newer usage employs the word as the equivalent of it is to be hoped, or let us hope: *Hopefully we are on the right track.* The newer sense is now very common but is still not accepted by many usage authorities.

host   Employed as a transitive verb meaning to serve as host for (a party, convention, or television program, for example), *host* is informal. In formal writing, *serve as host for* or *be host to* are preferable.

human   The noun is acceptably employed, on a formal level, in the sense of human being.

human, humane, humanitarian As descriptive words, *human* is essentially a classifying term relating to individuals or people collectively (*human achievement; human events*); *humane* implies having the qualities of kindness and compassion (*humane treatment*); and *humanitarian* applies to what actively promotes the needs and welfare of people (*humanitarian concerns*).

hung See **hanged, hung.**

I See **between you and me; me.**

if Both *if* and *whether* are used to introduce noun clauses, though *whether* is preferred by many writers and editors in formal writing: *By Friday he will learn whether* (or *if*) *he has succeeded.* When such a clause comes at the start of a sentence, *whether* is always the choice: *Whether he has succeeded is not certain.* Use of *if* in such an example very likely would confuse a reader and make a rereading of the sentence necessary.

if and when See "Redundant Expressions."

illicit See **elicit, illicit.**

illusion See **allusion, delusion, illusion.**

imaginary, imaginative Something *imaginary* has existence only in the imagination and is therefore unreal. *Imaginative* primarily describes persons having creative imagination or ingenuity, or things reflecting such qualities.

immigrate See **emigrate, immigrate, migrate.**

imminent See **eminent, imminent.**

impassable, impassive Something *impassable* cannot be traveled across or through. Someone *impassive* experiences no emotion or shows none and is characteristically expressionless.

imply, infer In modern usage these are carefully distinguished. To *imply* something is to state it indirectly, to hint or suggest it. *Implication* is the corresponding noun: the act of implying or that which is implied (an indirect indication or hint). *Imply,* in another sense, means to involve by logical necessity or to entail: *Continued success generally implies something more than luck.* To *infer* is to conclude (something) from evidence, or to deduce: *inferred from her actions that she didn't believe my story. Infer* is often misused for *imply,* in the sense of stating indirectly, just as *inference* is misused for *implication.* An *inference* is a deduction or conclusion, something that is inferred.

important, importantly *Important,* not *importantly,* is the choice in examples such as the following: *The move will hinder this project and, more important, will ruin the morale of the entire staff. More important* is a shortened form of *what is more important;* thus an adjective, *important,* following *is*—not the adverb *importantly.*

impracticable, impractical *Impracticable* describes

what cannot be done or carried out. *Impractical* can be used in the same sense, but more often is applied to what would be unwise to carry out or maintain in practice. The distinction is that between what is impossible and what is not desirable or worthwhile.

in, into, in to As a preposition, *in* primarily indicates position, location, or condition: *He was in the library. She was in a bad mood.* Used correspondingly, *into* indicates direction or movement to an interior location or, figuratively, change of condition: *She went into the lobby. He flew into a rage. In* is also possible in such examples, but conveys the desired sense less clearly and less forcefully. The two-word form *in to* is used in examples, such as the following, in which *in* is an adverb: *We went in to supper. You may go in to see them now.*

in addition to See **along with.**

include Unlike *comprise,* this verb does not imply that all components are enumerated; generally it implies an incomplete listing: *New York comprises the boroughs of Manhattan, the Bronx, Queens, Brooklyn, and Richmond. The cake's ingredients include butter and egg yolks.* When a complete listing is made, *comprise* is a better choice than *include.*

incredible, incredulous What is *incredible* is unbelievable. *Incredulous,* often misused in that sense, properly describes a person or something about a person that shows skepticism or disbelief.

indefinitely Although the word describes a condition or action that lacks precise limits, in many contexts it makes the implication of lengthy duration: *She expects to be stationed in Puerto Rico indefinitely.* In such examples, *indefinitely* suggests continued residence (or other action) in the foreseeable future and is acceptably so used except when lack of clarity might result.

individual As a noun, *individual* means person but should not be used as an all-purpose substitute for *person*. *Individual* is most appropriate in examples in which a single human being is distinguished from a group or mass, by contrast or stress on individuality: *the individual's right to a nonconformist view; an individual to the core* (an independent, strong-willed person). When those conditions do not exist in the example at hand, *person* is the better choice.

indoor, indoors *Indoor* is an adjective only, and *indoors* an adverb: *indoor sports; an indoor football field; went indoors; a field built indoors.*

infer See **imply, infer.**

inferior Persons and things are said to be *inferior to* others—not *inferior than.*

inflammable, inflammatory In their most common application, *inflammable* applies to what ignites readily and burns rapidly, and *inflammatory* to what stirs

strong emotion—a speech, for example. See also **flammable, inflammable.**

ingenious, ingenuous Both are said of persons and the attributes and creations of persons. *Ingenious* indicates inventive skill or imagination; *ingenuous,* the absence of worldliness or sophistication, or a tendency to be open and honest in dealing.

inhuman, inhumane, nonhuman The first two adjectives are close synonyms and refer to persons or things that are cruel and lacking in compassion. *Nonhuman* is basically a categorizing term applicable to things not human, but lacks a suggestion of their nature in other respects.

inside As a preposition, *inside* is capable of functioning without a following *of: remained inside the house.* In written usage such a construction is preferable to the variant *inside of the house.* With reference to time and distance, *inside of* is perhaps the more common construction, but *inside* is likewise able to express the desired sense: *inside* (within) *a mile; inside an hour.*

insignia Though plural in form, this noun is acceptably used with a singular verb: *This insignia is attractive.* The plural form, meaning more than one such badge or distinguishing sign, is either *insignia* or *insignias.* The English singular *insigne,* from Latin, is extremely rare in current usage.

insure See **assure, ensure, insure.**

intend This verb is often followed by an infinitive (*intend to go*) or by a clause introduced by *that* and with a subjunctive form of verb: *intended that he call her* (but not *intended for him to call her*).

intense, intensive *Intense* most often describes what is extreme in degree (*intense pain; intense emotion*), usually in the sense of being deeply felt; it can also indicate intensity, as in *intense effort* and *a very intense person*. In a corresponding sense, *intensive* is synonymous with concentrated and exhaustive: *intensive care; intensive study.*

interment, internment *Interment* refers to burial, *internment* to detaining or confining, especially in wartime, or to training or serving as an intern (in medicine).

internecine The word describes something mutually destructive, ruinous or fatal to both sides; or it can refer to internal struggle, within a nation or an organization, that is not necessarily fatal or mutually destructive, though intense.

interpretative, interpretive These are alike in meaning, and both are acceptable on a formal level.

into See **in, into, in to.**

intrigue As a transitive verb meaning to arouse interest or curiosity (*a tale that intrigued us*), the

word occurs on all levels. It is still resisted by some usage authorities, however, on the ground that it displaces words that would express the desired sense more precisely: *excite, interest, puzzle, fascinate,* and *titillate,* for example.

invent See **discover, invent.**

inward, inwards Only *inward* is the adjective: *an inward force.* The corresponding adverb is *inward* or *inwards: turned inward,* or *inwards.*

irregardless This double negative is not acceptable. Use *regardless.*

irrespective The phrase *irrespective of* (regardless of) is always written thus, not *irrespectively of.*

Israel, Israeli *Israel* is the name of the modern republic, and is sometimes used as an adjective relating to that nation. *Israeli* is more widely employed as an adjective in that sense; it (not *Israelite*) is the term for a native or inhabitant of modern Israel, with alternative plurals: *Israeli, Israelis.*

its, it's *Its* is the possessive form of the pronoun *it: a city and its people. It's* is the contraction of *it is* and *it has: It's not new; it's been done before.*

jealousy See **envy, jealousy.**

jibe See **gibe, jibe.**

judicial, judicious *Judicial* refers broadly to courts of law and the administration of justice: *judicial branch of government; the judicial process. Judicious* describes persons or things that show sound judgment: *judicious measures.*

jurist The term is more inclusive than *judge.* It denotes any person skilled in the law: an eminent judge, lawyer, or legal scholar, for example.

kind In formal written usage, *kind* is preferably employed in a consistently singular construction in examples such as *This kind of pen is quite useful.* (The demonstrative adjective *this* is singular, as are the following noun and verb, *pen* and *is.*) The alternative constructions, *these kind of pens are* and *this kind of pens are,* are more typical of spoken language, though they also have a long history of written usage. A preferable rendering of the example employing plural elements is *Pens of this kind are quite useful.* A more acceptable use of *kind,* with an accompanying plural noun and verb, occurs in interrogative constructions introduced by *what* or *which: What kind of pens are these?* Writers sometimes use *kinds* in sentences of this variety in an effort to justify accompanying plural elements—but *kinds* is possible only when the desired sense involves more than one class or variety. *Kinds* and plural verbs are required when *all* precedes *kinds: All kinds of aircraft are on display.*

(a) kind of, kind of   *A kind of* indicates a rough approximation of the category stated: *a kind of early printing press.* Such examples are acceptable on all levels of writing. An informal use of *kind of* expresses the sense of somewhat (*kind of tired*) or after a fashion; to a degree: *kind of nodded.*

knot   In nautical measure, *knot* is a unit of speed, with a built-in sense of "per hour." A ship is said to travel at ten knots (not knots per hour) and to cover ten nautical miles in an hour.

kudos   The term means acclaim or prestige resulting from achievement or position. It is construed as singular in choice of a verb: *Kudos was not his lot.* There is no singular term *kudo* in standard usage.

lack   See "Picking a Preposition."

last, latest   Both can describe what is final: *the last* (or *latest*) *train to Chicago. Last* makes the clearer implication that nothing else follows; *latest train* might also be one in a continuing series. Both also mean most recent: *the last* (or *latest*) *word from Saigon. Latest* expresses that sense more clearly, for it stresses the expectation of further news. *Last word* implies that no other word may be forthcoming. See also **first, last.**

latter   As a term corresponding to *former,* this word is applied only to the second of two. In referring to

the last element in an example containing three or more, use *last-named*, not *latter*. In general, use all these terms only when the desired reference is clear without a rereading of what has gone before. Otherwise, a better course is to repeat the name of the person or thing to which a term like *latter* refers.

lay, lie   The following examples illustrate these verbs in constructions in which errors commonly occur. *Lay* (to put, place, or prepare) always takes a direct object in the meanings indicated; *lie* (to recline or be situated) never does. Confusion occurs in part because the meanings are complementary, in part because of the overlapping of principal parts. The past tense and past participle of *lay* is *laid*. The past tense of *lie* is *lay*, the past participle is *lain*.

In the following, only *lay* and *laid* are possible, as indicated: *laid the letter on the desk; decided to lay the cards on the table; laid some cables and then the flooring; laid a burden on us; has laid the blame on her; laid plans and then a trap; laid much stress on several points; laid our case before the people; laid a bet; laid bare the scandal; laid claim to the property; had laid himself open to criticism; the hen that laid the eggs; a tale laid in Greece; a table laid for two; a ceiling laid with precious stones.*

In the next group, only *lie, lay, lain,* and *lying* are possible, as indicated: *decided to lie down for an hour; undressed and then lay on the couch; had lain*

there a few minutes when the bell rang; was lying half asleep; a dispute that lies unresolved; a site that lies between two small towns; property that lay between the frontier and an ancient fortress; accused of lying down on the job; lay in wait for them all night; advised us to lie low; a choice that lay with them alone.

learn, teach   In modern usage these are carefully distinguished. *Learn* is confined to the act of gaining knowledge. It is not acceptably used to express the act of instructing or imparting knowledge, a sense expressed only by *teach*.

leave, let   The verbs are interchangeable only when followed by a noun or pronoun and *alone: Leave* (or *let*) *them alone.* The meaning thus expressed is to refrain from disturbing or interfering with. Both *leave alone* and *let alone* convey it acceptably. For reasons concerned in part with style and in part with clarity, some writers prefer *let alone* in such examples and confine *leave alone* to those in which the meaning is to depart and leave (one) in solitude (a sense *let alone* cannot convey). *Leave* is never interchangeable with *let* when the desired meaning is to allow or permit. Only *let* is acceptable in the following: *Let her go. Let me be. Let go of the rail. Let us not argue. Let it lie.* Note that *let* is followed by objective pronouns in the preceding examples and in *Let George and me* (not *I*) *help.*

lend.   See **loan, lend.**

less   See **fewer, less.**

let   See **leave, let.**

level, levy   These are confused in one sense of *level:* to direct emphatically or forcefully toward someone. One *levels* criticism, charges, accusations, and the like at another person. One does not *levy* such things; but taxes and war are *levied.*

liable   See **apt, liable, likely.**

libel, slander   *Libel* refers to injury through written, printed, or pictorial statements, and *slander* to similar injury through utterance of defamatory statements.

lie   See **lay, lie.**

like   The verb *like* often occurs in constructions in which it is followed by an infinitive preceded by a noun or pronoun: *They would like us to report early* (but not *like for us to report early*). In conditional sentences, *would have liked* and *should have liked* are followed by a present infinitive: *She would have liked to remain* (not *to have remained*). But the perfect infinitive is possible when *like* is in the present tense: *She would like to have remained.* An unacceptable usage is that of *like* as a verbal auxiliary with a perfect infinitive: *I like to have died last night.* Make it *almost,* or *nearly, died.*

like, as   As prepositions, *like* and *as* express different senses. *Like* most often indicates resemblance to

the object mentioned: *run like a greyhound; a boy like him; not at all like her to give up.* (Note that the pronouns are in the objective case.) *As* indicates a role, capacity, or function: *serve as chairman.* In these usages, the words are not interchangeable. The distinction is illustrated by *act like a leader* and *serve as leader.* The object of *like* can be either a single word or a phrase: *felt like running away; looks like a good spring for gardening.*

A much less desirable use of *like* occurs when the word serves as a conjunction (to introduce a clause). In formal writing, the conjunctive *like* is usually acceptable only when it introduces an elliptical clause in which a verb is not expressed. The last example of the preceding paragraph is such a usage, as are: *The car looked like new. He took to politics like a fish to water.* If these examples were more fully expressed in the following ways, they would not be acceptable on a formal level: *looks like it will be a good spring; looked like it was new; like a fish takes to water.* To make them appropriate to formal writing, *like* must be replaced by *as, as if,* or *as though: as if it will be a good spring; as though it were new; as a fish takes to water.* Other typical examples: *Tell it as* (not *like*) *it is. The oatmeal tastes good, as* (not *like*) *cereal should. He had no authority but acted as if* (not *like*) *he did.*

Note that the last sentence could be recast: *but acted like one who did.* Here *like* is a preposition,

and the usage is fully acceptable. Fear of misusing *like* should not tempt writers to employ *as* when *like* (preposition) is called for: *She acted like* (not *as*) *an idiot. They treated him like* (not *as*) *a child.* See also **along with; as if, as though.**

likely When *likely* is employed as an adverb (meaning *probably*) in formal writing, idiom calls for it to be preceded by a qualifying word such as *quite, very,* or *most: He will very likely refuse to testify. Most likely it will rain tomorrow.* No such qualifying word is needed when *probably* replaces *likely* in such examples, nor is one called for when *likely* functions as an adjective following a linking verb such as *be, appear,* or *seem: It is likely to rain tomorrow. His refusal to testify now appears likely.* See also **apt, liable, likely.**

likewise The word is an adverb only, not a conjunction. Consequently it cannot take the place of connectives such as *and, as well as,* and *together with* in examples such as: *Her attractiveness and her good manners disarmed most of the questioners* (not . . . *attractiveness, likewise her good manners disarmed* . . .).

linage, lineage The noun meaning number of lines of printed or written material is usually spelled *linage,* though *lineage* is an acceptable variant. The noun pertaining to descent or derivation is spelled only *lineage.*

literally The following example illustrates a common

misuse of *literally* (meaning actually): *Enraged, he literally spit fire.* The opposite of *literally*—that is, *figuratively*—is what is meant by writers of such sentences. But since *figuratively* would not be a comfortable choice idiomatically, a different course is desirable. One is to delete *literally;* another is to use as a substitute for it a less extreme phrase such as *seemed to* or *all but,* one of which is usually appropriate.

loan, lend As a verb, *loan* is acceptable, but *lend* is preferable, according to many writers and editors, especially when a given example does not deal with a transaction of money: *lent her some patterns.*

loath, loathe, loth *Loath,* or *loth,* is an adjective meaning unwilling, reluctant, or disinclined. *Loathe* is a verb meaning to detest or abhor.

lot The noun, meaning a considerably large number of persons or things, is found on all levels of usage: *A lot of modern music seems lacking in warmth.* In formal writing, *much* and *a great deal* are more frequent. The variant noun construction, *lots of,* occurs most often in informal writing, as does the adverbial usage: *lots of modern music; a lot better; lots better.*

loud, loudly *Loud* is both adjective and adverb. As an adverb it is often interchangeable with *loudly* after common verbs such as *laugh, play, roar, say, scream, shout, sing,* and *talk. Loudly* is the established form after *boast, brag, insist, proclaim,* and *exclaim,* among

other verbs. In general, *loudly* is found more often than *loud* in formal usage, especially in writing.

luxuriant, luxurious   *Luxuriant* is the choice when the sense is that of abundant growth (*luxuriant beard*), ornateness (*a luxuriant literary style*), or highly productive (*a luxuriant talent*). A *luxurious* taste reflects love of luxury; *luxurious* surroundings are marked by luxury.

majority   The expression *great majority,* meaning most of, is always written thus, not *greater majority*. The expression *greater majority* is used only with reference to a comparison of two specific numbers. *Majority* is used with a singular verb when the reference is to a specific numerical figure: *Their majority is four votes*. When the meaning is the larger of two groups, the verb may be either singular (if unity or oneness is meant) or plural (if the members are considered as individuals): *The majority is determined to force a vote. The majority are of different minds on the issue.* When the term denotes most of a given group, it takes a plural verb: *The majority of the workers are without representation*.

male, masculine   As an adjective, *male* (like *female*) is largely confined to classifying by sex: *male population figures; male ward of a hospital. Masculine* is applied to characteristics generally associated with men: *masculine force; masculine vigor; a typical masculine sense of self-importance.*

mania, phobia Though often confused, the words are almost opposites. A *mania* is a desire or enthusiasm amounting to a craze. A *phobia* is a strong fear or aversion, often abnormal or illogical.

mantel, mantle *Mantel* is confined to fireplace terminology (facing and shelf). *Mantle* conveys all the many noun senses of these terms, including those of *mantel,* and it alone is the verb. Pertaining to fireplaces, *mantel* and *mantelpiece* are the more common spellings.

masculine See **male, masculine.**

masterful, masterly *Masterful* primarily describes what is forceful, vigorous, or domineering but can also mean skillful or expert, a sense that is expressed more precisely by *masterly*.

materialize In figurative usage this verb is sometimes employed to express the act of giving, or assuming, material or effective form. Plans and dreams can be said to *materialize* when they result in something real. But the verb is imprecise and pretentious as a mere substitute for *happen* or *occur,* which do not connote transformation into something actual.

may, might *Might* is the past tense of *may.* In modern usage, however, both verb forms are treated as subjunctives capable of expressing present and future time. When they are employed in the senses of possibility and permission, they are basically alike in mean-

ing, and differ in intensity rather than in time. In both senses, *may* is stronger than *might: He may go. He might go.* The example with *may* suggests greater likelihood. The distinction holds with respect to permission: *May he go? Might he go?* The *may* example is the more forceful and direct. See also **can, may.**

maybe, may be *Maybe* is the adverb meaning perhaps or possibly: *Maybe she will return. May be,* written as two words, is a verb form having a corresponding meaning: *It may be that she will return.*

me This is the objective case of the pronoun *I*. Its principal uses are illustrated by the following: *injured me seriously* (direct object of a verb); *did me many favors* (indirect object of a verb); *gave the package to me* (object of a preposition). *I*, not *me*, is required after the verb *be*, in formal writing: *It was I who called you.* Informally, and in speech on all levels, *me* is used acceptably after a form of *be*, as a concession to speech patterns that seem more natural to most users of language: *It's me. The caller was me.* Rules of grammar, which govern formal writing, specify *I* in both examples. See also **between you and me; myself.**

mean In expressing intention, *mean* is used with a clause introduced by *that: We did not mean that they should leave.* In written usage, particularly, the following variant of that sentence should not be used: *did not mean for them to leave.*

means When *means* is used in the sense of resources such as money and property, it takes a plural verb: *His means are small*. When *means* has the sense of a way to an end, it may be used in either singular or plural constructions. The determination of grammatical number is influenced by the modifying words preceding *means*. *The means* may be followed by either a singular or a plural verb. *A means, any means, each means, every means,* and *one means* are followed by singular verbs. *All means, several means,* and *such means* (not *such a means*) are followed by plural verbs.

meantime, meanwhile Each of these is a noun and an adverb, but in usage *meantime* is more often a noun: *In the meantime he waited. Meanwhile* is the more common as an adverb: *She went inside; meanwhile he waited.*

media This plural form of the noun *medium* is applied in a collective sense to means of mass communication. Each means, considered individually, is a *medium: Television is a highly influential medium* (singular). *Together, television and radio, newspapers, and periodicals make up what we call the media* (plural). When it is used as a subject, *media* (plural) always takes a plural verb: *The media are often the target of public criticism.* As a collective plural, *media* expresses the sense of a group of things. Because some writers do not realize this, they some-

times seek to express the group sense by using *medias* —but *medias,* a superfluous term, is not accepted in standard usage.

might   See **may, might.**

mighty   As an adverb meaning very or extremely, *mighty* is informal: *a mighty fine day.* In formal writing, make it *very fine.*

migrate   See **emigrate, immigrate, migrate.**

militate, mitigate   *Mitigate* (to moderate or alleviate) is the one of this pair of verbs that is often misused, as in *prejudice that mitigated against his advancement.* *Militate against* (to have an adverse effect) is the proper choice in such examples. *Mitigate* is correctly used in *a surprise that mitigated his deep disappointment.*

million   The plural is either *million* or *millions.* The first is almost invariably found when a specific number precedes: *fifty million Frenchmen.* *Millions* is used (with *of*) in the sense of an indefinitely large number: *millions of wasted opportunities.*

mishmash   This is the only acceptable spelling.

mitigate   See **militate, mitigate.**

mobile, movable   *Movable* is applicable to what is capable of being moved, but does not imply great facility for movement. In contrast, *mobile* stresses

such facility. For example, *mobile* equipment is that which is designed and built so as to be capable of being moved readily.

money   *Moneys,* not *monies,* is the preferred plural. It is used in referring to the mediums of exchange of two or more countries or, within one country, in designating particular forms of money or specific sums.

moral   See **ethical, moral.**

more, most   In comparisons of two persons or things, one is said to be *more* talented, *more* efficient, or the like (or *the more* talented, *the more* efficient). *Most* is the corresponding term in such examples when more than two are present.

more than one   Contrary to what logic would dictate, this expression is followed by a singular verb: *More than one man has tried and failed.*

Moslem, Muslim   *Moslem* is found largely in journalism and popular usage in general. *Muslim* is preferred by scholars and English-speaking adherents of Islam. *Muslim* is the only form used by the organization of American blacks, Nation of Islam.

most   As an adverb meaning almost, *most* is confined to informal usage: *Most everyone was present.* It is spelled thus—not *'most.* Of the two adverbial usages established on a formal level, one indicates a comparison: *the most skillful of all.* The other does not;

most functions as a mere intensive meaning *very*: *a most unfortunate occurrence*. Overuse of this last-named sense is often condemned as a stylistic weakness—as an affectation. See also **more, most.**

mostly   This adverb conveys only one sense: for the most part, or almost entirely: *She wrote some fiction, but her work was mostly in biography*. It cannot replace the adverb *most* in examples in which the sense is to the greatest degree, very, or extremely: *She was most* (not *mostly*) *famous as a biographer*.

motif, motive   *Motif* is the special word of this pair, applicable to a recurrent thematic element in the development of a work in architecture and the fine arts, music, or literature. That meaning can also be expressed by *motive,* though *motive* is used most often to denote something that serves to move a person to action.

movable   See **mobile, movable.**

Muslim   See **Moslem, Muslim.**

mutual, reciprocal   *Mutual* primarily refers to a relationship of two. Most often it describes intangibles of a personal nature, such as fear, respect, and obligation, and consequently expresses what two persons do, feel, or represent to each other. John Donne wrote: *The best league between princes is a mutual fear of each other*. In a few cases the word indicates a rela-

tionship between more than two. Examples are *mutual friend,* generally preferred to *common friend* in denoting a third party, and *mutual aid,* which often is not limited to two. *Reciprocal* most often is applied to two parties. But it usually describes terms with impersonal, tangible senses, notably *reciprocal trade* and *reciprocal tariff,* and strongly implies a balanced relationship in which one action is taken in return for another. It differs also in being applicable to a single action of one party, whereas *mutual* always implies a continuing interaction.

myself This pronoun sometimes replaces *me* and *I* in compound objects and compound subjects, but not acceptably so in formal writing: *They invited Mary and me* (not *myself*). *The mayor and I* (not *myself*) *are equally responsible.*

mysterious, mystic, mystical *Mysterious* has the widest application to anything that arouses wonder by being full of mystery and therefore difficult to understand or solve. *Mystic* and *mystical* are generally interchangeable as adjectives and are applied principally to highly unusual spiritual disciplines and religious practices, or to rites associated with the supernatural.

nauseated, nauseous A person who is *nauseated* experiences nausea. Something or someone that is *nauseous* causes nausea and is therefore sickening in

a physical sense or repulsive in an intellectual one. The second word is often misused for the first.

near See **close, near.**

nearest, next *Nearest* is the more general term; it indicates proximity in space, time, or kinship, but does not necessarily imply a sequence. *Next* always indicates direct succession in a series.

née This term is used when identifying a married woman by her maiden name. It literally means born; consequently it is followed only by a family name, the sole name a person has at birth: *Mrs. Helen Sloan, née Carver* (not *née Helen Carver*).

need *Need* is often employed as an auxiliary verb meaning be obliged or have to. As such it has several peculiarities. It is regularly followed by an infinitive (*need to sleep*), but in varying ways. When the example is a negative statement or a question, the infinitive that follows is sometimes expressed with *to,* and sometimes not: *You need not leave. Need we leave?* But: *You do not need to leave. Do we need to leave?* In all examples, *to* is always expressed when the infinitive follows the inflected forms *needs* and *needed: She needs to rest. They needed to stop.* In negative statements and questions, *need* as an auxiliary is not inflected in the third person singular, present tense, as it is in positive statements: *He need not try. He needs to try. Need it have occurred?*

neither   As adjective and pronoun, *neither* is applied to one of two persons or things: *Neither shoe fits properly. Neither feels comfortable.* When more than two are present, use *none: Tax revision, welfare reform, and energy proposals all have high priorities, but none is likely to get definitive action in this session of Congress.* In formal usage the adjective or pronoun *neither* takes a singular verb: *Neither house was open; neither is available for inspection.* This is true even when a plural noun follows the subject *neither: Neither of the buildings is close to completion.* When accompanying possessive pronouns or pronominal adjectives appear in such sentences, they agree in number with the singular verb: *Neither of the women has her identification papers in proper order.*

The adverbial use of *neither,* for *either,* is not acceptable on any level, when it forms a double negative: *I could not go, and he didn't neither.*

neither . . . nor   In this construction, *neither* is a conjunction, and *nor* is always the second word of the pair to signify continuing negation: *Neither men nor machinery could remove the chief obstacle.* The construction is almost invariably used with two elements (*men* and *machinery* in the preceding example). But either of the elements may be compound; that is, either may consist of two or more components that, taken together, make up a single element. Two or more such closely related components may be joined by *or* within this *neither . . . nor* formula: *Neither United Nations*

sanctions nor unofficial threats or promises are likely to change such a dictator's course.

The procedure for determining the number of a verb in such constructions is the same as that used in the case of *either . . . or*. For a discussion of this problem, and that of the agreement of accompanying personal pronouns and pronominal adjectives, see **either . . . or.**

never Applied to action in the past, this adverb means not ever or on no occasion: *During his stay in Washington he never visited any of the governmental buildings.* It implies action (or lack thereof) over a period of time and is not properly used to give a negative sense to a single action: *He was invited to yesterday's reception but never attended.* Make it *did not attend. Nor* is never paired with *ever* to emphasize the sense at no time whatsoever: *She promised never ever to do it again* (delete *ever*).

next   See **nearest, next.**

nite, nitely   These are not acceptable forms of *night* and *nightly*.

nobody   See **no one.**

noisome, noisy   These have no relationship in meaning. *Noisome* refers to what is extremely offensive or harmful: *a noisome odor. Noisy* refers only to noise. When *noisy* implies clamor or contention, in particular, *noisome* is often misused for it: *a noisy* (not *noisome*) *debate.*

nominal   When applied to amounts, as in *nominal charge* or *nominal sum,* the term means not merely low, but so low in relation to value that the amount in question is merely a token.

none   As a pronoun and subject, *none* is used with both singular and plural verbs, according to the meaning conveyed by *none*. When *none* stands for *no one* or *not one,* it is construed as singular and followed by a singular verb: *None is without some blemish. None of us is perfect.* A singular verb also occurs when *none* precedes a singular noun: *None of the laundry is really clean.* A plural verb is used when *none* has the sense of not any of a specified group of persons or things: *None were more deserving of pity than the survivors who returned hopelessly injured.* In many examples, a case can be made for either a singular or plural verb: *None of these proposals is* (or *are*) *a real solution.* Especially in earlier usage, a singular choice was invariably urged by conservative grammarians, but that position is much less widespread now. Whatever the choice, the singular or plural nature of the construction should be consistent throughout: *None has his work completed* (or *none have their*).

nonhuman   See **inhuman, inhumane, nonhuman.**

no one   When used as subjects, *no one* and *nobody* take singular verbs, and accompanying modifiers are also singular: *No one* (or *nobody*) *has complete control of his* (or *her,* or *his or her*) *future.*

nor This conjunction is used primarily to express the sense of continuing negation. In varying examples it stands for *and not, or not, likewise not,* or *not either.* It is often paired with *neither,* and *nor,* not *or,* invariably follows *neither: She insisted that she was neither for it nor opposed. Nor,* not *or,* is always the choice to signify continuing negation in sentences having successive independent clauses: *She said she was neither for the proposal nor was she opposed. He had no experience in cost accounting, nor did the subject interest him.* Often such examples are expressed within a single independent clause, however; then *or,* rather than *nor,* is used following the opening negative statement, when it is clear that the negative sense carries over to the element introduced by *or: She was not strongly for or against the proposal. He had no experience or interest in cost accounting. He would not accept the explanation or even consider it.* See also **either . . . or; neither . . . nor; nor.**

normalcy There is no disputing the wide use of this word on a formal level or the fact that the usage has dictionary sanction. Among many writers, however, there is still considerable resistance to the noun. In part the adverse feeling traces to the belief that *normalcy* is a needless alternative to *normality* and *normal,* coined outside the usual pattern of the language. In part it also stems from the word's association with Warren Harding, who used it in a famous campaign speech preceding his ill-fated Presidency: *America's*

present need is not heroics but healing; not nostrums but normalcy. He was not the coiner of the word, however; it was in standard usage before the address in Boston and so it remains, despite the controversy.

nothing When *nothing* is used as a subject, it takes a singular verb, even when it is separated from the verb by a qualifying passage introduced by *but, except,* or a like term that contains a plural noun or pronoun: *Nothing but bales of cotton was visible on the waterfront. Nothing except a few of their primitive tools survives today*.

nowhere This is the only acceptable form of the word. *Nowheres* and *noplace* are not in standard usage.

number Referring to quantity, *number* is used with a singular verb when preceded by *the*. In the expression *a number of,* meaning a large, indefinite quantity, a plural verb follows: *The number of applicants was smaller this year. A number of applicants were disqualified by the new rule*.

O, oh *O* is the more special of these, except on those rare occasions when it is used as a variant of *oh*. In general the two have separate functions and are not interchangeable. The present-day writer has use for *O* principally in the exclamations *O dear!* and *O my!* (in which *oh* is also possible). In literature and in religious contexts, *O* is employed in direct address to

express earnestness or solemnity: *O mighty ocean! O God on high!* In such usage *O* is always dependent on the words that follow it; unlike *oh,* it does not stand alone. *O* is always capitalized (usually as the first word of a sentence) and never followed directly by punctuation. The interjection *oh* has both wider use and greater range. Usually it expresses strong emotion but can also indicate merely a reflective pause. Most often it is part of a sentence, but it can stand alone as a one-word (elliptical) sentence. *Oh* is capitalized only when it begins a sentence; it is followed directly by a comma or, when the emphasis is strong, by an exclamation point: *Oh, I see. Oh! What a relief.*

obligate, oblige   The two verbs are frequently used in passive constructions, and they are generally interchangeable when the prevailing sense is that of actual constraint. In other words, a person is *obligated,* or *obliged,* when under direct compulsion to follow a given course. A person is *obliged* (not *obligated*) upon feeling a debt of gratitude and nothing more: *We were obligated* (or *obliged*) *to follow all the terms of the contract. We were much obliged to them for their kindness.*

oblivious   As an adjective corresponding to the noun *oblivion,* this word basically means forgetful of something that one has known in the past: *stayed at home, oblivious of the fact that he had tickets for a play that night.* But *oblivious* is also acceptably used in a

broader sense equivalent to not conscious or aware of: *pursued her work oblivious of* (or *to*) *the distractions around her.*

observance, observation *Observance* refers to the keeping or celebrating of holidays, anniversaries, and customs, and to abiding by laws and regulations. *Observation* refers to close watch or study (of a person's actions, for example, or of current affairs or a branch of learning).

obsolescent, obsolete Something *obsolete* is no longer in use or in fashion, or no longer useful owing to outmoded design or construction or because of hard wear. Something *obsolescent* is in the process of passing out of use or usefulness, and is thus becoming obsolete.

occur See **happen, occur, take place.**

oculist, ophthalmologist, optician, optometrist *Oculist* and *ophthalmologist* are names for a physician who specializes in diseases of the eye. *Optometrist* names one skilled in testing the eyes and prescribing corrective lenses. *Optician* is the name for one who makes or sells optical goods.

odd Among the word's uses is that of indicating an indefinite amount in excess of a specified round number. The number and *odd* are usually joined by a hyphen, and invariably so when otherwise the meaning of *odd* might be misconstrued: *100-odd teachers.*

of When it indicates possession or association, *of* is followed by either an uninflected noun (*friend of my brother; parts of a machine*) or by a noun or pronoun in the possessive case (*friend of my brother's; son of hers*).

off When it is used as a preposition, *off* expresses its various meanings without being joined with *of*. In the following typical examples, use *off*, not *off of*: *stayed off the grass; lived off roots and herbs* or *off her pension; anchored a mile off shore. Off from* is as unnecessary as *off of* in examples such as *stepped off the curb. From*, not *off*, is the only acceptable preposition in expressions indicating a source: *got a loan from him*.

official, officious *Official* is the general term used to indicate a position of authority or proper authorization: *official responsibilities; an official representative; official permission. Officious* describes a person who is excessively forward in offering services or advice to others, especially where they are unneeded or unwanted, and implies a tendency to be meddlesome.

oh See **O, oh.**

O.K. or OK This most popular of American coinages is used and understood throughout the world, but is best kept for informal writing and business correspondence. In general, the most acceptable usages are the noun, meaning approval, agreement, or consent (*got her O.K.*) and the verb: *O.K. this arrange-*

ment. The adjective has a more informal sound: *a partner who was O.K.* (preferable to *an O.K. partner*). The adverbial use is least desirable: *The engine is running O.K.* A variant form of the expression is written *okay* (lower-case *o*); another variant, *okeh*, is now seldom found. The plural noun forms are *O.K.'s, OK's* and *okays.* The inflected verb forms are *O.K.'d, OK'd, okayed; O.K.'ing, OK'ing, okaying; O.K.'s, OK's, okays.*

older, oldest See **elder, eldest.**

on, onto, on to Both *on* and *onto* indicate motion to a position, and in many examples they are interchangeable. But *onto* more clearly expresses movement toward the object specified: *leaped onto the platform; leaped on the platform. Leaped on* can also mean action in a given place. In constructions in which *on* is an adverb and *to* a preposition, they are not joined as one word: *move on to* (not *onto*) *other problems; hold on to* (not *onto*) *what we have.* In such usage, *on* may be considered part of a verb.

on, upon, up on Both *on* and *upon* can indicate a position of rest or movement in a given position or toward a specified object. *On* primarily implies rest: *The pillow lies on* (or *upon*) *the bed. Upon* is stronger in indicating movement toward: *He jumped upon the platform. Jumped on the platform* is less clear in that sense. *Jumped on* and *jumped upon* both convey the idea of movement in a single position. When *up* func-

tions adverbially and *on* as a preposition, the words are not joined: *climbed up on the roof.* Here *up* is, in effect, part of the verb, stressing elevation whereas *upon* would indicate only contact.

one another See **each other, one another.**

one in every A singular verb is employed in this phrase: *One in every four of these switches is defective.* The singular verb is in agreement with the subject *one.*

one of these (those) The following examples illustrate a common construction that often gives difficulty: *It was one of these medicine bottles that have special caps to protect children. She is one of those women who like to walk their dogs in the park.* The form usually recommended is as given: the relative pronouns *that* and *who* are construed as plural (with reference to *bottles* and *women*), and the verb forms, *have* and *like,* are correspondingly plural. Sometimes the examples are written thus: *one of these bottles that has a special cap; one of those women who likes to walk her dog* (or *dogs,* if she has more than one). The alternative constructions are open to question grammatically, since *bottles* and *women* are the true antecedents, not *one,* in the view of most. But writers occasionally choose the singular form to emphasize the sense of *one.* Whatever the choice, the elements should be consistently plural or singular throughout.

oneself   This is the usual form of the pronoun, which may also be written *one's self*.

only   Often more than style is at stake in the proper placement of the adverb *only;* clarity is also an important consideration. Quite different senses are conveyed by these sentences: *Only I work here. I only work here.* Proper placement of *only,* adjoining the word it actually limits, is illustrated by the two examples (*I* in the first, *work* in the second). Other examples of recommended placement are: *She had only a few minutes. They arrived only an hour ago. A cure is possible only if you cooperate.*

Though *only* has a long history of use as a conjunction, meaning but or except that, the use does not occur often in good writing, but rather in everyday speech: *They would have gone, only his wife became ill.* In formal writing, *only* would be replaced by *but* or *except that,* or the second clause would be reworded: *had not his wife become ill.*

onto   See **on, onto, on to.**

onward, onwards   The adjective is only *onward: an onward movement.* The adverb is either *onward* or *onwards: moving steadily onward* or *onwards.*

ophthalmologist, optician, optometrist   See **oculist.**

or   When all elements of a sentence connected by *or* are singular, the verb they govern is singular: *This*

version or the other has to be correct. A tax increase or a subsidy or a reduction in services is indicated by today's testimony. When the elements are all plural, the verb is correspondingly plural. When the elements do not agree in grammatical number, or when one or more is a personal pronoun, the verb agrees in number with the element to which it is nearer or nearest: *Cold symptoms or headache is the usual first sign. Nausea or fainting spells are often early indications. Baseball or football or similar games have little place in their program. He or I am most likely to be chosen.* In examples in which a pronoun causes awkwardness, it is better to rephrase even a sentence that abides by the rules as outlined above. This is a case in which being correct and being desirable are not necessarily compatible. See also **either . . . or; neither . . . nor; nor.**

oral, verbal *Oral* is the more precise term for specifying that something (an agreement or contract, for example) is by word of mouth. *Oral* refers only to what is spoken, whereas *verbal* can also apply to what is written. Nevertheless, the phrases *verbal agreement* and *verbal contract* generally signify something unwritten and are understood accordingly.

other than, otherwise The phrase *other than* is used both adjectively and adverbially to express difference or opposition: *firearms other than pistols; acted other* (or *otherwise*) *than perfectly.* It should not be used as the equivalent of *apart from* or *aside from* in examples

such as: *He said nothing more, apart* (or *aside*) *from noting a minor change* (not *other than to note*). *She has a bad headache, but apart from that* (or *otherwise*) *her condition is favorable* (not *other than that*). See also **each other, one another.**

ought *Ought* is employed as an auxiliary verb and is not inflected. It is used with an infinitive, the choice of which is important in indicating time. Present time is expressed by a present infinitive: *They ought to comply.* Past time is conveyed by a perfect infinitive: *They ought to have complied.* A negative sense is indicated by using *not* immediately following *ought: ought not to have complied.* Other auxiliary verb forms, such as *did, could, had,* and *should,* are never used with *ought: She ought to go* (not *had ought*). *They ought not to complain* (not *hadn't ought* or *shouldn't ought*). Sometimes the infinitive (verb) following *ought* is omitted and only *to* is expressed, if the sense is clear from the context: *Shall we try again? We ought to.* Sometimes the reverse procedure holds true; the infinitive without *to* is used in negative sentences: *ought not complain; ought not have complied.* But the writer must not omit *to* in combinations such as the following: *She ought and can call. She ought and could have called.* The word *to* is necessary in these positive sentences, and structural revision is also in order. Make them read: *She can and ought to call. She could and ought to have called.* As corrected, the last example permits *could* and *ought* in a single sentence; as we have

noted, however, *could* and *ought* are never joined as *couldn't ought*.

ourself, ourselves   *Ourself* is a singular form approximately equivalent in meaning to *myself*. It is used only when *we* is employed in the sense of *I*—when a monarch employs *we* or an editor uses the same term in speaking for a publication. Thus an editor might write: *We ourself favor the incumbent mayor for reelection, but we shall also present other opinions.* Though the average writer has little use for *ourself,* it is important to understand that the word cannot be substituted for *ourselves.* The latter term is the usual form of the first person plural pronoun, used in sentences such as the following: *We should not permit ourselves such liberties. We ourselves are not directly involved. We have not been ourselves since the accident.* (In none of the examples can *ourself* replace *ourselves.*) *Ourselves* should not replace *us* and *we* in compound objects and subjects, as in the following: *They have invited the Smiths and us* (not *ourselves*). *We* (not *ourselves*) *and the Smiths are invited.*

outdoor, outdoors   *Outdoor* is an adjective: *outdoor lighting. Outdoors* is an adverb (*went outdoors*) and a noun: *enjoying the great outdoors. Outdoors* is sometimes written *out-of-doors;* much less often, *outdoor* is written *out-of-door.*

outside   In formal writing, *outside* (preposition) is preferable to *outside of* in indicating physical limits,

scope, or an exception: *stayed outside the house; a matter outside our jurisdiction; received no word outside what you already know.*

over   As a preposition meaning more than (a specified amount), *over* is well established on all levels of usage: *cost over three dollars; over age sixty-five.* It is clearly out of place in an example having a sense of decrease: *attendance figures down five per cent over last year's* (properly *down . . . from*).

overlay, overlie   Though both verbs are transitive, and are related in meaning, they are carefully distinguished in usage. *Overlay* expresses the sense of superimposing; a carpenter *overlays* plywood with veneer, and a writer might *overlay* a narrative with much symbolism. *Overlie* refers to lying over or resting upon (something), as one layer of rock *overlies* another. The past tense and past participle of *overlay* is *overlaid.* The past tense of *overlie* is *overlay,* the past participle is *overlain,* and the present participle *overlying.* Both verbs are often used in the passive voice: *wood that was overlaid with silver; bedrock overlain with sand.*

overly   This adverb, meaning to an excessive degree, is established on all levels of usage though it is disliked by many writers on the stylistic ground that it is a superfluous word. Many adjectives and adverbs formed with *over-* express the same sense more con-

cisely: *overcautious* (for *overly cautious*) and *over-fast* (for *overly fast*).

pair   In formal usage, the plural is *pairs: three pairs of shoes.* Informally, the same sense is conveyed by *three pair.* When *pair* is used as a subject it always takes a singular verb when the meaning stresses one-ness or unity of components: *This pair* (of socks) *is not mine.* A plural construction occurs when the members are considered individually: *The pair were seldom in agreement on anything.*

palate, palette   *Palate* denotes the roof of the mouth. *Palette* is a board for mixing colors.

partially, partly   Often these adverbs are interchangeable; in many cases a choice is determined by prevailing idiom. In general *partially* is found most often before a word describing the condition of a person: *partially blind; partially dependent.* *Partly,* which has much wider application, could replace the other term in the second example. Other examples: *a house partly* (or *partially*) *completed; mail sorted partly* (or *partially*) *by hand; partly to blame; partly at fault.* Only *partially* has the sense of showing favorable prejudice or bias, but that meaning is now expressed more often by the noun *partiality.*

party   In formal usage, the word as the equivalent of person is confined to legal material. Informally *party*

is applied to a particular person, often in a jocular sense: *a strange old party*.

pass, past The past tense and past participle of the verb *pass* is *passed: They passed* (or *have passed*) *our home. Time had passed slowly. Past* is the corresponding adjective (*in centuries past*), adverb (*drove past*), and preposition (*past midnight; past the crisis*).

pedal, peddle As a noun, *pedal* most often denotes a lever operated by the foot; as an adjective, it refers to a foot, as in *pedal extremities;* as a verb it applies to riding a bicycle and to operating levers in other machines and in musical instruments. *Peddle* is a verb only (to sell wares). The corresponding noun is *peddler* (or *pedlar* or *pedler*).

people The plural of this noun is usually also *people*. When the noun refers to a nationality, however, or to a body having a common religion, culture, language, or inherited condition of life, the plural is *peoples: Germanic peoples; nomadic peoples*. The possessive form in such cases is *peoples': the Semitic peoples' goals*. When *people* is the plural form, the possessive is written *people's: the people's best interests*.

people, persons, public *People* (not *persons*) is the choice in referring to a large body collectively and indefinitely—people in general: *People do strange things. Persons* is applicable to a specific, relatively small number: *Ten persons are affected by the change.*

Persons is considered by some usage authorities the better word in such an example, but *people* is also acceptable. *The people* and *the public* are often interchangeable, but only *the people* has the political sense of an electorate.

per cent, percentage Both terms express quantity with relation to a whole. *Per cent* (which may also be written *percent*) is specific and used with a number or numeral. *Percentage* is nonspecific; it is never preceded by such a figure, but should be qualified by an adjective such as *small* or *large,* since *percentage* does not necessarily connote smallness. The grammatical number of the noun that follows these terms, or is understood to follow them, determines the number of the verb: *Twenty per cent of the estate has been distributed. The first five per cent of the profits* (a sum, singular) *is tax-exempt. Fifty per cent of these claims are fraudulent. A small percentage of the mail orders were unfulfilled.*

perfect In a few of its meanings bearing on scientific and technical subjects, this adjective is construed rigidly: *a perfect specimen* (lacking nothing essential); *a perfect gem* (without a defect). In those senses it would be illogical to call one animal, plant, or stone *more perfect* than another since *perfect* (like the adverb *perfectly*) is an absolute term. In most usage, however, *perfect* and *perfectly* are not used in absolute senses but in those that only approach the ab-

solute. When *perfect* is the equivalent of *altogether excellent,* it is acceptably used with *more* and *most: no more perfect day; the most perfect tribute imaginaable.*

persecute, prosecute   To *persecute* is to ill-treat someone, or to annoy persistently. In a corresponding sense, to *prosecute* is to bring legal action against a person.

person   In formal usage, a consistently singular construction is required in examples such as: *A person should be permitted to make up his* (or *her* or *his or her,* but not *their*) *own mind.* See also **people, persons, public.**

personage, personality   In the senses in which the words correspond, *personage* refers to a person of distinction, and *personality* to one of prominence or notoriety. *Personage* is quite formal; *personality* is largely informal.

personnel   Like most collective nouns, *personnel* may be construed as singular (and take a singular verb) when unity of the group is stressed, and as plural when the component members are considered individually. The term is never used with a specific number as in *six personnel of the police department.* Make it *members, employees,* or *representatives.*

persuade   See **convince, persuade.**

phobia   See **mania, phobia.**

piteous, pitiable, pitiful All three describe something that arouses pity. *Pitiable* and *pitiful* also apply to what arouses or deserves disdain or contempt.

place, put The verb *place* usually implies care and precision in bringing something to a desired position. *Put* makes no such suggestion of exactness.

plan This verb plus an infinitive is the usual construction in expressing intention: *plan to leave.* An alternative, *plan on leaving,* is not recommended for formal writing.

plead In legal usage, a person *pleads guilty* or *pleads not guilty;* the expression *plead innocent* is not used, though it often appears in general usage.

plenty The word *plenty* is always used as a predicate (following a verb): *This is plenty.* It is not employed before a noun, as in *have plenty money.* Make it *have plenty of money.* Sometimes the noun *plenty* appears acceptably in the expression *in plenty: goods in plenty.* An informal adverbial use occurs in expressions such as *plenty tired* and *plenty hot,* in which *plenty* means very or sufficiently.

plus When it expresses the sense of *added to, plus* is a preposition, not a conjunction. Consequently a verb that follows *plus* is not invariably plural. The grammatical number of the verb is determined by that of the subject: *Two* (the numeral, construed as singular) *plus two equals four. His skill* (singular) *plus their*

material resources makes them a formidable foe. Their possessions (plural) *plus his ingenuity constitute a considerable advantage.* The element introduced by *plus* does not affect the verb. A recent use of *plus* as a conjunction is not acceptable in formal writing: *She has a great deal of talent, plus she is willing to work hard.* Instead of *plus,* use *and, in addition, besides,* or *moreover.*

politics Though plural in form, this noun is usually used with a singular verb in present-day writing. A singular verb occurs especially when *politics* is used in the sense of a science or profession and when it is followed by a singular predicate noun: *Politics is a strange business.* A plural construction is used when *politics* means opinions or principles: *His politics are his own business.*

poor, poorly *Poor* is an adjective only, not an adverb. It cannot qualify a verb, as in *did poor* and *never played poorer. Poorly* and *more poorly* are required in such examples.

pore, pour *Pore* means to read or study carefully. *Pour* applies to the flowing of liquid and to sending or going forth: *poured the milk; rain that poured down; troops who poured into the capital's streets.*

possible See **feasible, possible.**

practicable, practical *Practicable* means capable of being done. *Practical* carries the idea beyond possi-

bility or capability by connoting that what is done is worthwhile in the given circumstances or that it has value in proportion to required means and is economical or efficient in execution.

practically, virtually Both can express the sense of in every important respect, to all intents, or in effect. Because *virtually* means that and nothing more, it is preferred by many writers and editors: *virtually* (or *practically*) *completed*. In that example and many others, *practically* could be misconstrued as completed in a practical way—since that is a primary and often used sense of *practically*.

precede, proceed *Precede* means to come before in time, order or rank, or physical position, or to preface or introduce. *Proceed* means to go forward or onward or to undertake an action.

precipitant, precipitate, precipitous *Precipitant* and *precipitate* are both applied, as adjectives, to rash, overhasty human actions and to the related sense of headlong movement. *Precipitous* can be used in those senses also, but primarily it describes things whose steepness suggests a precipice: *a precipitous descent*. These distinctions apply also to the corresponding adverbs ending in *-ly*.

predominant, predominate The adjective that describes something that has greatest importance, influence, or force, or that is most common or con-

spicuous, is *predominant*. The corresponding noun is *predominance*. The verb meaning to be most important or outstanding, or to have authority or controlling influence, is *predominate*. In most examples the adverbs formed from these words are interchangeable: a *predominantly* (or *predominately*) *male occupation*; *predominantly* (or *predominately*) *blue in color and small in size*.

prefer This verb is often followed by an infinitive: *prefer to leave early*. When the object is not an infinitive, the object is usually followed by *to*, never by *than: prefer tennis to golf; prefer leaving early to getting in a traffic jam*. When an infinitive is the object, the usual construction for an elaborate sentence is *rather than* (not merely *than*) plus a second infinitive, sometimes without *to: prefer to leave early rather than get in a traffic jam*.

premiere The verb usage (to present or have the first performance) is not established in formal writing.

preparatory to The phrase means *in preparing for*, and in careful usage is restricted to what calls for actual preparation. It does not mean merely *before* or *prior to*.

prescribe, proscribe Prescribe expresses the act of establishing rules or directions, or of recommending remedies. *Proscribe* means to denounce or prohibit. The nouns *prescription* and *proscription* have corresponding senses.

presently   The safest course is to use this adverb only in the sense of *in a short time, soon,* or *directly*. It is also widely employed in the sense of *currently* or *now,* but that usage is not approved by many writers.

presume   See **assume, presume**.

prevent   This verb is most often followed by *from: prevents us from seeing properly*. When, instead, a gerund (the *-ing* form of a verb) follows, the noun or pronoun preceding the gerund is in the possessive case: *prevents our seeing properly; prevented the emissary's going; prevented Smith's leaving*.

preventative, preventive   Both forms of the adjective are acceptable. *Preventive* is the more common.

principal, principle   *Principal* is both an adjective meaning leading or chief and a noun, most often denoting a leader or person in charge; or, in finance, the capital or main body of an estate, and a sum owed as a debt. *Principle* is only a noun applicable to basic truths, rules of human conduct, and fundamental laws governing the operation of a thing.

proceed   See **precede, proceed**.

prophecy, prophesy   The *-cy* form is a noun meaning prediction. The *-sy* form is the corresponding verb meaning to predict or foreshow.

proportion   The noun *proportion* deals principally with relationship—of a part to the whole, between

things or their parts, and between quantities in the sense of a ratio. It can also mean harmonious relation, or balance. The plural *proportions* is also acceptably used in the less specialized sense of dimensions or size: *a job of such proportions.*

proscribe   See **prescribe, proscribe.**

prosecute   See **persecute, prosecute.**

protagonist   Applied to a drama or other literary form, this noun denotes the leading character. It is improper to use the plural form *protagonists* with respect to a single such work. The noun in an extended sense can refer to any leading figure (in a cause or movement, for example) but does not necessarily mean that the person is the opposite of the noun *antagonist* (adversary). In this sense *protagonist* is not always the equivalent of the words *advocate, champion,* or *partisan.*

proved, proven   Both are past participles of the verb *prove,* but *proved* is the preferred one in actual verb usage: *She had proved her point. Their worth was proved on many occasions. Proven* is the more common when used as an attributive adjective before a noun: *a proven record; a proven remedy.* It is also the form used in the phrase *not proven.*

provided, providing   As conjunctions these mean on the condition: *There will be no trouble provided the*

contract is fulfilled. Provided is preferable to *providing* in this sense, especially in formal writing. Both are often used with *that: provided that the contract is fulfilled.*

public See **people, persons, public.**

put See **place, put.**

quick, quickly Though both are adverbs in good standing, *quickly* is found more often in formal writing and *quick* in speech and dialogue.

quite In its primary senses the adverb means to the greatest extent or entirely (*quite alone*) and actually or truly (*quite happy*). But it is also used acceptably in the less rigid sense of somewhat or rather: *quite cool for August.* The expressions *quite a* and *quite an,* indicating indefinite quantity (*quite a few*), are also acceptable on all levels, but only informal when they indicate extraordinary quality: *quite an actor.*

quote The noun *quote,* for *quotation,* is for informal writing. See also **cite, quote.**

rack, wrack As noun and verb, *rack* is the more common, associated with the senses of framework, torture machine, mental torture, and straining with great effort. Thus, *nerve-racking, on the rack, rack one's brain,* and *rack up* (in sports). *Wrack* (verb) is the form for causing ruin, but the corresponding noun

for destruction is either *wrack* or *rack*. *Wrack and ruin* has the variant form *rack and ruin*.

raise, rear   Both verbs are acceptable in formal writing in expressing the sense of bringing up (children).

raise, rise   In the sense of moving upward or to a higher position, *raise* is transitive and *rise* intransitive: *Raise the window. The window rises easily.* As nouns, both words mean an increase in salary; *raise* is the more common in American English and *rise* in British.

rare, scarce   *Rare* implies special quality and value enhanced by permanent shortness of supply. *Scarce* describes things not plentiful at the moment, though they may have no great and lasting value in themselves.

rarely   In the expressions *rarely ever* and *seldom ever, ever* is redundant and should not be used, especially in writing: *They rarely* (or *seldom*) *go.* But the following combinations are possible: *rarely* (or *seldom*) *if ever; rarely* (or *seldom*) *or never;* but not *rarely* (or *seldom*) *or ever.*

rather   In modern usage, *rather* is usually preceded by *would* or *should* in expressing preference: *would rather stay home.* The construction *had rather* is an acceptable alternative in such examples.

ravage, ravish   *Ravage* has the wider application; it means to destroy or devastate. *Ravish,* sometimes mis-

used in that general sense, properly refers to the act of violating by rape or to enrapturing.

re This preposition and the variant form *in re* mean in reference to. They have little place outside business correspondence and legal writing.

rear See **raise, rear.**

reason Since *because* and *why* are inherent in the noun *reason,* the expressions *the reason is because* and *the reason why* are better avoided in formal writing: *The reason for her hesitating was that she was unable to see* (preferable to *The reason why she hesitated was because she was unable to see*).

reciprocal See **mutual, reciprocal.**

reclaim, re-claim The verb meaning to reform (a person), make (land) suitable for cultivation, and procure (usable things) from refuse or waste products is *reclaim.* To *re-claim* is to claim again or back.

recount, re-count *Recount* means to narrate the facts of. *Re-count* means to count again.

recourse, resource The act of turning to a person or thing for aid and the person or thing turned to are inherent in *recourse: He had recourse* (not *resource*) *to the courts. The law was his only recourse* (not *resource*). *His knowledge of the law was among his resources.*

recover, re-cover   To *recover* is to regain; to *re-cover* is to cover anew: *re-covered the sofa.*

recreate, re-create   To *recreate* is to refresh or take recreation; to *re-create* is to create anew.

reform, re-form   *Reform* applies to improvement by eliminating defects, and *re-form* to the act of forming again or becoming formed again.

regard, respect   The expression *in* (or *with*) *regard to* is written thus (singular *regard*). But the corresponding expression is *as regards. Respect,* not *regard,* is the better choice in examples in which the noun means a particular feature: *They differ in some respects.* The verb *regard* (meaning to consider in a particular way) is used with *as: regarded her as a friend* (not *regarded her a friend* or *regarded her to be a friend*).

regretful, regrettable   A *regretful* person feels regret or sorrow. Something *regrettable* calls forth regret. The distinctions also apply to the adverbs *regretfully* and *regrettably: a regrettably long wait.*

relay, re-lay   *Relay* means to send along: *relayed the message. Re-lay* means to lay again: *re-laid the tiles.*

reluctant, reticent   A *reluctant* person shows unwillingness in a given respect. A *reticent* one shows uncommunicativeness by being silent or restrained or reserved. *Reluctant* is the desired adjective in expressions such as *reluctant to discuss the matter.*

repel, repulse Both verbs mean to drive back or off, as in *repel* (or *repulse*) *a commando raid. Repulse* also applies to rebuffing or rejecting by discourtesy; *repel* alone means to cause distaste or aversion: *repulsed this newcomer whose forwardness repelled them all.*

replete This adjective means abundantly supplied with—not merely complete with or equipped with.

replica Strictly, this refers to a copy of a work of art by the original artist. But it is also acceptably applied to any close reproduction, including one in miniature, such as a model.

repulse See **repel, repulse**.

resign, re-sign To *resign* is to quit or to force (oneself) to acquiesce. *Re-sign* means to sign anew.

resource See **recourse, resource.**

respect See **regard, respect.**

respectfully, respectively *Respectfully* means with respect or esteem: *treated the hostages respectfully; respectfully yours. Respectively* means singly in the order designated: *willed cash and securities to Joan and Ellen, respectively.*

restive, restless Both adjectives are applicable to uneasiness. *Restive,* however, especially suggests impatience under restriction or pressure and resistance

to control, in which sense the word is more nearly interchangeable with *unruly* or *balky*.

reticent See **reluctant, reticent.**

revenge See **avenge, revenge.**

right, rightly Both are adverbs, but *right* has the wider application. They are often interchangeable when *correctly* is the sense: *answered her right* (or *rightly*). *Rightly* is used most often when the desired sense is either *properly* or *uprightly: quite rightly refused the request; can rightly claim title to the land.* In the last example, *rightfully* could also be used; *right* would be impossible in either one.

ring When the verb pertains to sound, the past tense is *rang,* not *rung,* particularly in written usage: *when the telephone rang.* The past participle is *rung: when it had rung several times.*

rise See **raise, rise.**

rob, steal Errors occur most often in passive usage. Persons and establishments are *robbed;* property, including money and goods, is *stolen,* not *robbed.*

round The adverb and preposition are spelled thus, not *'round: as they gathered round; make the turn round the bend; worked round the clock.*

rung See **ring.**

said, same   In the following, *said* (adjective) and *same* (pronoun) refer to someone or something mentioned earlier: *The said tenant is given two keys and is expected to return same.* The example, from a lease, illustrates two usages that should be confined to legal and commercial writing. *Said* is almost never needed; if clarity demands it, *said* can be replaced by *aforementioned* or *specified.* For *same,* use *them* (or another pronoun in a different example) or repeat the noun (here, *keys*).

sanatorium, sanitarium   Though these may be used interchangeably, there is some distinction in their primary meanings. A *sanatorium* (also spelled *sanatarium*) is devoted to treatment of chronic diseases and to medically supervised recuperation. A *sanitarium* is a health resort.

sank   See **sink.**

savings   The plural noun *savings* should not be preceded by the article *a: a savings of three dollars.* Make it *a saving* or delete *a.*

scan   This verb can be used acceptably in senses that are poles apart: to examine (something) closely and to look over or leaf through hastily. Examples are *scan a road map* (closely); *scan a newspaper or the headlines* (hastily). Care must be taken to see that the intended sense is clear.

scarce   See **rare, scarce.**

scarcely   Since this adverb has a sense verging on the negative, it is not used with another negative in a single statement: *could scarcely make it out* (not *couldn't scarcely*); *listened with scarcely a change of expression* (not *without scarcely*). In examples such as the following, *scarcely* is followed by *when* or, less often, *before* but not by *than: They had scarcely departed when the storm broke.*

Scot   *Scot* and *Scotsman* (the preferred terms), together with *Scotchman,* all denote a native or inhabitant of Scotland. The corresponding plural terms are *Scots* and (*the*) *Scotch.* The adjectives preferred in Scotland are *Scottish* and *Scots; Scotch* is also in common usage (but not *Scot,* which is not an adjective). Certain combinations have been established by idiom. We speak of Scotch broth, Scotch whisky, Scottish rite, and Scots Guards.

seasonable, seasonal   Use *seasonable* when the thing it describes is appropriate to a season (*light frost, seasonable in the North in early fall*) or timely (*seasonable rains welcomed by farmers*). Use *seasonal* to describe what depends on and is controlled by seasons or a given season: *seasonal employment; seasonal variations in precipitation.*

seeing as how   See **being as.**

seldom   See **rarely.**

senior citizen   See "Euphemisms and Genteelisms."

sensual, sensuous   Both adjectives apply to gratification of the senses but differ in the level of the senses affected. *Sensual* has strong reference to physical (especially sexual) appetite; *sensuous,* though neutral by definition, is more often associated with aesthetic pursuits.

series   Depending on how it is construed, *series* can take either a singular or a plural verb. When it has the singular sense of one set, it is followed by a singular verb, even though it is also followed more immediately by *of* and a plural noun: *The series of plays is open to the public.*

serve, service   *Service* is the more specialized of these verbs, used especially in the sense of making (something) fit for use, as by repairing or maintaining: *serviced the household appliances.* But most services —of broadcasters, newspapers, the medical profession, and utility companies, for example—are expressed by *serve: served the city.*

set, sit   The verb *set* is most often transitive (it takes a direct object), whereas *sit* is largely intransitive. The most common errors involving the pair are uses of *set* for *sit.* In the following, forms of *sit* are correct and *set* would be incorrect: *Sit with us. The bird sat on a low branch. The town sits in a valley. Her duties and a hostile environment sat heavily on her. Neither the dinner nor the speeches that followed sat well with me.* Either verb is possible in these examples: *The*

hen sets (or *sits*) *on eggs. The coat sets* (or *sits*) *well.*

sew, sow One *sews* an article of clothing and *sews up* a business deal or the rights to something. One *sows* seed or the like.

sewage, sewerage The waste material carried off in sewers is usually called *sewage,* though *sewerage* is also possible in that sense. *Sewerage* more often denotes a system of sewers and the process by which the system removes waste.

shall, will In formal writing these verbs are employed as auxiliaries according to a formula that distinguishes mere future time from the expression of a variety of conditions. In the first person, singular and plural, *shall* indicates simple futurity (unstressed intention or normal expectation): *I shall leave tomorrow.* In the second and third persons, the same sense of futurity is expressed by *will: He will come this afternoon.* Use of the auxiliaries is reversed when the writer wants to indicate any of the following conditions: determination, promise, obligation, command, compulsion, permission, or inevitability; *will* is employed in the first person, and *shall* in the second and third. Thus, *I will leave tomorrow* (meaning: am determined to leave, or obligated, compelled, or fated). *He shall come this afternoon* likewise can express any of the conditions enumerated, such as promise, permission, command, or compulsion.

In actual practice, the restrictions on the use of *shall* and *will,* in indicating mere futurity, are observed by most careful writers and should be the rule in all writing on a formal level. But the roles of the auxiliaries in the expression of the various conditions is not widely understood by the average reader. Consequently a more realistic (and recommendable) course is to use other constructions. For example, to indicate determination, compulsion, or obligation, use *must* or *have to;* or use an intensifying word, such as *certainly* or *surely,* with *shall* or *will* to express one of the other conditions. In informal usage, *will* is generally employed in all three grammatical persons to express futurity and any of the conditions listed. On a variety of usage levels, *shall* is sometimes employed, regardless of grammatical person, to emphasize resolve, as in *We shall overcome* and Churchill's memorable speech after Dunkirk: *"We shall fight on the beaches, we shall fight on the landing grounds . . . ; we shall never surrender."*

shambles The word can denote a slaughterhouse or a place or scene of bloodshed. It is even more widely, and acceptably, used in the extended sense of a scene or condition of complete disorder or ruin.

shine The past tense and past participle are *shined* or *shone: The sun* (or *moon* or *a diamond* or *a light*) *shone brightly. The truth shone through. He shined a light in the closet. They shined their boots. She had shined as both scholar and athlete.*

short See **brief, short.**

should, would Of these auxiliary verbs, only *should* is employed to express obligation or necessity. Both are used in sentences expressing simple conditions (contingency of one clause or phrase on another), but *would* is much more common in American usage: *If she had objected, we would* (or *should*) *have made other plans. I would* (or *should*) *not have proceeded without her consent.* To indicate condition (but not obligation), *would* is used in such examples in all three grammatical persons, whereas *should* is limited to the first person. In the same way, either *would* or *should* is used in the first person as an auxiliary with *like, be inclined, be glad, prefer,* and related verbs: *I would* (or *should*) *like to change my vote.* Again *would* is more common in American usage. In such examples, the present and perfect infinitives are frequently found: *I would* (or *should*) *have preferred to stay. I would* (or *should*) *like to have stayed.* But not *I would* (or *should*) *have liked to have stayed.*

sick The idea of experiencing nausea is expressed acceptably by *sick at* (or *to*) *one's stomach.*

Sierra The preferred form for reference to a mountain range such as the Sierra Nevada is the full name or *the Sierras* (not *Sierra mountains*).

similar This is an adjective only. It can follow a linking verb and thus modify the subject to which it is

linked: *The mechanism seems similar to ours.* But it cannot acceptably modify a nonlinking verb, a job for an adverb: *The mechanism works similarly to that in our refrigerator.*

simultaneous This adjective, like *similar,* is often misused in examples that require the adverb *simultaneously.* Only the adverb is acceptable in *physical examinations conducted simultaneously with student registration.*

since Though clauses introduced by *since* (referring to time) are in the past tense, the corresponding verb in the clause joined by *since* must be in a perfect tense: *It has been* (not *was*) *two years since I last visited my home. It had been two years since she departed.* See also **ago.**

sink In formal writing, the preferred past tense is *sank: as the ship sank from view. Sunk* is the preferred past participle: *after it had sunk from view.* The alternative past participle, *sunken,* is more often used as an adjective: *sunken cheeks; sunken treasure.*

sit See **set, sit.**

slander See **libel, slander.**

slow, slowly Both are adverbs. Where they are interchangeable, *slowly* is generally preferred in formal writing; *slow* occurs more often in speech, in commands and exhortations (*drive slow*), and when em-

phasis is desired. Established idiom is important in determining a choice. In the following senses, only *slow* conveys the meaning, and it should be used on all levels: *My watch runs slow* (loses time). *The trains are running slow* (behind schedule). *Go slow* or *Take it slow* (referring to a course of action, not to speed of a vehicle).

smell When the verb means to have or emit an odor, it is a linking verb followed by an adjective: *The milk smells good,* or *fresh,* or *sour.* An adverb may occur in constructions such as *smells strongly of vinegar.* When *smell* means to have or emit an unpleasant odor (to stink), it may be modified by an adverb: *The fish smells disgustingly.* Here the adverb indicates a degree of foul smell; in contrast, *smells disgusting* merely specifies an odor, as in the first example.

sneak The only acceptable past tense is *sneaked: as he sneaked* (not *snuck*) *behind the screen.*

so When the conjunction *so* introduces a clause that gives the purpose of, or reason for, an action stated earlier, it is usually followed by *that,* in formal writing: *He worked late so that he could complete the shipment.* Informally, the same thought is often expressed by *so* used without *that.* *So* is used alone when the clause that it introduces states a result or consequence of something preceding: *He had to complete the shipment, so he worked late.* See also **as ... as, so ... as.**

so-called   This hyphenated adjective precedes a noun that is not enclosed in quotation marks, even when sarcasm is intended: *this so-called leader*. Alternative ways of expressing the same thought are *this "leader"* and *this leader, so called*.

some   As an adverbial substitute for *somewhat,* this word is used informally: *feeling some better*. In formal writing, make it *somewhat better*. In those examples in which *somewhat* cannot replace *some,* the desired meaning (of indefinite degree or extent) must be expressed by other wording in formal usage: *plays golf sometimes* (for *plays golf some*).

somebody, someone, some one   In formal usage, *somebody* and *someone* take singular verbs, and accompanying pronouns and pronominal adjectives are also singular: *Someone has lost his way.* (*Her* or *his or her* can replace *his,* but *their* cannot.) *Somebody* and *someone* refer indefinitely to some person unspecified or unknown. The reference is general, whereas *some one* (two words) refers specifically to a person or thing singled out of a group: *Some one of them will be called on to explain.* In such an example, *someone* cannot be used.

someday, sometime   These adverbs express future time indefinitely, not specifically: *They hope to return home someday* (or *sometime*). The two-word forms *some day* and *some time* are for reference to a specific day or time: *We should choose some day* (or *some*

time) *when reduced fares are in effect*. In such examples *someday* and *sometime* cannot be used. See also **sometime.**

some place, someplace In formal writing, *somewhere* is the proper choice rather than one of these in making an indefinite reference. But when reference is made to a specific place, rather than to one not specified or definitely known, the two-word form *some place* is acceptable on all levels: *seeking some place* (not *someplace*) *better served by public transportation.*

sometime When this word serves as an adjective, it means former: *a sometime public official*. It should not be used as a synonym of *occasional,* as in *an economist and sometime writer on public finance*. See also **someday, sometime.**

some way, someways, someway The adverbs *someway* and *someways* are for informal usage. In formal writing, the desired sense is expressed by *somehow: must raise the money somehow*. The two-word form *some way,* indicating a more specific course, is acceptable on all levels, as in *some way that is less difficult. Someway* cannot be used in such an example.

somewhere The adverb is written thus, not *somewheres*. See also **some place, someplace.**

sooner In sentences such as the following, *no sooner*

is followed by *than,* not by *when: She had no sooner departed than her true identity became known.*

sort When the noun *sort* means a group or collection, it is a synonym of *kind.* The information provided in the entry for *kind* also applies to *sort.* See also **kind; type.**

sow See **sew, sow.**

special, specially See **especial, especially.**

spoonful The plural is *spoonfuls.*

stamp See **stomp.**

stanch, staunch *Staunch* is the usual spelling of the adjective, though *stanch* is possible: *staunch friends. Stanch* (less often *staunch*) is the verb meaning to stop a flow.

stationary, stationery *Stationery,* denoting writing materials, is a noun only. *Stationary* is usually an adjective referring to fixed position or condition.

steal See **rob, steal.**

stomp The verbs *stomp* and *stamp* are interchangeable in the sense of trampling or violent treading: *stomped to death; stomping horses.* Either is acceptable in such examples. In formal usage, however, only *stamp* is acceptable in the sense of striking the ground with the human foot, as in anger.

strait In modern usage *strait* is never interchangeable with *straight*. It is a noun denoting either a passage of water or a position of difficulty or need: *in dire straits*.

strata This is the plural of *stratum*. We speak of a *stratum* (layer) of rock and of a *stratum* (category) of society, literature, or the like. *Strata* is properly preceded by *all, the,* or another modifier appropriate to a plural form, but never by *a*. To denote more than one *stratum,* only *strata* is acceptable; *stratas* is not a standard form.

sunk, sunken See **sink.**

superior A person or thing is said to be *superior to* (not *superior than*) another.

swim In modern usage the past tense is *swam,* the past participle *swum: swam a mile before breakfast; had never swum that early before.*

tablespoonful The plural is *tablespoonfuls.*

take See **bring, take.**

take place See **happen.**

tasteful, tasty In usage, *tasteful* is applied to that which shows a sense of what is proper or seemly, and *tasty* to what has a pleasing flavor.

teach See **learn, teach.**

tear   The past participle of the verb is *torn: He has torn the page. The page is torn. Tore* is the past tense: *He tore the page.*

teaspoonful   The plural is *teaspoonfuls.*

tend to   When this phrase expresses the sense of applying attention (*tended to his chores*), it is informal. *Attend to* is the formal equivalent.

than   In formal writing, *than* is generally construed as a conjunction rather than as a preposition in constructions that make comparisons. Accordingly, the inflected word following *than* is not necessarily in the objective case; case is determined by the word's grammatical function: *She dances better than I do.* The same rule applies to elliptical clauses introduced by *than,* in which unexpressed words are plainly indicated: *She dances better than I* (subject of unexpressed *do*). *She is a better dancer than I* (subject of unexpressed *am*). *The children liked no one more than her* (that is, *than they liked her*). In informal usage, the word following *than* is more often in the objective case. In some examples, an argument can be made for either the nominative or the objective case; both *They had no more devoted follower than she* and *They had no more devoted follower than her* are acceptable. The objective case always occurs in the expression *than whom: Lee, than whom no more admired general ever lived.*

that   For a discussion of ambiguity resulting from omission of *that* (conjunction), see "Faults of Omission."

that, which, who (whom)   All these are relative pronouns, whose function is to introduce subordinate clauses. Rules of usage guide the writer in choosing the right relative pronoun for a given example.

That has for its antecedent persons, animals, and things; *which* now refers only to animals and things; and *who* and *whom* refer to persons (and occasionally to animals).

The choice in formal writing is determined by the nature of the clauses introduced by the pronouns. *That* is used almost exclusively to introduce restrictive clauses, that is, clauses that define and limit the antecedent by providing information necessary for a real understanding of the sentence: *The book that you ordered has just arrived*. Such clauses are never set off by commas; a good test of a restrictive clause is that the relative pronoun can be unexpressed. *Who* and *whom* also may be used in restrictive clauses: *I met the girl (whom) you spoke of. Who, whom,* and especially *which* are employed to introduce nonrestrictive (nondefining) clauses, or those that provide incidental or nonessential information: *The book, which received excellent reviews, is much in demand. Later I spoke to my teacher, who has a German accent*. Such nonrestrictive clauses are set off by commas; in theory they are capable of being enclosed within parentheses. *Which* is

always used for clauses of both types when the relative pronoun is preceded by *that* used as a demonstrative pronoun: *We often long for that which is impossible.*

Sometimes it is hard to decide whether a clause is restrictive or nonrestrictive, and use of either *which* or *that* can be justified. But *that* should be employed when a clause is clearly restrictive; those who invariably choose *which* in all examples because they think it alone is appropriate in formal writing are misguided. Sometimes careful discrimination between *which* and *that* is essential to clarity: *The typewriter, which needs cleaning, is on the front table. The typewriter that needs cleaning is on the front table.* Unlike the first example, the second strongly implies the presence of more than one typewriter. See also **this.**

this Both *this* and *that,* as demonstrative pronouns, represent, in single summarizing words, thoughts expressed earlier: *She had good intentions, but that* (or *this*) *cannot excuse the wrong she did.* Either *that* or *this* is acceptable in most such examples. In formal writing, however, many authorities consider *that* the better choice in referring to what has gone before (a prior action or its basis, as in the example); *this* is preferably employed in referring to what is about to be stated: *That is what she intended, but this is what she did. This* tends to be much overworked in such sentences without regard to consideration of time. Neither *that* nor *this* should be used when the one

chosen is so far removed from the thought it represents that the reference is unclear; in such cases, restate what is meant. The use of *this* should also be avoided to refer to a person: *This is a public official of real integrity* (preferably *he* or *she is,* or *here is*).

though   When *though* is an adverb meaning however or nevertheless, it usually occurs at the end of a sentence or clause: *Its owners said the great liner could never sink; it did, though.* Such usage is more typical of speech and informal writing than of formal writing, in which *however* or *nevertheless* would be more likely to occur. A more clearly informal usage is the spelling *tho* for *though* in all the word's various senses. See also **although, though.**

thrash, thresh   *Thrash* is applied principally to the acts of beating, defeating, and lashing out with the arms or legs, and *thresh* to beating grain. To discuss or go over (something) is to *thresh over* it. The act of resolving by intensive discussion is expressed by either *thresh out* or *thrash out.*

through   As an adjective meaning finished, *through* has a less formal sound than its synonym *finished* but may be used on all levels: *Call when you are through.* The word is largely confined to informal usage in the senses of having no further relationship and having no further effectiveness: *He and I are through. As a serious contender he's through.* The spelling *thru* is also informal.

thus, thusly *Thus* is always the choice. *Thusly* is not only a needless variant of *thus* (itself an adverb) but also a nonstandard one.

tie The past tense and past participle of the verb is *tied,* the present participle *tying: tied the parcels; tying the score in the baseball game.*

till, until These are usually interchangeable, and each is found in formal writing. The shortened form *'til* is a third possibility but hardly a necessary one. *'Till* is nonstandard and should be avoided.

together with See **along with.**

tonite This variant spelling of *tonight* is not acceptable in formal usage.

too The use of *too* preceded by *not* or another negative is an acceptable means of conveying humor or sarcasm through understatement: *He was not too bright. They were not too pleased by the slight.* But *not too,* used indiscriminately to mean not very, is not appropriate in formal usage: *His health isn't too good* (preferably *very good* or *is none too good*). *Not too,* in such casual usage, can create ambiguity; the intended sense is generally not very, but the construction can be construed as meaning not excessively: *We cannot say too much for her effort.*

tore See **tear.**

tortuous, torturous Keep these straight by remem-

bering that *torturous* is associated with the pain and anguish of torture. *Tortuous* means winding, highly involved or complex, or not straightforward (and thus deceitful or devious).

toward, towards Either form is acceptable, though *toward* is more common in American formal writing.

transient, transitory *Transient* usually describes persons who remain in a given place only a short time: *a transient guest in a hotel; transient labor. Transient* can also mean short-lived or impermanent, inherently or otherwise, but that sense is generally expressed by *transitory: transitory exercise of power.*

transpire Apart from scientific usage, this verb should be employed in the sense of becoming known or coming to light. It is more widely employed to mean happen or occur, but that usage is considered improper by many authorities.

troop, troupe As noun and verb, *troupe* is applied only to stage performers. *Troop* has wider application, to persons, animals, or things, especially when they are on the move. It has particular reference to soldiers and Boy Scouts and Girl Scouts.

try In formal usage, *try* is followed by *to,* not by *and,* in expressing an attempt to accomplish something: *Try to finish on time.*

turbid, turgid *Turbid* means muddy, cloudy, dense,

or muddled. *Turgid* describes what is swollen, bloated, or excessively ornate in language or style.

type   As a noun denoting a group, *type* is used most precisely when it refers to a specific, clearly definable category; resemblance between members is marked, and so is difference from other groups. In contrast, *kind* and *sort* refer to less sharply definable categories. In expressions such as the following, *type* is always followed by *of* in formal usage: *this type of flower.*

unaware, unawares   *Unaware* is the adjective, followed by *of* (expressed or implied): *She seemed unaware of the danger. Unaware, she hastened ahead.* The adverb *unawares* qualifies a verb: *The storm caught them unawares. They made the discovery unawares.*

underestimate   Like *minimize,* this verb is often misused and conveys a meaning exactly opposite to that intended: *His worth cannot be underestimated.* To express the sense of great worth, make it *cannot be overestimated.*

underwater   The word is both an adjective (*underwater exploration*) and an adverb (*exploration performed underwater*). The adjective usually occurs before the noun it modifies. In examples such as the following, the two-word form is used: *Much of the town was under water after torrential rains.* The ad-

verbial example could also be written *performed under water*.

under way The phrase is written thus (two words).

undoubtedly See **doubtless, undoubtedly.**

unexceptionable, unexceptional These are not interchangeable. *Unexceptionable* means not open to objection or above reproach. *Unexceptional* means either not exceptional (and therefore usual or ordinary) or not permitting exceptions to a rule.

uninterested See **disinterested, uninterested.**

unique Something *unique* is in a class by itself, being the only one of its kind or without an equal. In careful usage, the adjective is construed as absolute; the quality it expresses cannot be said to vary in degree or intensity, and is consequently incapable of comparison. Therefore expressions such as *more unique* and *most unique,* indicating comparison, should be avoided, as should *rather* (or *somewhat*) *unique* and *very unique*. Each of these modifiers may be used with adjectives such as *unusual, remarkable, rare,* or *exceptional,* which are not absolute. *Unique* may be modified by terms that do not imply degree in the sense noted; each of these is acceptable: *really* (or *quite,* meaning truly) *unique; almost* (or *nearly*) *unique; more* (or *most*) *nearly unique*.

until See **till, until.**

up, upon   See **on, upon, up on.**

upcoming   In formal writing, *forthcoming, coming, approaching,* and *anticipated* are preferable to *upcoming.*

upward (or **upwards**) **of**   This expression means more than or in excess of. It should never be used to convey the sense of somewhat less than, about, or almost.

us   See **we.**

usage, use   *Usage,* a specialized term, has particular reference to what is customary practice or procedure and to the employment of language. When the desired meaning is related to employment or usefulness in a much more general way, *use* is the proper choice: *gave her car hard use; a new use for nylon.*

use(d) to   To express the meaning of regular practice or custom in past time, the verb *use* occurs in the inflected form *used,* or as *use* when coupled with *did.* For example: *He used to walk to work. He used not to ride* (or *did not use to ride*). *Did* (or *didn't*) *he use to ride?*

various   This is an adjective only: *wrote to various officials; her reasons were various.* It is not acceptably used as a plural collective pronoun, as in *wrote to various of the officials.*

verbal   See **oral, verbal.**

virtually See **practically, virtually.**

wake, waken See **awake, awaken.**

want The phrase *want for* is standard usage in expressing need: *She did not want for funds.* The same phrase is unacceptable in the sense of wish or desire: *She wants him to leave* (not *wants for him to leave* or *wants he should leave*).

way Referring to distance in general, the singular noun *way* is the only acceptable form in an example such as *a good way* (not *ways*) *to go.*

we The choice between the nominative pronoun *we* and the objective *us* is governed by the grammatical function of the pronoun in a given example. The same method of determination applies when *we* and *us* are followed by nouns, as in: *We officers were not consulted* (subject of verb). *They gave us officers no hearing* (indirect object).

well, well- The adverb *well* appears in many modifiers that are hyphenated when they stand before nouns: *the well-known actress.* A hyphen is not used when the modifier follows a verb: *The actress is well known for Shakespearean roles.*

were As the past subjunctive of the verb *be, were* appears in statements expressing conditions that are clearly hypothetical or contrary to fact: *if I were you.* Such statements frequently express a wish: *I wish that the operation were over.* Often they are introduced by

if and *as if* (or *as though*): *If the economy were more healthy, we would proceed. She acted as though everything were settled.* In formal writing, *were* is required in such examples; in speech and informal writing, the indicative form *was* is often found. But more errors probably occur through misguided use of *were.* Such misuse is especially common in mere conditional statements (not contrary to fact) and in indirect questions. In each of the following, *was,* not *were,* is proper: *They said that if the report was true, changes would be necessary. I tried to determine whether the emergency was over. They asked if he was agreeable.*

what The relative pronoun *what,* as the subject of a sentence or clause, can be either singular or plural in construction, according to the sense involved. It is construed as singular when *what* is the equivalent of *that which* or *a* (or *the*) *thing that;* it is plural when *what* stands for *things that* or *those which.* How *what* is construed governs the grammatical number of the verb or verbs that follow. For example: *He is involved in what seems to be an outright fraud. They are making what appear to be signs of welcome. What impresses me most is his honesty. What were intended as gestures of friendship appear to have aroused suspicion.* Note that in the last two examples, the verbs preceding and following *what* agree in number. In some examples, either a singular or a plural construction of *what* is possible, especially when the elements

following the second verb can be construed collectively or abstractly and *what* has the meaning that which: *Sometimes what really commands respect is power and the willingness to use it effectively.* Or two plural verbs could be used.

when This word and *where* should not be used to define other words, as in *a rupture is when* (or *where*) *there is a tear in bodily tissue.* A noun is defined in terms of another noun: *A rupture is a tear.*

whence Since *whence* has a built-in sense of *from,* it is not preceded by *from* except redundantly: *the land whence* (not *from whence*) *he came.*

where Use *where* with *from* to indicate motion from a place: *Where did she come from?* Use *where* alone in a corresponding sentence to indicate direction or motion to a place: *Where did she go* (not *go to*)? Use *where* alone to indicate location or position of rest: *Where is she now* (not *where is she at now*)? *Where* is improperly used as a conjunction, in place of *that,* in sentences such as *I see where* (properly *that*) *he has resigned.* See also **when.**

which In sentences such as the following, *which* means a thing or circumstance that: *He seemed unhappy, which was understandable. Which* refers to an entire preceding clause instead of to a single word. This usage is acceptable when the reference is clear, as in the preceding example. It should be avoided

when the reference is unclear. Ambiguity occurs most often when *which* follows a noun that could be construed as the antecedent: *She refused our offer, which caused much surprise.* If the surprise stemmed from the refusal rather than from the nature of the offer, rephrasing is desirable: *She refused our offer, and that caused much surprise.* See also **that, which, who (whom).**

while   As a conjunction, *while* is used most often, and most safely, to indicate a period of time: *He slept while I worked.* It is also acceptably used to mean although: *While we dislike her, we did respect her talent.* It is acceptable too in the sense of whereas, to imply opposition or difference: *The main figure is red, while the background is blue.* In such examples, when something other than time is intended but a reference to time can easily be read into them, *while* should be replaced by a more specific conjunction: *While he had rifles of his own, he believed strongly in control of firearms* (preferably *Although he had*). *He spent his youth in Ohio, while his father grew up in England* (preferably *whereas his father grew up*). *While* should never be used as a mere substitute for *and,* as in *They took steak, my brother had veal, while I ordered fish.* See also **awhile, a while.**

whiskey, whisky   *Whiskey* is the more common spelling in American usage, particularly for American and Irish liquor. *Scotch whisky* and *Canadian whisky* are spelled thus.

who, whom   In written usage, especially on a formal level, the grammatical distinctions between these pronouns are closely observed. *Who* (and *whoever*) are nominative forms employed to represent a subject or a predicate after a form of the verb *be*. *Whom* (and *whomever*) are corresponding objective pronouns, used principally to represent an object of a verb or of a preposition. In speech and informal writing, *who* often replaces *whom* in questions (*Who did they choose?*) and in sentences in which the object of a preposition precedes the preposition: *He wanted to know who he should speak to.* In both examples, on a formal level, *whom* is required. Misuse of *whom,* when *who* is indicated, is a more glaring error; it occurs most often when the pronoun is misconstrued as the object of a verb when in fact it is the subject of a clause: *I talked to a man who I think is much interested in the job.* The choice between *who* and *whom* depends always on the pronoun's function in its clause, even though the entire clause may be the object of a verb or of a preposition: *Who shall we say is calling? They will accept whoever is chosen. They will accept whomever the delegates name. We should give our support to whoever is selected. We should give our support to whomever the delegates express a preference for.* See also **than; that, which, who (whom).**

whose   *Whose* functions as the possessive form of both *who* and *which*. As such it can refer to things as well as to persons: *It is the only work whose author-*

ship is in doubt. The alternative possessive form *of which* is also possible in referring to things: *the only work the authorship of which is in doubt*. In that example, as in most others, the alternative is too cumbersome to be desirable.

why   See **reason**.

wide   See **broad, wide**.

will   See **shall, will**.

-wise   In certain combinations, such as *taxwise* and *timewise, -wise* means with reference to. The usage is informal outside business writing, where its conciseness is considered an asset. On other levels, such combinations are objectionable particularly if they are formed indiscriminately and overused, thus giving the effect of commercial jargon.

with   See **along with**.

would   *Would have* is frequently misused for *had* in conditional clauses introduced by *if*. The following illustrate correct forms: *They could have come if they had wanted to* (not *if they would have wanted to*). *If they had come, this would not have occurred* (not *if they would have come*). *Had* is also the proper auxiliary in clauses following *wish*: *I wish that she had called* (not *that she would have called*). See also **should, would**.

wrack   See **rack, wrack**.

wrong, wrongly   In the meaning erroneously, *wrong* is the more common adverb, but *wrongly* is used before a verb or participle that it modifies: *advised us wrong; spelled it wrong; a wrongly conceived arrangement.*

Xmas   Although the word is by no means the creation of modern advertising, it is now largely confined to that medium and to commercial writing. It is not appropriate to formal usage.

yet   As an adverb meaning up to the present, thus far, or in the phrase *as yet,* this word is used with a perfect tense rather than with the simple past tense: *She has not called yet. Have you made plans yet?*

yourself, yourselves   In formal usage, these are not interchangeable with *you* in sentences such as *They are expecting the Smiths and yourself. Yourselves and our neighbors come from the same town.* Make it *you* in both examples.

How it is Written

Forms of Address

Forms of address do not always follow set guidelines; the type of salutation is often determined by the relationship between correspondents or by the purpose and content of the letter. However, a general style applies to most occasions. In formal salutations, when the addressee is a woman, "Madam" should be substituted for "Sir." When the salutation is informal, "Mrs." or "Miss" or "Ms." should be substituted for "Mr." If a woman addressee has previously stated a preference for a particular form of address this form should be used.

	Form of Address	Salutation
Academics		
assistant professor, college or university	Dr. (*or* Mr.) Joseph Stone Assistant Professor Department of ___	Dear Professor Stone:
associate professor, college or university	Dr. (*or* Mr.) Joseph Stone Associate Professor Department of ___	Dear Professor Stone:
chancellor, university	Chancellor Joseph Stone	Dear Chancellor Stone:

dean, college or university	Dean Joseph Stone *or* Dr. (*or* Mr.) Joseph Stone Dean, School of ____	Dear Dean Stone: Dear Dr. (*or* Mr.) Stone:
president, college or university	President Joseph Stone *or* Dr. (*or* Mr.) Joseph Stone President, ____	Dear President Stone: Dear Dr. (*or* Mr.) Stone:
professor, college or university	Professor Joseph Stone *or* Dr. (*or* Mr.) Joseph Stone Department of ____	Dear Professor Stone: Dear Dr. (*or* Mr.) Stone:

Clerical and Religious Orders

abbot, Roman Catholic	The Right Reverend Joseph Stone, O.S.B. Abbot of ____	Right Reverend Abbot:
archbishop, Armenian Church	His Eminence the Archbishop of ____	Your Eminence: *or* Your Excellency:
archbishop, Greek Orthodox	His Eminence Archbishop Joseph Stone	Your Eminence:
archbishop, Roman Catholic	The Most Reverend Joseph Stone Archbishop of ____	Your Excellency:

323

archbishop, Russian Orthodox	His Eminence the Archbishop of —— *or* The Most Reverend Archbishop of ——	Your Grace: Right Reverend Joseph:
archdeacon, Episcopal	The Venerable Joseph Stone, Archdeacon of ——	Venerable Sir: Dear Archdeacon Stone: Dear Father Stone:
archimandrite, Russian Orthodox	Very Reverend Father Joseph Stone	Very Reverend Father: Very Reverend Father Stone:
archpriest, Russian Orthodox	Very Reverend Father Joseph Stone	Very Reverend Father: Very Reverend Father Stone:
bishop, Episcopal	The Right Reverend Joseph Stone Bishop of ——	Right Reverend Sir: Dear Bishop Stone:
bishop, Greek Orthodox	The Right Reverend Joseph Stone	Your Grace:
bishop, Methodist	Bishop Joseph Stone	Dear Bishop Stone:
bishop, Roman Catholic	The Most Reverend Joseph Stone Bishop of ——	Your Excellency:
brotherhood, Roman Catholic, member of	Brother Joseph Stone, C.F.C.	Dear Brother: Dear Brother Joseph:

canon, Episcopal	The Reverend Canon Joseph Stone	Dear Canon Stone:
cantor	Cantor Joseph Stone	Dear Cantor Stone:
cardinal	His Eminence Joseph Cardinal Stone	Your Eminence:
clergyman, Protestant	The Reverend Joseph Stone *or* The Reverend Joseph Stone, D.D.	Dear Mr. (*or* Dr.) Stone:
elder, Presbyterian	Elder Joseph Stone	Dear Elder Stone:
dean of a cathedral, Episcopal	The Very Reverend Joseph Stone Dean of ____	Very Reverend Sir: Dear Dean Stone:
metropolitan, Russian Orthodox	His Eminence the Metropolitan of ____ *or* The Most Reverend Metropolitan of ____	Your Grace: Right Reverend Joseph:
monsignor, Roman Catholic	Reverend Monsignor Joseph Stone	Reverend Monsignor: Dear Monsignor: Dear Monsignor Stone:
patriarch, Armenian Church	His Beatitude the Patriarch of ____	Your Beatitude:
patriarch, Greek Orthodox	His All Holiness Patriarch Demetrios	Your All Holiness:
patriarch, Russian Orthodox	His Beatitude the Patriarch of ____	Your Beatitude:

325

		Your Holiness:
pope	His Holiness Pope John XXIII *or* His Holiness the Pope	
president, Mormon Church	President Joseph Stone Church of Jesus Christ of Latter-day Saints	Dear President Stone:
priest, Greek Orthodox	Reverend Father Joseph Stone	Dear Reverend Stone: Dear Reverend Father:
priest, Roman Catholic	The Reverend Joseph Stone, S.J.	Dear Reverend Father: Dear Father: Dear Father Stone:
priest, Russian Orthodox	The Reverend Joseph Stone	Reverend Father: Reverend Father Stone:
protopresbyter, Russian Orthodox	Very Reverend Father Joseph Stone	Very Reverend Father: Very Reverend Father Stone:

Clerical and Religious Orders

rabbi	Rabbi Joseph Stone *or* Joseph Stone, D.D.	Dear Rabbi (*or* Dr.) Stone:
sisterhood, Roman Catholic, member of	Sister Mary Stone, C.S.J.	Dear Sister: Dear Sister Mary:
supreme patriarch, Armenian Church	His Holiness the Supreme Patriarch and Catholicos of all Armenians	Your Holiness:

Diplomats

ambassador, U.S.	The Honorable Joseph Stone The Ambassador of the United States	Sir: Dear Mr. Ambassador:
ambassador to the U.S.	His Excellency Joseph Stone The Ambassador of _____	Excellency: Dear Mr. Ambassador:
chargé d'affaires, U.S.	Joseph Stone, Esq. American Chargé d'Affaires	Dear Sir:
chargé d'affaires to the U.S.	Joseph Stone, Esq. Chargé d'Affaires of _____	Dear Sir:
consul, U.S.	Mr. Joseph Stone American Consul	Sir: Dear Mr. Consul:
minister, U.S.	The Honorable Joseph Stone The Minister of the United States	Sir: Dear Mr. Minister:
minister to the U.S.	The Honorable Joseph Stone The Minister of _____	Sir: Dear Mr. Minister:
secretary general, United Nations	His Excellency Joseph Stone Secretary General of the United Nations	Excellency: Dear Mr. Secretary General:
U.S. representative to the United Nations	The Honorable Joseph Stone United States Representative to the United Nations	Sir: Dear Mr. Stone:

327

Federal, state, and local officials (government)

alderman	The Honorable Joseph Stone	Dear Mr. Stone:
assistant to the President	The Honorable Joseph Stone Assistant to the President The White House	Dear Mr. Stone:
Attorney General, U.S.	The Honorable Joseph Stone Attorney General of the United States	Dear Mr. Attorney General:
attorney general, state	The Honorable Joseph Stone Attorney General State of _____	Dear Mr. Attorney General:
assemblyman, state	The Honorable Joseph Stone _____ Assembly State Capitol	Dear Mr. Stone:
cabinet member	The Honorable Joseph Stone Secretary of _____	Dear Mr. Secretary:
assistant secretary of a department	The Honorable Joseph Stone Assistant Secretary of _____	Dear Mr. Stone:
undersecretary of a department	The Honorable Joseph Stone Undersecretary of _____	Dear Mr. Stone:
deputy secretary of a department	The Honorable Joseph Stone Deputy Secretary of _____	Dear Mr. Stone:
chairman, House Committee	The Honorable Joseph Stone Chairman, Committee on _____ United States House of Representatives	Dear Mr. Chairman:

328

chairman, joint committee of Congress	The Honorable Joseph Stone Chairman, Joint Committee on Congress of the United States	Dear Mr. Chairman:
chairman, Senate Committee	The Honorable Joseph Stone Chairman, Committee on —— United States Senate	Dear Mr. Chairman:
chief justice, U.S. Supreme Court	The Chief Justice of the United States The Supreme Court of the United States	Dear Mr. Chief Justice:
associate justice, U.S. Supreme Court	Mr. Justice Stone The Supreme Court of the United States	Dear Mr. Justice:
commissioner (federal, state, or local)	The Honorable Joseph Stone	Dear Mr. Stone:
delegate, state	The Honorable Joseph Stone House of Delegates State Capitol	Dear Mr. Stone:
governor	The Honorable Joseph Stone Governor of ——	Dear Governor Stone:
judge, federal	The Honorable Joseph Stone Judge of the United States Tax Court	Dear Judge Stone:
judge, state or local	The Honorable Joseph Stone Judge of the Superior Court of ——	Dear Judge Stone:
lieutenant governor	The Honorable Joseph Stone Lieutenant Governor of ——	Dear Mr. Stone:
mayor	The Honorable Joseph Stone Mayor of ——	Dear Mayor Stone:

Postmaster General	The Honorable Joseph Stone Postmaster General of the United States	Dear Mr. Postmaster General:
President, U.S.	The President The White House	Dear Mr. President:
former President, U.S.	The Honorable Joseph Stone	Dear Mr. Stone:
representative, state	The Honorable Joseph Stone House of Representatives State Capitol	Dear Mr. Stone:
representative, U.S.	The Honorable Joseph Stone United States House of Representatives	Dear Mr. Stone:
secretary of state, state	The Honorable Joseph Stone Secretary of State State Capitol	Dear Mr. Secretary:
senator, state	The Honorable Joseph Stone The State Senate State Capitol	Dear Senator Stone:
senator, U.S.	The Honorable Joseph Stone United States Senate	Dear Senator Stone:
Speaker, U.S. House of Representatives	The Honorable Joseph Stone Speaker of the House of Representatives	Dear Mr. Speaker:
Vice President, U.S.	The Vice President United States Senate	Dear Mr. Vice President:

Professions

attorney	Mr. Joseph Stone Attorney at Law *or* Joseph Stone, Esq.	Dear Mr. Stone:
chiropractor	Joseph Stone, D.C. (office) *or* Dr. Joseph Stone (residence)	Dear Dr. Stone:
dentist	Joseph Stone, D.D.S. (office) *or* Dr. Joseph Stone (residence)	Dear Dr. Stone:
physician	Joseph Stone, M.D. (office) *or* Dr. Joseph Stone (residence)	Dear Dr. Stone:
veterinarian	Joseph Stone, D.V.M. (office) *or* Dr. Joseph Stone (residence)	Dear Dr. Stone:

Military

admiral vice admiral rear admiral	Full rank, full name, abbreviation of service branch	Dear Admiral Stone:
airman first class airman airman basic	Full rank, full name, abbreviation of service branch	Dear Airman Stone:

331

cadet (air force, army)	Cadet Joseph Stone, United States Air Force Academy, United States Military Academy	Dear Cadet Stone: *or* Dear Mr. Stone:
captain, (air force, army, coast guard, marine corps, navy)	Full rank, full name, abbreviation of service branch	Dear Captain Stone:
chief petty officer (coast guard, navy)	Full rank, full name, abbreviation of service branch	Dear Mr. Stone: *or* Dear Chief Stone:
chief warrant officer, warrant officer (air force, army, marine corps, navy)	Full rank, full name, abbreviation of service branch	Dear Mr. Stone:
colonel, lieutenant colonel (air force, army, marine corps)	Full rank, full name, abbreviation of service branch	Dear Colonel Stone:
commander (coast guard, navy)	Full rank, full name, abbreviation of service branch	Dear Commander Stone:
commodore (navy)	Full rank, full name, abbreviation of service branch	Dear Commodore Stone:
corporal (army), lance corporal (marine corps)	Full rank, full name, abbreviation of service branch	Dear Corporal Stone:

ensign (coast guard, navy)	Full rank, full name, abbreviation of service branch	Dear Mr. Stone: *or* Dear Ensign Stone:
first lieutenant, second lieutenant (air force, army, marine corps)	Full rank, full name, abbreviation of service branch	Dear Lieutenant Stone:
general, lieutenant general, major general, brigadier general (air force, army, marine corps)	Full rank, full name, abbreviation of service branch	Dear General Stone:
lieutenant commander, lieutenant, lieutenant (jg) (coast guard, navy)	Full rank, full name, abbreviation of service branch	Dear Mr. Stone: *or* Dear Lieutenant Stone:
major (air force, army, marine corps)	Full rank, full name, abbreviation of service branch	Dear Major Stone:
midshipman	Midshipman Joseph Stone United States Coast Guard Academy United States Naval Academy	Dear Midshipman Stone:
petty officer (coast guard, navy)	Full rank, full name, abbreviation of service branch	Dear Mr. Stone:
private first class, private (air force, army, marine corps)	Full rank, full name, abbreviation of service branch	Dear Private Stone:

seaman, seaman apprentice, seaman recruit (coast guard, navy)	Full rank, full name, abbreviation of service branch	Dear Seaman Stone:
master sergeant (air force, army, marine corps)	Full rank, full name, abbreviation of service branch	Dear Sergeant Stone:

Note: Other compound titles in enlisted ranks are not shown here. They all follow forms indicated for this example.

specialist (army)	Full rank, full name, abbreviation of service branch	Dear Specialist Stone:

Social notes

Each of us has "social business" to conduct. We invite people to parties, answer invitations, send gifts, thank others for gifts, offer sympathy to the bereaved, and congratulate those who have cause for gladness.

For some of us, writing social notes comes easily and naturally. For others, each note is written with great difficulty and uncertainty. The sample notes in this section are designed to serve as models to be used by people who find social notes difficult to write.

All social notes and their acknowledgments should be handwritten, but for easier reading they have been typed in the following examples.

None of the notes in this section would be considered formal, but different degrees of informality are used. In each of the notes, the writer would use a more chatty tone with a good friend than with a casual acquaintance. Even when the tone is not chatty, the wording should not be too stiff or artificial. At times social notes must be written to complete strangers, and it is important to convey a feeling of warmth in your note.

Most of these notes are brief. They are not letters, although many of the messages could be included in longer letters.

A word about stationery

Social notes should be on personal stationery of good quality and simple design. The stationery may

have your name or initials; it may have a picture or design; or it may be unadorned. Business stationery is not usually appropriate for these notes.

Invitations and replies

Many people today use the printed invitations one finds in stationery stores to invite people to parties and dinners. Other people choose to write out the invitations in full. Try to keep invitations short so that the essential details are prominent. The invitation should include the following information:

> Date
> Time
> Host or hostess
> Occasion or purpose
> Location
> R.S.V.P.

At times it will be necessary to include a map or directions. These are usually enclosed on a sheet inserted into the folded invitation. If the guest does not know your address, you should be sure it is on the invitation as well as on the envelope. If you want people to telephone their replies, you should show your telephone number on the invitation unless you are certain that the phone number is known.

Acceptances and refusals follow the invitations given here as examples. If you must refuse an invitation that you really want to accept, your genuine regret should show.

Dear Lucie and John,

We are having a buffet dinner at our home next Friday evening, March 22, at 7:30. We hope you can be there.

Sincerely,

Ellen Miller

R.S.V.P.

Dear Ellen,

Thank you for inviting us to the buffet. We gladly accept the invitation.

Sincerely,

Lucie and John

Dear Ellen,

Thank you for the invitation to the buffet. We wish we could accept it, but we have already made plans for that evening. Perhaps we can get together some other time soon.

Sincerely,

Marcia and Lewis

Dear Ellen and Paul,

Mark will be home from college for the holidays. To celebrate, we are giving a luncheon on Saturday, December 19, at one o'clock at Gerard's Restaurant, 110 East Road. We hope you are able to join us.

Sincerely,

Lucie Johnson

R.S.V.P.

Dear Lucie,

   We are looking forward to seeing
Mark again and gladly accept your
invitation. Thank you for including us.

                    Sincerely,

                    Ellen and Paul

Dear Lucie,

   Thank you for inviting me to the
luncheon to celebrate Mark's homecom-
ing. I wish I could be there, but I
expect to be away on vacation at that
time. Please remember me to Mark. I
hope to see him the next time he
comes home.

                    Sincerely,

                    Polly

Dear Mrs. Wilson,

Now that the big project has been completed successfully, it is time to celebrate. We are inviting the entire staff and their families out to the house for a barbecue on Sunday, June 10, at 12:30. I hope that you, your husband, and your children can come.

Our address is 78 Wildwood Drive, Smithtown, N.J. 01234. A map is enclosed to help you find your way.

Yours truly,

Frank Fisher

R.S.V.P.

Dear Mr. Fisher,

Thank you for the invitation. Our family is looking forward to the barbecue.

Sincerely,

Lois Wilson

Dear Mr. Fisher,

Thank you for the invitation. We wish we could accept it, but we have already made some family commitments for that afternoon.

Sincerely,

Joan Wood

Sometimes the host or hostess wants a guest to feel free to bring a friend to the party. The invitation should be worded so that the guest will feel comfortable about inviting someone but will not feel uncomfortable about coming alone.

Dear Ellie,

Since so many of our friends were unable to go to Houston for Bob's wedding, we have decided to have a small reception here so that our friends can meet Laura, our new daughter-in-law.

The party will be held at the Green Lake Country Club, Saturday, July 31, at 8:30 p.m. We hope that you will be able to come.

Please feel free to bring an escort if you choose.

Sincerely,

Gloria and Rick

R.S.V.P.

Dear Gloria and Rick,

Thank you for the invitation to the reception. I'll be glad to attend. It was very thoughtful of you to ask me to bring an escort. I have invited Bill Jones to accompany me.

Sincerely,

Ellie Smith

In some instances, a host or hostess wants the prospective guests to reply by telephone.

Dear Ruth and Allan,

I am planning a surprise fortieth birthday party for Len on Saturday, April 9, at 8:00 p.m. Our neighbors, the Browns, have kindly offered their home for the occasion. Their address is 987 Pebble Road, Milltown. Please call me at 246-3579 between 9 and 5 to let me known if you will be there.

Sincerely,

Jane Arthur

At times a person finds that he or she is giving a party for both friends and strangers. Invitations to the same party should be worded differently to each group. The following letters illustrate how a man invites both *his* friends and family and *his daughter's fiancé's* friends and family to the same party.

Dear Anne and Joe,

    I am giving a party at my home on May 12, a Saturday evening, at 8:00, to celebrate Lenore's engagement to Andrew Miller. It will give our friends an opportunity to meet Lenore's fiancé. I hope you will be there.

              Sincerely,

              Jerry Stone

R.S.V.P.

Dear Mr. and Mrs. Miller,

I am giving a party on May 12, Saturday evening at 8:00, to celebrate the engagement of my daughter Lenore to your nephew Andrew Miller. It would give us great pleasure if you could attend. The address is 21 Old Creek Drive, Welltown. I am enclosing a map and directions.

Yours truly,

Jeremy Stone

R.S.V.P.

Replies would also be worded differently by friends and strangers.

Dear Jerry,

We are delighted to come to Lenore's engagement party. We would not miss the chance to celebrate the happy event.

Sincerely,

Anne and Joe

Dear Jerry,

We wish we could attend the engagement party for Lenore and Andrew. Unfortunately, we cannot be there. Since Sam's niece is to be married that same evening, we must decline your invitation. Our love and best wishes to the happy couple.

Love,

Ellie and Sam

Dear Mr. Stone,

We are very happy to accept your invitation to the engagement party for Lenore and Andrew.

Sincerely,

Betty and James Miller

Dear Mr. Stone,

Thank you for your invitation to the engagement party for Lenore and Andrew. Unfortunately, we shall be unable to attend, since we expect to be away at the time.

We look forward to meeting you at another time.

Sincerely,

Sylvia and Marty Miller

Occasionally only half of a married couple can accept an invitation. If the occasion does not demand a balance of men and women, one reply may be used to accept the invitation on the part of one person and refuse it for the other.

Dear Jerry,

Thank you for the invitation to the engagement party. Although Stan will be able to attend, I will not. I am leaving next week to visit my mother in Florida. She has not been feeling well. Stan will have to represent us both and convey our best wishes for the children's future happiness.

Sincerely,
Barbara

When you invite people to visit, the tone of the note is determined by how well you know them. There are times when you may extend an invitation to someone you have not met. Then the tone should certainly be warm and welcoming.

If the invitation includes several people, it should clearly say that it does.

Invitations for a visit should be accepted or refused as soon as possible. If you are unable to accept the invitation for the time indicated but would like to visit at another time, your reply may suggest this.

Dear Sue and Bob,

It seems like ages since you moved to Washington. We miss you and would love to have you and the children stay with us during the Christmas vacation. If you can come for a visit, please let us know so that we may get some tickets for a show or two.

Sincerely,
Molly and Ned

Dear Molly and Ned,

We have been thinking of coming back for a visit, but until your letter we could not decide. Now we have an additional reason to come home, and we accept your invitation gladly.

All of us look forward to seeing you and the children. We do miss you, even though life in Washington has been exciting for us. As soon as we know exactly what travel arrangements we can make, we'll let you know.

Thank you so much.

Sincerely,
Sue and Bob

Dear Molly and Ned,

How tempting your invitation sounds! Unfortunately we can't get away at Christmas time. Our parents are coming here for a visit then.

Perhaps we can visit at some other time. We do miss you and would love to see you.

> Sincerely,
>
> Sue and Bob

Dear Jennifer,

Mark speaks of you often and with great warmth. He has asked me to invite you for a visit, and I do so gladly. We should like it very much if you could spend Memorial Day weekend with us.

If you can, be sure to pack a swimsuit and tennis racket. We usually give a party that weekend, so be sure to include something dressy.

We are looking forward to meeting you. Please let us know if you can visit.

> Sincerely,
>
> Cynthia Blaine

Dear Mrs. Blaine,

It would be lovely to spend Memorial Day weekend with you. Mark often speaks of his parents, and I feel that I almost know you.

Thank you again for the invitation. I am looking forward to meeting you.

Sincerely,

Jennifer Green

Dear Mrs. Blaine,

Thank you for the invitation. Unfortunately I am not free Memorial Day weekend.

Mark speaks of his parents often. I look forward to meeting you at another time.

Sincerely,

Jennifer Green

Dear George,

I bought some land for a weekend place. Although the house isn't finished yet, my son, Tom, and I have been camping out there weekends. There is good camping, fishing, swimming, and hiking.

Why don't you and your boys join us next weekend? Bring your own camping and fishing equipment. I'll take care of the food.

If you can come, let me know and I'll send you directions.

Sam

Dear Sam,

Thanks for the invitation. The boys are excited and we're all looking forward to a weekend of camping.

Yours,

George

Dear Sam,

The invitation to camp out sounds so good that I hate to turn it down. But I do have to say no. Beth invited her family here for a barbecue that Saturday. It's her father's birthday.

Can we have a rain check? I'd like to go up there with the boys some other weekend.

Sincerely,
George

Dear Mr. and Mrs. Blaine,

We are delighted that the children have decided to marry. Mark is such a fine boy that we are glad to have him in the family.

It is unfortunate that you live so far away that we have not met. We should like to remedy that by inviting you to visit us for a weekend. We have a very comfortable guest room.

Could you come here for the Thanksgiving weekend? If that weekend is impossible for you, please suggest one that would be possible.

Sincerely,
Wilma Green

Dear Mrs. Green,

It is very gracious of you to invite us for the Thanksgiving weekend. We have heard a great deal about you and are looking forward to meeting you.

We can leave here late Wednesday afternoon and stop somewhere en route to allow us to reach your house at about noon on Thursday. Would that be satisfactory?

Sincerely yours,

Cynthia Blaine

Dear Mrs. Green,

It is very kind of you to invite us for the Thanksgiving weekend. Unfortunately, we cannot make it then. We are free both the weekend before that and the weekend after. Would either of those be good for you?

We look forward to meeting you soon.

Sincerely,

Cynthia Blaine

Congratulations and good wishes

There are many occasions for congratulating people: marriages, births, promotions, awards, etc. A thoughtful person remembers to extend congratulations when the occasion calls for it. Notes of congratulations need not be long.

Dear George,

    I just heard the good news about your promotion. Congratulations on the well-deserved recognition.

                Sincerely,

                Sam

Dear Mr. Smith,

    Congratulations on becoming a vice president. Those who have worked with you over the years believe that you are well suited to your new responsibilities.

                Sincerely,

                Leslie Davis

Dear Paul,

We understand that you have just received the man-of-the-year award. Congratulations! You have certainly earned the honor.

Sincerely,

Jessie and Joe Turner

Dear Kim,

Your mother just told us that you are about to receive your Ph.D. degree. Congratulations. It is an excellent achievement.

We wish you a successful career in your chosen field.

Sincerely,

Joyce and William Wilde

Dear Lyle,

We saw your name today in the news-paper as one who has passed the bar exam. Congratulations and our good wishes for your success as an attorney.

Sincerely,

Anne and Harvey Butler

Dear Joyce and Bill,

Is it really twenty-five years since your wedding? The time has certainly flown by.

We want to offer our best wishes for your silver anniversary and for happiness in the next twenty-five as well.

Sincerely,

Cynthia and Arthur Blaine

Dear Mr. and Mrs. Wilde,

Congratulations on your twenty-fifth wedding anniversary. May you continue to have a good life in the years to come.

Sincerely,
Kim Collins

Dear Sam and Ellie,

We just heard that you have become grandparents. Congratulations! Please extend our best wishes to the new parents and baby.

Sincerely,
Cynthia and Arthur

Dear Jennifer and Mark,

Congratulations on your new baby. We wish you all health and happiness and the things you wish for yourselves.

Sincerely,
Sylvia and Martin Miller

Dear Lucie and Jack,

    Your wedding announcement just appeared in the newspaper and we had to write immediately to tell you how happy we are for you both. We wish you a life full of all the good things that you wish for yourselves.

                Sincerely,

                Ann and Harvey Butler

For many years it was considered proper to congratulate a man on his engagement, but simply to offer wishes for happiness to a woman. Many customs are changing, but it is still considered more appropriate to avoid using the word "congratulations" in a note to a woman concerning her engagement.

The tone of the note may depend on whether you do or do not know the fiancé or fiancée of the person to whom you write.

Dear Beth,

Mr. Harris and I are delighted to learn of your engagement. We wish you much happiness in your forthcoming marriage and hope we may have the pleasure of meeting your fiancé soon.

Sincerely,

Sarah Harris

Dear Lawrence,

Congratulations! James and I have learned that you and Beth are to be married soon. She is a lovely young woman. We wish you both a long and happy life together.

Sincerely,

Peggy Moore

Notes accompanying gifts

Any note of congratulations may accompany a gift. If you do not want to write out an entire note, one line will do.

Dear Beth and Lawrence,

We are sending you this cake plate along with our best wishes for your new life together.

Sincerely,

Constance and Colin Foster

To Melissa,

With my love and best wishes.

Sally

Congratulations and good luck!

George

For the new baby with our love,

Ellie and Sam

Thank-you notes

Thank-you notes are part of life's social exchange. They are sent to people who have entertained you, who have given you gifts, or who have shown some special kindness to you. Ideally, thank-you notes should be sent out within a day after the occasion for thanks. That is not always possible. After a large party at which many gifts have been received, it is impossible to send thank-you notes to everybody at once. Then, you must try to send them as soon as possible.

In any event, it is especially important to send notes promptly to people who have sent presents by mail delivery service. These people want to know that the presents have actually arrived.

When you thank someone for something, try to mention exactly what you are thanking the person for.

Dear Mr. and Mrs. Foster,

    Thank you so much for the beautiful cake plate and for your good wishes.

        Sincerely,

        Beth and Lawrence

Dear Sally,

The stemware arrived today. It is beautiful. Thank you. Come soon and let us toast you with one of the goblets.

Love,

Beth and Lawrence

Dear Mr. and Mrs. Welles,

Thank you for the lovely flowers you sent for my recital. The occasion itself was exciting to me, but your flowers made me feel like a star.

Sincerely,

Janice Taylor

Dear Aunt Martha,

Thank you for the delightful evening at the opera. I enjoyed myself thoroughly and appreciate your having asked me.

Sincerely,

Laurie

Dear Mrs. Green,

Your dinner party last night was delightful. Thank you for inviting us. We shall remember it for a long time to come.

Sincerely,

Mary and Harry Bell

Dear Laurie,

The beautiful dress for Betsy arrived today. It is lovely and the color is perfect for the baby. Thank you for thinking of her.

Sincerely,

Ginny

Dear Bill,

You turned a long weekend in a strange town into a pleasant one. Thanks for the tickets to the ball game and the play. I enjoyed them thoroughly.

Sincerely,

Chuck

Dear Mr. Chandler,

Thank you for the book that you sent me when I was in the hospital. It was enjoyable light reading and kept my mind off the nuisance of being ill.

Sincerely,

Harvey Bell

Dear Mrs. Fisher,

It was very generous of you to take the time to show me around a strange city. Thank you very much for making me feel so much at home.

Sincerely,

Joan Jones

Dear Mrs. Green,

Thank you for the lovely weekend we spent at your home. It was delightful to meet you and your family and to feel the warmth of your hospitality.

Sincerely,

Cynthia Blaine

Inquiry into whether a gift has been received

When you have sent a gift and have received no note or telephone call, you may need to find out whether the gift has actually arrived. It is wise to avoid assuming that the person has received the gift and not acknowledged it. Department stores, the post office, and delivery services have on occasion lost packages.

After a sufficient time has elapsed, you may have to write this most difficult letter. Be sure your return address is on the envelope. If you have sent both the package and the letter to the wrong address, your returned letter may be the only way you have to learn of your mistake.

Needless to say, if you receive such a letter, you should answer it immediately either by mail or by telephone.

Dear Sandra,

Last month I sent a complete layette for your new baby. Have you received it? If not, I want to begin to make inquiries at the department store as soon as possible.

Please let me know promptly.

Love,

Aunt Meg

Dear Aunt Meg,

Thank you for your note. No, the layette never arrived. I am glad that you thought to write and ask me about it.

After you check at your department store, please let me know if I must make any inquiries as well.

Love,

Sandra

Dear Aunt Meg,

I am thoroughly embarrassed! Your beautiful layette arrived some time ago, and Melissa has been using it.

I had not realized that so much time had elapsed without my having thanked you. Please forgive me. I am truly grateful for your kindness in sending the gift.

Love,

Sandra

Condolence notes

Condolence notes are sent when someone has died. Usually, you know both the deceased and the bereaved. Sometimes, you know only one.

Condolence notes should be short except when you are writing to someone close to you. Then a longer, more personal, letter may be sent.

Dear Mr. Brown,

James and I are sorry to hear of your loss. We extend our condolences to you and your family.

Yours truly,

Constance Foster

Dear Mr. Brown,

I was grieved to learn of your loss. Those of us who worked with your father knew him to be a man with a warm sense of humor and good common sense. We shall miss him. Please accept my sympathy.

Sincerely,

Joan Jones

Dear Sally,

    We are so sorry to learn of your
loss. Although we never knew your
mother, your many stories made it clear
that she was an extraordinary person.
    Our loving sympathy goes out to you.

                    Sincerely,

                    Belle and Ben Nolan

The résumé

A résumé is a short description of your history in work and at school. Many white-collar jobs require a résumé from any prospective employee. At times, your résumé will be mailed to a prospective employer. What the résumé reveals about you may determine whether or not you are actually interviewed for a job.

The résumé should be neatly typed. If you are not a good typist, there are services that will retype the material you have written. Spelling and grammar should be correct. It is advisable to have someone else read over what you have written before you send it out. Once you are satisfied that what you have written is in good order, you will want to have copies made. Copies should be made on good quality paper. There are many small shops that reproduce résumés by photo offset or xerography. It is not in your best interest to send out copies of your résumé on the gray or pink slippery paper available in many library duplicating machines.

The format of a résumé

Résumés have a fairly standard format. At the very top, give your name, address, and telephone number. Many people include their age and marital status, although it is not necessary to include them. You must judge whether your age and marital status will assist you in your job search or work against you.

The next item in the résumé is a brief paragraph that may be labeled "Objectives." In the paragraph, you indicate what job you are looking for and your major qualifications for such a job. Or you may simply use this paragraph to state your basic strengths and the nature of your past work.

Following this is the record of your work experience. This record is the main part of the résumé (except if you are looking for your first full-time job). Your work experience is listed with your most recent job first. The job before that is listed next, and so on with your first job listed last:

1977 to present
1973 to 1977
1970 to 1973

Usually, you give your title for each job and the name of the company (and division when relevant). Sometimes you may not want to reveal the name of your current employer in your résumé. Then you may write a descriptive phrase, such as "independent engineering consultant firm."

Résumés are generally kept to one page. If you have worked for a very long time at a variety of different jobs, it may be necessary to prepare a two-page résumé.

After the record of your work experience, list your schooling, any degrees, relevant noncredit courses, hobbies, honors, and affiliations that you consider

worth including. For example, physical fitness is an asset: if you jog, swim, play tennis or golf, or engage in any other fitness activity, it may be worth noting. If you belong to professional societies, you should definitely list them. If you belong to social, civic, or volunteer organizations, list them only if you believe your membership in them is an asset. Do list any awards or honors you have received whether or not they are job-related. Such honors indicate that you are esteemed by others.

What if you are looking for your first job?

If you are looking for your first full-time job, you must review your work history somewhat differently. If you have held some sort of part-time or summer job or worked at volunteer jobs, these should be included. If you have participated in school extracurricular activities, these are worth mentioning. Your school record is also an indication of your ability and seriousness of purpose.

In seeking a first job, you must state your field of knowledge, that you are reliable, and that you can work well with others.

Whether you are looking for your first job or your fourth job, the time span from the end of schooling to the present should be accounted for on your résumé. You may be sure that a gap of a year or two will be noticed. If you have taken off a year and traveled around the world, say so. If you have attempted unsuccessfully to start your own business, say so. It is

far better than allowing a prospective employer to wonder what you were doing with your time.

Below are two sample résumés. The first is for a person looking for a first job. The second is for a person who has held several jobs. The résumé indicates that each job has involved more responsibility and skills than the previous job.

```
Leslie White
987 East Road
Elmwood, New Jersey 03103
987-6543
```

Objective

```
To find an entry-level job in sales
with a large international company.
Would like to utilize my knowledge
of French.
```

Work experience

```
Summers 1978, 1977

Group leader in a European teen-travel
summer trip. We traveled on bicycles
and by boat. Many of the arrangements
had been made in advance, but I often
had to make substitute arrangements
because of unforeseen events.
```

Summer 1976

Spent three months in France working as a volunteer on a farm. Did so to improve my spoken French.

Part-time employment 1977, 1978, 1979

Salesperson, college bookstore during school year.

School record

1979   B.A. magna cum laude with honors in French Literature and Language. Minor in History. Princeton University

1975   Elmwood High School, class salutatorian. Honors in language and science.

Extracurricular activities

Member of soccer team in high school and college.
Contributor to school magazine in college.
President of French Club in high school.

Speak and write French fluently.
Have working knowledge of Spanish.

Courtney Black
123 Lincoln Street
Deerfield, Illinois 60015
789-3456

Objectives

To find a job that would utilize a
broad range of my managerial and business skills and offer the potential for
advancement in a large company.

Record of work experience

1977 to present Public Relations
Director for a small manufacturing
company

Am responsible for creating and maintaining a favorable public image by
preparing and disseminating news releases, arranging press conferences,
contests, conferences, and other
activities that keep the company in the
public eye. Supervise a staff of six
and work with various other departments: art, advertising, production,
etc. Maintain close working relations
with various people in the media and
local government.

1973 to 1977 Publicity Writer for the
Widget Company

Wrote copy for publicity releases and
other public-relations material. Know
paper, printing, art styles. Many of
my releases appeared in trade journals
and local newspapers. Two-person office
made for more responsibility than a
publicity writer normally encounters.

1970 to 1973 Copy editor for Deerfield
<u>Gazette</u>

Corrected copy and did proofreading for
the local paper. Did some rewrite and
occasional reporting.

<u>Educational</u> <u>background</u>

M.B.A. University of Illinois, 1976.
Took night courses for master's degree.

B.A. University of Illinois, 1970.
Major in Journalism. Received award
for Most Promising Student.

Extracurricular: Worked on college
newspaper; member of swim team.

Affiliations and hobbies

Member of Illinois Society of Publicity
Writers
Vice President of Alumni Association,
University of Illinois

Hobbies include swimming, tennis, and
directing amateur theater productions.

Business letters

The formats of the following four letters are typical of those used in business correspondence, although other variations certainly exist. For example, in the sample executive letter the date could have been centered on the page instead of aligned with the right-hand margin.

Most letters are single-spaced, with double spacing between paragraphs. In the full block and modified block formats the first line of each paragraph aligns with the left-hand margin. In the modified semiblock and executive formats the first line is indented five to ten spaces.

When stationery without a printed letterhead is used, the mailing address of the sender is typed in two lines, centered, at the top of the page:

9988 Beacon Street
New York, New York 12345

Full Block

1	15 Lines	**7**	Complimentary Close
2	4, 6, or 8 Lines	**8**	Body of Letter
3	Double Spaces	**9**	Salutation
4	4 Lines	**10**	Inside Address
5	Identifying Initials	**11**	Date
6	Writer's Name and Title		

Full Block

Houghton Mifflin
Company

11 December 14, 1972

2

Ms. Margery Grant
10 President, Alumnae Association
Copley College
Copley, MO 99887

9 Dear Ms. Grant:

Thank you for your letter of November 20, 1972, in which you questioned the absence in the dictionary of the word <u>misandrist</u>, "one who hates men," as the counterpart of the established word <u>misogynist</u>, "one who hates women." <u>Misandrist</u> would seem to be a likely candidate for inclusion in the lexicon, in view of the accepted word <u>misandry</u>, "a hatred
8 of men."

The reason <u>misandrist</u> has not been entered in our dictionary is that no citations for its use have yet been reported. If sufficient evidence of its occurrence in reputable sources can be found, it will doubtless **3** be included in future editions of the dictionary.

We appreciate your pointing out this lexical asymmetry to us. Our citation readers will be on the lookout for <u>misandrist</u>.

7 Very truly yours,

4

6 Sally Spencer
Managing Editor

SS:ad

5

DICTIONARY DIVISION
One Beacon Street   Boston, Massachusetts 02107   (617) 725-5000   Cable HOUGHTON
BOSTON   ATLANTA   DALLAS   GENEVA, ILL.   HOPEWELL, N. J.   PALO ALTO   LONDON

Modified Block

1	15 Lines	**7**	Writer's Name and Title
2	Date	**8**	Complimentary Close
3	4, 6, or 8 Lines	**9**	Body of Letter
4	Double Spaces	**10**	Subject Line
5	4 Lines	**11**	Salutation
6	Identifying Initials	**12**	Inside Address

Modified Block

Houghton Mifflin
Company

1

2

July 12, 1976

3

Mr. Frank James
12 Oak Publishing Co., Inc.
9988 Forest Avenue
Dellwood, OH 12345

11 Dear Mr. James:

10 Subject: Price Stickers

We now have the capability of affixing price stickers mechani-
cally. In order to utilize the equipment that enables us to do
this, it will be necessary for price stickers to meet certain
specifications.

9 We would appreciate it if in the future you would supply stickers
of the following description: maximum roll diameter, 8"; roll
core I.D., 1-1/2"; spacing between stickers, 1/8"; blank lead on
each roll, 24".

4

If you have any questions or foresee any problems, please do not
hesitate to get in touch with us.

8 Sincerely,

5

7 F. P. Mapleson
Account Operator,
Operating Department

FPM:lo

6

DICTIONARY DIVISION
One Beacon Street   Boston, Massachusetts 02107   (617) 725-5000   Cable HOUGHTON
BOSTON ATLANTA DALLAS GENEVA, ILL. HOPEWELL, N. J. PALO ALTO LONDON

Modified Semiblock

1	15 Lines	**7**	Writer's Name and Title
2	Date	**8**	Complimentary Close
3	4, 6, or 8 Lines	**9**	Body of Letter
4	Double Spaces	**10**	Salutation
5	4 Lines	**11**	Attention Line
6	Identifying Initials	**12**	Inside Address

Modified Semiblock

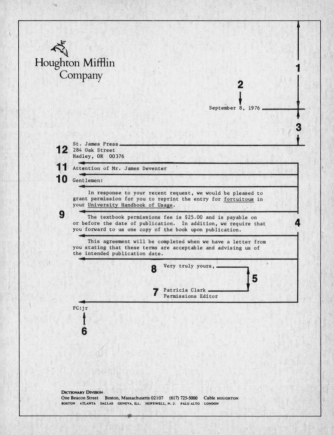

Houghton Mifflin
Company

2

September 8, 1976

1

3

12 St. James Press
284 Oak Street
Hadley, OR 00376

11 Attention of Mr. James Deventer

10 Gentlemen:

In response to your recent request, we would be pleased to
grant permission for you to reprint the entry for <u>fortuitous</u> in
your <u>University Handbook of Usage</u>.

9 The textbook permissions fee is $25.00 and is payable on
or before the date of publication. In addition, we require that
you forward to us one copy of the book upon publication.

4

This agreement will be completed when we have a letter from
you stating that these terms are acceptable and advising us of
the intended publication date.

8 Very truly yours,

5

7 Patricia Clark
Permissions Editor

PC:jr

6

DICTIONARY DIVISION
One Beacon Street   Boston, Massachusetts 02107   (617) 725-5000   Cable HOUGHTON
BOSTON   ATLANTA   DALLAS   GENEVA, ILL.   HOPEWELL, N. J.   PALO ALTO   LONDON

Executive

Executive

Houghton Mifflin Company

1

2

December 19, 19—

3

12 Dear Mr. Fitzpatrick:

Upon receipt of your Roxite C-1 Vellum Red, we made our normal testing of the material. Our laboratory results show that a cracking problem develops in the bend test.

These bend tests put the cloth below normal specifications required in such a grade of cloth. Note the enclosed 11 sample strips of the cloth after testing.

Our laboratory technician stated, however, that the cracking will cause only minor damage to the appearance of the 4 book. The condition will not cause any structural deficiency.

We will need to know as soon as possible whether you approve or disapprove of the use of this cloth.

10 Very truly yours,

5

9 Account Manager

6

Mr. Joseph Fitzpatrick
8 Argo Publications
975 Park Boulevard
Athens, MT 45678

enclosures

7

DICTIONARY DIVISION
One Beacon Street Boston, Massachusetts 02107 (617) 725-5000 Cable HOUGHTON
BOSTON ATLANTA DALLAS GENEVA, ILL. HOPEWELL, N. J. PALO ALTO LONDON

Use of library and reference materials

The card catalog

The card catalog is your best tool for finding books in the library. In some libraries, the card catalog may also help you locate records, filmstrips, microfilms, microfiches, etc. In other libraries, these materials may have their own reference systems. But books will be listed in the card catalog.

What exactly is a card catalog? A card catalog is an index of books, arranged alphabetically in a set of file drawers usually with 3″ x 5″ cards. Each file drawer is usually labeled to show what portion of the alphabet it contains. The cards list the information about the books: author, title, subject or subjects covered in the book. Some cards give cross-references to other cards. A few cards are information cards: they do not direct you to a particular book, but tell you where to find cards for items that may be hard to locate.

No matter where a book is situated in the library, the card will direct you to it. Although the cards are listed alphabetically, the books are not arranged alphabetically on the shelves. Libraries in the United States usually organize their books by one of two systems: the Dewey Decimal System, or the Library of Congress System. Both systems classify books into the major

fields of knowledge, and will be explained in the section "Organization of the Library." Thus, mathematics books will be in one section, history books in another, and so on. Within each broad area of knowledge there are subdivisions. While these systems create an orderly arrangement for the library, without the card catalog it would be very difficult for the average individual to find the required books. The card catalog is an efficient way of directing people to the books they want. Cards are added to the catalog for new books as the books are acquired; cards are eliminated for books that are discarded. Material on the cards can help a person decide if that book will be helpful.

Organization of the cards

The cards in the card catalog are alphabetized word by word. That means that all the cards beginning, for example, with "New" will be placed before the cards beginning with "News" or "Newton." Thus the order will be:

> New astronomy theories
> New Jersey
> New mathematics
> New ports
> New theories of science
> New York
> Newark
> Newport
> News

News gathering
Newton, Isaac
Newtonian physics
Newts

The word-by-word method of alphabetizing differs from the method used by dictionaries. In dictionaries, each word or phrase is alphabetized as if it were written as one word. In a dictionary system, "Newark" would come before "New Jersey" and "New York."

Also, in a card catalog, all abbreviations are listed as if they were spelled out. Thus, "Mt." would be listed as if spelled "mount" and "St." would be listed as if spelled "saint." "Mc" and "M'" would be listed as if spelled "Mac." Articles (a, an, the) are not considered if they appear at the beginning of a title. (*The House of Seven Gables* would be alphabetized at *House,* not at *The.*)

If there are books *by* a person and *about* that same person, all the books *by* that author would be listed before all the books *about* the author.

In situations that are very complicated, an information card in the drawer will often clarify matters. For example, there are many kings named Henry from many countries. There are also people whose last names are Henry. How do you figure out which comes first? An information card will usually explain the order used in the catalog.

What do the cards tell you?

So far, we have investigated how the cards are arranged in the catalog. But the cards are designed to direct you to the books themselves. To find the books, you need to understand what can be learned from the cards.

In the first place, a card in the catalog tells you that the book you want is in the library's collection. The card will not tell you if someone else has the book out on loan, and in many libraries, will not indicate whether the book is at the bindery for repairs. The card will let you know whether the book may be borrowed or must be used in the library, in which case the card is stamped "Reference." In some cases, the most recent edition of a book is a reference book, but an older edition of the same book may be taken out on loan. Then there are usually two cards in the catalog. One is stamped "Reference," the other is not. Or the word "Reference" is inked out on the older card.

Other items that may be learned from a catalog card are: the author's full name, date of birth, date of death, title and subtitle of book, copyright date of the book, number of pages, and publisher. You can learn whether the book has illustrations, a bibliography, an introduction by someone other than the author. Some cards will give the date when a book was first published if the book is a new edition or revision. At the bottom of the card, there are notations that

indicate where other cards may be found in the catalog for that same book. These notations can be helpful if you want to pursue the subject matter in other books.

The most important thing that you can learn from the card is the book's *call number,* which will direct you to the shelf on which the book can be found. The call number may look like this: 828.609 (B) if the book is classified by the Dewey Decimal System, or like this: PR3533.w33 if the book is classified by the Library of Congress system. Some books may have no call number. Works of fiction—especially contemporary fiction—are often arranged by author's last name in a separate fiction section in a library. Some catalog cards may have *Fic.* or *F.* in the corner where one would normally find the call number. Other libraries place nothing at all on the fiction cards.

Biographies may be treated as a separate category in some libraries. The call number on a biography book may simply be a *B* (for biography) followed by the first initial of the last name of the person about whom the book is written. Thus, a biography *about* Sigmund Freud would have B-F where the call number would normally appear. A biography *by* Sigmund Freud *about* Woodrow Wilson would have B-W for the call number.

Before we pursue the question of library organization, let us consider some sample catalog cards.

Author cards

Librarians consider the author card to be the basic catalog card. Most books have authors. Sometimes the author is one individual. Sometimes several people, a committee, foundation, magazine, or even the U.S. Government may be the "author" of a book.

The author card lists the author's name, last name first. On the line below, it lists the title of the book. If there are ten books in the library by one author, there will be ten author cards, one for each book. Those cards will be listed alphabetically by their titles.

For example, if you wanted to find books written by Herman Kahn, you would look up "Kahn, Herman" and find:

```
Kahn, Herman
   Thinking about the unthinkable.  Horizon
Press [c1962]  254 p.




        Includes bibliographical references.


1. Atomic warfare        2. U.S.--For. rel.
I Title
```

After that card, you might find:

```
Kahn, Herman    1922-              301.2-K

  The year 2000; a framework for speculation
on the next thirty-three years by Herman Kahn
and Anthony J. Wiener, with contributions
from other staff members of the Hudson Institute.
Introd. by Daniel Bell.  New York, Macmillan
(c1967), 431 p. illus.



I.  Twentieth century      Forecasts 1. Hudson
Institute   II. Title
```

The first book, *Thinking About the Unthinkable,* was written in 1962 by Herman Kahn. It has 254 pages and bibliographical references. Other catalog cards may be found at: Atomic warfare, U.S.-Foreign relations, and *Thinking About the Unthinkable.*

Most important of all, the card tells you that the book will be found on the shelf with other books having the number 355|K. (The K is for Kahn).

The second book by Herman Kahn has a different number: 301.2–K. It falls into a different subject area. It was written by Herman Kahn and other people. Its copyright date is 1967. The book has 431 pages and is illustrated. Other catalog cards for the same book may be found at: Twentieth century, forecasts, Hudson Institute, and *(The) Year 2000.*

Some authors do not write under their own names. The library may list the book at the pseudonym or at the real name. The card catalog will clarify the name and the spelling that the library uses.

```
Twain, Mark

     see

Clemens, Samuel Langhorne
```

All the catalog cards for Mark Twain will be found under "Clemens." And you will find, when you look at the Clemens cards, that not all the fiction by Mark Twain is to be found in the fiction section. Some will be found in the American Literature section. The call number will direct you to the correct section.

Not all writers who use pseudonyms are listed at their real names. When you look up an author, look under the name that you are familiar with. The card catalog will inform you whether the author is listed by his or her pseudonym or real name.

The United States government and its branches may be the "author" of a book. If you try to look up "Library of Congress" in the card catalog, a cross-reference card will tell you to look under "U.S. Library of Congress." There you will find books with "U.S. Library of Congress" as the official author. Following all the author cards, you will find books *about* the Library of Congress. Some of the books about the Library of Congress may have been compiled by the U.S. Library of Congress staff. Others may have been written by individuals.

Title cards

Suppose that you know the title of a book, but don't know who wrote it. The card catalog can help you find it. Titles are also listed in the card catalog in alphabetical order.

The title card gives the title above the author's name. The title is usually typed in. Then the author's name is given, and the title is repeated again. A title card is really the basic author card with the title shown at the top.

If you wanted to find a book named *My Antonia,* you would look under *My.*

```
   My Antonia

Cather, Willa Sibert

   My Antonia.   Houghton Mifflin Co.

Boston.      371 p.
```

There is no call number on this card because it is a work of fiction and will be found in the fiction section under Cather.

Sometimes several short novels are bound into one volume. The volume may have the title of one of the short novels. How do you find the other short novels? Try the card catalog. For example, if you wanted to find *Neighbour Rosicky,* look up *Neighbour*:

```
        Neighbour Rosicky

Cather, Willa Sibert

        Neighbour Rosicky (In Obscure destinies.)
```

The short novel *Neighbour Rosicky* may be found in the volume *Obscure Destinies*. Although the card catalog may help you find short novels, it will usually *not* help you find short stories, poems, plays, and essays. To find these you need reference books. (See the next section, "Basic Reference Materials.")

The main thing to remember when looking for a title card is to ignore the article at the beginning of the title. Look for *A Tale of Two Cities* at "Tale," not at "A." Look for *The Uses of Enchantment* at "Uses" not at "The."

Suppose you are not sure if the name by which you know a book is an author's name or the title. For example, if you wanted to find *The Guinness Book of World Records,* look it up under *Guinness.*

```
                              Reference
Guinness book of world records. Sterling
    Pub. Co. 19--    illus. ports

  Title varies: The Guinness book of

superlatives.



  1. Curiosities.    (1) Title: The Guinness
book of superlatives
```

The authors' names are omitted from this card, but a card for an older edition reveals that the authors were Norris McWhirter and Ross McWhirter.

Some books—such as reference books—have no official author, since they are compiled by groups of people. When they are published, these books can be located by their titles.

Subject cards

Most researchers find that the subject cards are the most useful cards in the catalog. Often there are some cards that refer you to books that cover the broad subject and other cards that refer to books on subdivisions of the subject. There may also be an information card that leads you to related topics.

Suppose that you are doing some research on costumes. Perhaps you must design and make costumes for a play that takes place in eighteenth-century England. You look up the subject COSTUME in the card catalog. Note that the subject card is the basic author card with the subject printed (or typed) in capitals at the top of the card.

```
COSTUME

Evans, Mary   1890-           391-E
   Costume through the ages.  Philadelphia,
Lippincott (c 1950)   360 p. illus. ports.



   "Revised edition."
   Includes bibliographies.


1. Costume   2. Costume - Hist.   I Title
```

The first book you see is *Costume Through the Ages* by Mary Evans. It has illustrations and portraits, and it is a revised edition. That suggests that it was sufficiently interesting to bring out a revised edition. It also has bibliographies. But since the copyright date is 1950, any books listed in the bibliographies will have been printed before 1950.

Other books are listed under the general subject COSTUME. There is also a cross-reference card:

```
COSTUME

   see also

CHURCH VESTMENTS
CLOTHING AND DRESS
FASHION
UNIFORMS
```

These other subjects may or may not be useful in your research. You make a note of the subjects that may help.

After the general subject COSTUME are books on particular aspects of the general subject. For example:

COSTUME—GREAT BRITAIN
COSTUME, THEATRICAL

Both of these subcategories will be helpful in the particular research you are doing, and you note the books listed under each one.

For example, this card may appear:

```
COSTUME, THEATRICAL

   Voland, Virginia              792.42-V
     Designing women; the art and practice of
   theatrical costume design.  Garden City,
   Doubleday (c 1966) 197 p.
```

The book seems to be one that may help you actually make the costumes once you have decided what the costumes are to look like. You make a note of it.

The card catalog can lead you to books, but it cannot help you decide if the books are what you need. To know if a book is useful, you must examine it. Sometimes a copyright date will let you know that a book was written too early to help you in your particular research.

From the card to the shelf

When you use the card catalog, take along a pencil and paper. Small slips of paper are especially useful. They may be rearranged once you have noted each book on a slip.

On the slip of paper, jot down the call number of the book you want, the author's name, and enough of

the title to help you find the book. If you are in a small library, you may find only a few books that you need. If you are in a large library, you may have many slips that lead you to many books.

Your slips may look like this:

792.42 -V

Voland, V.

Designing woman

391 - E

Evans, M.
Costume through the ages

391-R

Rudofsky, B.

The unfashionable
human body

391-T

Truman, N.
Historic costuming

The next step is to arrange the slips by call numbers. Put all the 391 slips into one pile. Put all the 792.42 slips into another pile. Keep your slips arranged by call number. Save the slips until your entire research project is completed.

If you must make your notes on a large sheet of paper instead of on small slips, make separate columns for each call number. Some complicated topics may have many more than two call numbers. You need the call numbers to find the books on the shelf.

Organization of the library

When you walk into a library, take a moment to notice how it is organized. Are all the books on one floor, or does the library have several floors? Where is the reference section? Where are the magazines and

periodicals? Do the books have Dewey Decimal System call numbers (e.g. 792.42) or Library of Congress call numbers (e.g. PN 1993.5)? Note that the Dewey Decimal System call numbers begin with arabic numerals. The Library of Congress call numbers begin with letters.

The floor plan of each library is distinct. Most libraries are logically arranged with the 200 books after the 100 books, and the 300 books after the 200 books (or the B books after the A books and the C books after the B books). But space does not always permit the logical order. The librarian can tell you where a particular call number can be found.

Oversize books may be shelved in a separate section. A catalog card is usually stamped "Oversize" if a book is too big to fit on the appropriate shelf. When you make out your call slips, be sure to make a note of any oversize books.

The call numbers stand for certain categories. The categories in the Dewey Decimal System differ from the categories in the Library of Congress system.

Dewey Decimal System basic categories

000	Generalities—bibliographies, encyclopedias, libraries, etc.
100	Philosophy and related disciplines
200	Religion
300	Social science—statistics, political science, economics, law, education, etc.

400	Language—linguistics, other languages
500	Pure sciences—mathematics, astronomy, physics, chemistry, earth science, biological science, botany, zoology, etc.
600	Technology—medicine, engineering, agriculture, domestic science, business, etc.
700	The arts—architecture, sculpture, drawing, painting, photography, music, recreational arts
800	Literature and rhetoric—American and English literature, literature from other languages
900	General geography, history, etc.

Each category is subdivided further (401, 426, 492, etc.) and decimal numbers may be added to make further distinctions (426.12, 792.42, etc.). On the shelf, all the books are arranged in numerical order. Books without the decimal are arranged before books with the decimal (792, 792.12, 792.42, etc.)

Library of Congress System basic categories

A	General works
B	Philosophy and religion
C	History and auxiliary sciences
D	History and topography (except America)

E & F	America
G	Geography and anthropology
H	Social sciences
J	Political sciences
K	Law
L	Education
M	Music
N	Fine arts
P	Language and literature
Q	Science
R	Medicine
S	Agriculture
T	Technology
U	Military science
V	Naval science
Z	Bibliography and library science

Note that the letters I, O, W, X, and Y are not included. If further categories become necessary, they may some day be used.

Categories in the Library of Congress System are further subdivided with a second letter, then a numeral of one to four digits, then a decimal followed by a numeral or a letter and a numeral. Sometimes there is a further subdivision of categories introduced by a second decimal.

On the shelf, books are arranged alphabetically by letter categories (P, PN, PS, etc.). Within each of the

letter categories, books are arranged in numerical order from 1 to 9999 (PN1, PN86, PN1993, PN1993.5, PN1994, PN6110, etc.)

Author numbers

In a small library, the first initial of the author's last name is added to the book number. For example, the book by Mary Evans on costumes had the call number 391–E. In a larger library, there may be a great many authors with books in the 391 category who have last names beginning with E. Larger libraries use author numbers. Author numbers usually begin with the first initial of the author's last name followed by one or more arabic numerals and sometimes a lower-case letter.

Author numbers are usually shown below the Dewey Decimal Number or the Library of Congress Number:

338.15   or   PN86
B21   K57

In a library that uses author numbers, the author number will appear on the catalog card as well as on the book. When you make up your call slips, you need to include both numbers—the book number and the author number. The two numbers together are then considered to be the call number.

Whatever system your library uses, the card catalog will direct you to the site of the book. The call number

of a book will be the same in any library that uses the same classification system. Thus, if you have made out a call slip for a book in a library that uses the Library of Congress System, you will find that the book in another library will have the same call number, providing that the second library also uses the Library of Congress System.

Right now there are two systems that are widely used in the United States. Some libraries are trying to convert from the Dewey Decimal System to the Library of Congress System. Such conversions require a great deal of time and money. The larger the library, the greater the cost.

If you do find yourself regularly using two libraries (such as a local library and a university library) that use the two different systems, it may be worthwhile to see that your call slips have both sets of call numbers on them. It is, however, easier to restrict yourself to libraries that use one system or the other for one research project.

Basic reference materials

After you have searched through the card catalog, you have not yet exhausted the resources of the library. Most libraries have reference sections—separate rooms, or areas—containing books that are often consulted as references. Some items may very clearly be reference books: encyclopedias, dictionaries, almanacs, atlases, etc. Other items may not fit as obvi-

ously into the category of reference books: anthologies, books of documents, etc. In addition, some valuable reference material may be found not in the reference section but in the general collection.

It is also important to recognize that there are many useful kinds of reference material to be found outside of libraries. A brief list of nonlibrary reference sources follows the discussion of library materials.

Library reference sources

There are two kinds of library reference sources. One kind supplies the required information—you look in the book and find what you want to know. The other kind directs you to the required information in another book, magazine, newspaper, etc. Both kinds are needed for most reference projects. Read the introductions to the reference books carefully. Each book organizes material in its own way. Each has its own abbrevations and cross-references.

Not all reference materials are useful for all projects. But here is a checklist of the most helpful sources for a research project, followed by a more detailed list.

1. Indexes to newspapers, periodicals—general and special interest
2. Indexes to material that is shorter than book length (poetry, stories, essays, etc.)
3. Bibliographies—general and special interest
4. Guides to location of books
5. Encyclopedias—general and special interest

6. Dictionaries and word books—general and special purpose
7. Almanacs and yearbooks
8. Biography books
9. Geography books
10. Business directories
11. Statistics materials
12. Document anthologies
13. Guides to trivia and curiosities
14. Guides to audiovisual material
15. Books of quotations
16. The librarian

Indexes to newspapers and periodicals

An index is a guide to direct you to material on a subject or by an author. Using an index involves two processes. The first is finding out whether and where an article has been published. The second process is sometimes more difficult—finding a copy of the required newspaper or magazine. Large libraries may have bound volumes of periodicals and microfilm or microfiche copies of newspapers.

Most magazines have their own yearly indexes. Once a year, they prepare an alphabetical list of the articles that have appeared over that year.

Readers' Guide to Periodical Literature—directs you to articles in the most widely read magazines in the United States. Regular supplements are available to bring you up to date. *Access*—directs you to some

periodicals not indexed in *Readers' Guide*. There are also indexes to direct you to more specialized journals in particular fields. A short list of examples includes:

Agricultural Index
Applied Science and Technology Index
Art Index
Business Periodicals Index
Education Index
Humanities Index
Index to Legal Periodicals
Music Index
Social Science Index
Ulrich's International Periodical Index (Lists the names of periodicals in many languages. It does not index specific articles.)

Very few newspapers are indexed. It may be possible to find information on world or national events in one of the following newspaper indexes:

Index to the Christian Science Monitor
The New York Times Index
The Times Index, London
The Newspaper Index (indexes a few large American newspapers)

If your library has the material to which the indexes refer, it is probably on microfilm or microfiches.

Local newspapers vary greatly in their manner of filing material about old stories and in their willingness to let people not on staff use the files.

Indexes to material shorter than book length

Short works are difficult to locate. They generally come in anthologies. The anthology title does not necessarily indicate what specific works are contained therein. If you want to find a poem, short story, play, or essay, you may find the relevant anthology or anthologies by using an index.

For poetry

Granger's Index to Poetry
Poems are listed by author, first line, title, and subject.

For short stories

Short Story Index
Short stories are indexed by author, title, and subject. Some periodicals are included, as well as anthologies.

For essays

Essay and General Literature Index
Essays and literary criticism are indexed by author and subject.

For plays

Ottemiller's Index to Plays in Collections, 1900–1975
Indexes plays by author and title.
Play Index (by year)

Bibliographies

Indirectly, you can locate many bibliographies through the card catalog. When you find a book on a subject you are investigating, that book may have a

bibliography. No bibliography in a book will be more up-to-date than that book.

> *Bibliography of Bibliographies*   Lists many bibliographies.
>
> *Bibliographic Index*   Also a bibliography of bibliographies.
>
> *Subject Guide to Books in Print*   List of American books still in print. The list is arranged by subject and may prove useful as a means of finding titles of books on a particular subject.
>
> *Cumulative Books Index*   Lists English-language books, by subject, author, and title.

There are also many special-subject lists of books. A few examples are:

> *The Reader's Advisor*
> *Sources of Information in the Social Sciences*
> *Harvard Guide to American History*
> *Science and Engineering Reference Sources*

Guides to finding books

It is unreasonable to expect any library to carry all the books on every subject. You may have compiled a good bibliography, but then you may not find the books in your library. What do you do?

1. Find out if your library participates in an interlibrary loan program. If so, there may be a catalog of the books available on loan from another library.

2. Look it up in *Books in Print*. You will find out if it can be purchased by you or by the library.
3. Try *Paperbound Books in Print*. If you have to buy the books yourself, you may find paperbacks more economical.
4. *Guide to U.S. Government Publications* will provide a list of books available from the U.S. Government Printing Office.

Encyclopedias

Encyclopedias provide good background material. They are a fine place to begin research on many topics. Often, an encyclopedia provides a short bibliography as well.

There are two kinds of encyclopedias—general and special purpose. Either kind may be organized alphabetically or by subject.

General encyclopedias

New Columbia Encyclopedia—a good one-volume reference work
Cadillac Modern Encyclopedia (one volume)
Collier's Encyclopedia
Encyclopedia Americana
Encyclopaedia Britannica
Encyclopedia International
Lincoln Library of Essential Information
World Book Encyclopedia
Compton's Pictured Encyclopedia

If you can read another language, you may want to try one of the excellent encyclopedias available, such as the German *Brockhaus' Konversations-Lexicon,* the French *Grand Larousse Encyclopédique,* or the Spanish *Enciclopedia Universal Illustrada Europeo-Americana.*

Special-purpose encyclopedias

When it comes to special-purpose reference books, it is sometimes hard to draw the line between encyclopedias and dictionaries. Both should be consulted (see the next section) if both exist in a special field. A few examples of special-purpose encyclopedias follows:

Encyclopedia of Education
Encyclopedia of Mammals
Encyclopedia of Philosophy
The Encyclopedia of Sports
The Oxford Companion to World Sports and Games
International Encyclopedia of the Social Sciences
Mammals of the World
McGraw-Hill Encyclopedia of Science and Technology
The International Cyclopedia of Music and Musicians

Dictionaries and word books

Dictionaries are consulted for a variety of reasons: for definitions, pronunciations, synonyms, word histories, etc.

General dictionaries

Good general-purpose dictionaries are available with the following imprints:

> American Heritage
> Funk & Wagnalls
> Merriam-Webster
> Random House

Note: Any dictionary may use the name *Webster.*

Word books

For *slang,* you may want to consult a specialized dictionary such as:

> *Dictionary of American Slang* by Wentworth and Flexner
>
> *A Dictionary of Slang and Unconventional English* by Eric Partridge

For *pronunciations:*

> *A Pronouncing Dictionary of American English*

Handbooks put out by radio and television networks for their staff are also good sources.

For *synonyms:*

> *Webster's Dictionary of Synonyms*

Any thesaurus bearing the name *Roget*—some are alphabetical, others are organized by subject.

For *word division and spelling:*

> *The Word Book*
> *The Medical & Health Sciences Word Book*

For *word backgrounds and historical usages:*

> *A Dictionary of American English on Historical Principles* by Craigie and Hulbert
> *A Dictionary of Americanisms on Historical Principles* by M. M. Mathews
> *An Etymological Dictionary of the English Language* by Skeat
> *The Oxford English Dictionary* (often called the *OED*)
> *Origins*—for etymologies
> *Dictionary of Word and Phrase Origins* by Morris and Morris

Also *concordances* to the Bible, to Shakespeare, and to other works will help you find specific uses of the words within the works. A concordance is a book that lists *all* the words used in a particular book and indicates exactly where each word is used each time it is used.

Special-purpose dictionaries

Note that it is often hard to draw the line between encyclopedias and dictionaries when it comes to special-purpose items. A few examples of special-purpose dictionaries are:

The American Political Dictionary

Black's Law Dictionary

A Comprehensive Dictionary of Psychological and Psychoanalytic Terms

Concise Chemical and Technical Dictionary

Dictionary of American History

Dictionary of Architectural Science

Dictionary of the Bible

A Dictionary of Classical Antiquities

A Dictionary of Comparative Religion

Dictionary of Education

A Dictionary of the Social Sciences

Grove's Dictionary of Music and Musicians

Harvard Dictionary of Music

McGraw-Hill Dictionary of Scientific and Technical terms

Modern Science Dictionary

Stedman's Medical Dictionary

Foreign-language dictionaries

Often, you may need dictionaries that are bilingual. There are bilingual dictionaries in virtually all the more common languages: French, Spanish, Italian, German, Russian, Greek, Latin, Hebrew, Japanese, etc. Often it is possible to find dictionaries in the languages that are less frequently known. Dictionaries in other languages with the definitions in that language are useful only for people who have a good knowledge of that language.

Almanacs and yearbooks

For the most recent facts, figures, and general information, almanacs and yearbooks are excellent.

Almanacs

> *Information Please Almanac*
> *The World Almanac and Book of Facts*

Yearbooks

Several encyclopedias put out yearbooks to update the information in the encyclopedia and to add new data. There are also yearbooks put out for many different industries or fields of interest.

Biography books

For brief, condensed facts and dates about people there are many reference books. If you are not sure about the correct biography book to look at, try:

> *Biographical Dictionaries Master Index*
> *Biography Index*

Some of the more popular biographical reference books are:

> *Chambers Biographical Dictionary*
> *Dictionary of American Biography*
> *Dictionary of National Biography* (for English history)
> *The International Who's Who* (living people)
> *Webster's Biographical Dictionary*
> *Who's Who* (living people)

> *The McGraw-Hill Encyclopedia of World Biography*
>
> *Who's Who in America*
>
> *Who Was Who* (dead people)

In addition, there are many specialized *Who's Who* books that are regional, professional, and even ethnic or religious. There are also books of biographies of authors, scientists, etc. For example, *Asimov's Biographical Encyclopedia of Science and Technology*.

Short biographies can also be found in encyclopedias and in dictionaries of specialized fields.

Geography books

There are two basic kinds of geography books: atlases and gazetteers. Atlases may contain maps of the modern world, or of particular historical periods, or of extraterrestrial locations. Gazetteers generally contain facts and figures (population, area, etc.) about places.

Atlases

> *Encyclopaedia Britannica World Atlas*
>
> *Goode's World Atlas*
>
> *Hammond Atlas*
>
> *The International Atlas*
>
> *National Geographic Atlas of the World*
>
> *The Times Atlas of the World*

Some historical atlases are:

> *Atlas of American History*
>
> *Atlas of the Classical World*

Atlas of World History
Historical Atlas

For nonmap information:

> *The Columbia Lippincott Gazetteer of the World*
> *Political Handbook & Atlas of the World*
> *Webster's New Geographical Dictionary*
> *The Statesman's Year Book*

Many other map sources are available outside of libraries.

Business directories

For information about companies, industries, etc.

> *Thomas Register of American Manufacturers*—many volumes such as "Products and Services," "Index of Brand Names," "Catalog of Companies."
> *Moody's* puts out a series of directories on special subjects.

Many industries put out handbooks. They are often called Red Books, Blue Books, or Year Books. Many are published annually and contain the names and addresses of companies and their main officers. Many trade magazines put out annual directories.

Statistics

Statistics may be found in almanacs, yearbooks, and various other reference books. Some excellent sources are:

> *Statistical Abstract of the United States*
> *The Statesman's Year Book*
> *Statistical Yearbook United Nations*

U.S. Bureau of the Census puts out statistics on many subjects.

Document anthologies

If you need to find the text of the Magna Charta or Washington's Farewell Address, look in a book of documents. These go by many names, "documents," "readings" "anthologies," etc. Some examples:

> *Documents of American History*
> *The World of Mathematics* (4 volumes)·

Guides to trivia and curiosities

Often we need to find out some odd bit of information. There are many books available that provide such information. Among the most useful are:

> *Kane Book of Famous First Facts and Records*
> *Guinness Book of World Records*
> *The People's Almanac*

Guides to audiovisual material

There are an increasing number of books available that will lead you to filmstrips, records, tapes, films of various speeds. Ask your librarian to help you locate these.

Books of quotations

Some books offer well-known quotations:

Contemporary Quotations by Simpson (after 1950)

Dictionary of Quotations by Evans

Familiar Quotations by Bartlett

Home Book of Quotations by Stevenson

Hoyt's New Cyclopedia of Practical Quotations

The Oxford Dictionary of Quotations

The librarian and guides to reference books

A good librarian is probably your most important reference source in a library. A good librarian is trained to use the library to the best advantage. The librarian should know the particular items available in the particular library and how to find them. Often the librarian knows what may be available in other libraries and in sources outside the library.

Do not be afraid to ask basic questions: "How can I find the poem 'Casey at the Bat'?" "Do you have any maps of the Holy Roman Empire?" "Where can I find the source of this quotation?" "Why can't I find last year's issues of that journal on the shelf?" (It may be at the bindery.)

If the libraries cannot help you, ask to see *Guide to Reference Books* by Winchell and the follow-up of the same name by Sheehy.

Beyond the library

The good researcher knows enough to go beyond

the library for many kinds of research. Here are some other sources of information:

Other kinds of libraries

Do not overlook the *children's library*. Often it has books that are good for basic background information. Children's libraries are likely to have single-subject books that might not be available in adult libraries. There may be books on specific animals, plant families, scientific phenomena, historical figures, etc. One must be cautious in using material from a children's library, but such material often balances what can be found in adult libraries.

Company libraries or reference rooms are more likely than a large library to have material on subjects of particular interest to that company's work. If your company does not have at least a reference shelf, it should begin to develop one. At times, you may be able to arrange to use other companies' libraries.

Museum libraries may have highly specialized materials that are helpful. Even a small museum may have a library that is complete in the field of that museum's specialization.

Private libraries may be general or specialized. They may belong to business associations or unions or professional groups. Terms of use differ from one private library to another.

College and university libraries are often for the specific use of faculty and students. Sometimes, however,

arrangements can be made by firms or individuals to use the libraries on a regular or temporary basis.

Specialized collections of maps, costumes, recordings, pictures, etc., may be available in your area.

The telephone

First of all, use the *yellow pages* of your telephone directory. There may be many valuable leads in the yellow pages.

Information can be obtained over the telephone for many projects. Some libraries and newspapers have telephone information services. Various public and private agencies may answer questions on the telephone.

Government and public institutions

Try the offices of the city, town, county, or state government. There are many maps, records, and often special information bulletins available.

Government agencies of all levels have a wealth of information. It is up to you to locate the agency and call or write for the information you need.

Chambers of commerce are often glad to supply material and answer questions about their area. They will often direct you to other people or organizations who can supply what they cannot supply.

Private companies and agencies

Private companies can supply annual reports—a source of a great deal of economic information. Some libraries have collections of annual reports, but you

can also obtain them by writing to the companies.

Private companies are often willing to supply other information about the industry or industries at large. Large companies often have pamphlets available about basic industrial techniques or products. Some of the material must be evaluated because the companies are trying to maintain a good public image and may not be presenting opposing views.

Private organizations often exist for the purpose of encouraging or discouraging certain practices. They are willing to supply information presenting their point of view. Again, this material must be carefully evaluated because it is often one-sided.

Private agencies and business organizations may have printed information available. For example, the New York Stock Exchange has a great deal of material on the operations of the stock market. Often, such agencies and organizations will answer questions, as well.

Trade magazines

Most industries have trade magazines that service that industry. Trade magazines have useful articles. They usually put out yearly directories of the companies in that industry, and they may have indexes on the articles published over the year. They may also put out specialized handbooks of interest only to that trade. Most of these trade magazines would not be in a small public library. They may be available on the shelves of

businesses in that field. And often back copies can be obtained from the publisher.

Occasionally staff of trade magazines will answer questions or direct you to people who can answer them.

Interviews

Do not ignore the possibility of interviewing people. Some informants may be more reliable than others. You will have to evaluate the information by checking it against what you have learned from other sources.

Maps

Maps may be obtained from a variety of sources.

Rand McNally Co. puts outs out books of maps and individual maps.

The Automobile Association of America makes maps available to members.

National Geographic Magazine prepares both contemporary maps and historical maps.

Travel agencies, foreign consulates, chambers of commerce and other organizations may offer maps.

Using a dictionary

Dictionaries are among the most useful reference tools. Every home and every office should have at least one good desk dictionary. That desk dictionary should be sufficiently up-to-date to include words that have

recently become part of our language.

Most people talk about "the dictionary" as if there were only one dictionary in the United States. There are in fact many different dictionaries, from small paperbacks to large unabridged dictionaries that endeavor to record the entire English language.

Each dictionary organizes information in its own way. All dictionaries list words, pronunciations, and definitions. Most dictionaries offer a great deal more. It is worth your while to spend some time studying the dictionary or dictionaries available to you. The better you understand what can be found in a dictionary and where to find it, the more useful the dictionary will be.

Your dictionary should tell you:

- How to spell the word (if it is one word, a hyphenated compound, two words, lower-case or capitalized);

- If there are other permissible spellings of the word (variants);

- If there are different words spelled the same way (homographs shown by superscript numbers);

- The syllabication of the word;

- The pronunciation of the word (and if there are any alternate pronunciations);

- The grammatical part of speech the word is or can

be (noun, plural noun, verb, adjective, adverb, pronoun, conjunction, preposition, interjection);

- Inflected forms (plurals of nouns, principal parts of verbs, comparatives and superlatives of adjectives and adverbs);

- Usage labels for the word or senses of the word (when, how, where, or in what field the word or sense is used);

- Different senses or meanings of the word (the definition proper);

- Idiomatic usage of the word;

- Other words derived from the word (run-on entries);

- The history of the word (etymologies);

- Words that are similar but not identical in meaning and that are interchangeable in some but not all contexts (synonym lists and synonym paragraphs);

- How to use the word correctly in different situations (usage notes);

- Prefixes, suffixes, and combining forms;

- Biographical entries;

- Geographic entries with population figures of cities, states, and countries;

- Other proper nouns;

- Abbreviations;

- Illustrations, maps, and diagrams;

- Special charts and tables.

Front matter

Almost every dictionary has a front section that tells you how to use that dictionary. It is worth reading and referring to from time to time. The more you understand the dictionary, the more you can make it work for you.

Alphabetical order and guidewords

In a dictionary all entries are alphabetized as if they were spelled as one word. In this system of alphabetizing, *New York* would be alphabetized as if it were *Newyork*. It would come after *Newark* and *Newport*. This is not the same as the word-by-word system used in alphabetizing catalog cards. The word-by-word system would not work well for a dictionary. A person may look up a word just to learn whether it is spelled as one word, two words, or as a hyphenated compound. The "whole-entry" system of alphabetizing works best for the needs of a dictionary user.

Words are alphabetized as they are spelled. Thus *Saint Bernard* (the dog) and *Saint-Denis* (the French city) are to be found at *saint. St. Bernard Pass* (in Switzerland) and *St. Denis, Ruth* (the dancer) are

found in alphabetical order beginning with *st*. Often a dictionary will cross-refer some of these confusing entries.

To find the page in the dictionary more easily where the word you need is alphabetized, you use the *guidewords*. They are printed in heavy type at the top of each page in a dictionary and are often separated by a slash. The first guideword shown is the first entry that begins on that page. The second guideword shown is the last entry that begins on that page. All the words on that page come in alphabetical order between the first guideword and the second guideword.

Pronunciation and pronunciation keys

All dictionaries give pronunciations. But different dictionaries use different systems for giving pronunciations. It is very important to acquaint yourself with the particular system your dictionary uses. Each has a pronunciation key showing what symbols they use for each sound and example words for the sound of each symbol. If you refer to this, you will be able to pronounce the word correctly.

Your dictionary can answer a great many questions, far more than how to spell, define, and pronounce words. The more items you search for in your dictionary, the more useful you will find it to be.

Organization of research papers

A research paper may be undertaken as a school assignment, a job assignment, a professional opportunity (giving a paper or publishing an article), or for other reasons.

At times, a very specific topic is assigned to you. At other times, you may choose any subject that interests you. Often, you are asked to look into a general subject area and choose a specific topic within it.

Certain techniques will be useful to you in preparing research papers on any subject. These techniques can be applied to most subjects and will be suitable for a wide variety of source materials.

Basic research procedures

There is a great deal of work to be done before you begin to write. A good way to begin is to formulate a tentative title. The title may be worded as a phrase or a question:

> What will the world's population be in the year 2000?
>
> The role of the sales manager in generating sales
>
> Jazz harmonies in Gershwin's music
>
> Changes in our city's central business district in the twentieth century
>
> Effects of a full moon: real or imaginary?
>
> How miracle wheat has altered a small nation's economy

The tentative title may or may not be the final title of your paper. The tentative theme may be too broad or too narrow. It may be a topic that you do not have the facilities to research. The title is merely a first statement of the general area of your research.

By definition, all research papers are based on some kind of data. All research papers also require that the writer collect, organize, present, and evaluate the data. Some papers rely very heavily on other people's evaluations. Other papers rely more heavily on the writer's own evaluations. In either case, it is not enough simply to reproduce sources.

The source materials

Before you commit yourself to a topic, consider the materials you will need: books, magazine articles, newspaper clippings, maps, recordings, sheet music, statistics, informants, etc. Begin to examine the library and make preliminary inquiries into other sources. Can you find what you need? If not, you will have to look farther afield, or you may have to restate your topic.

On the other hand, you may encounter too much material. It may be necessary to limit your topic to a more manageable subject.

Breaking down the topic

At this point, make some preliminary notes for an outline. The outline notes may be revised, expanded, or totally reorganized once your research is under way.

The data you encounter may not be what you expect to find, or it may set you thinking in a different line of reasoning. But you need some notes to start you off.

Take one topic as an example:

What will the world's population be in the year 2000?
   Reasons for asking the question
   Predictions:
      On what basis are they made?
      Do experts agree?
      Are there areas of general agreement?
      Are there areas of major disagreement?
   The unpredictable:
      What events could alter predictions?
      How likely are those events?
      Have events altered past predictions?
   Your own evaluations based on the source materials.

As you begin to read, you may want to shift your outline to stress a particular aspect of the topic:

   Shifts in the ratio of older people
   Relation of population growth to earth's resources
   Differences in population trends in developed and
      developing nations

The specific topic may be related to your reasons for undertaking the paper. One area may be interesting if you are writing the paper for an ecology course in school while another area may be more productive if

you are in an industry that produces goods for one segment of the population.

Planning the work

It is best to begin by reading a general book or article about your topic. Encyclopedia articles, textbooks, and sometimes children's books can provide good background sources of a topic. You may be fortunate enough to find an article that provides a good overall picture of the subject.

Once you have found a background source, further research may be structured in several ways. Different aspects of a topic may be studied one after another. More general material may be examined before more specific material. Material that is easier to understand may be examined before more difficult material, or data may be examined at random.

Practical considerations often impose a sequence of study. It may be necessary to devote one segment of time to investigating magazine articles, another segment to newspaper clippings, and so on. Books that must be read in a library may take up specific portions of time, while books that can be used in a home or office may be scheduled more freely. Research that requires travel must be planned for carefully. Sometimes it is necessary to wait for a reserved book or an interlibrary loan. Such books do not always arrive at the most desirable time. A research plan must take all these factors into account.

Another important consideration is time. Time must be allotted realistically. Some extra time should always be allowed for the unexpected.

Taking notes

As you work, you will need to keep notes of what you learn. It is advisable to equip yourself with two kinds of index cards (either two sizes or two colors). One set of cards will be used to record your sources. Each card will represent a different source. The second set of cards will be used to take notes of specific information gained from a source. These cards will contain much of the substance of your paper. They will record quotes, opinions, analyses, and other data. They may also contain your own opinions of what you encounter.

In addition to the cards, some of your "notes" may be photocopies of library materials that you will need for reference. Most libraries now have machines for reproducing printed material. Some libraries also have facilities for copying microforms. Copying machines help you duplicate charts, tables, statistics, as well as long quotations that you may want to use or consult.

A tape recorder can be useful for interviews. If you do use a recorder, advise your informant that you are doing so before you begin.

For research that involves visual material, a camera or a sketch pad may be necessary. Careful notes should be kept of the nature of each photograph or sketch.

Source cards

An index card should be made out for every source you consult. You may not quote every book and article, or even refer to each specifically, but you will probably want to include each in your bibliography.

Source cards will provide the data for bibliographies and footnotes. You can record your own general comments about each source on the card. And, because you have the full data on the source card, you will not need to repeat the full information on each information card.

For a *book,* include the following
- author's full name
- full title and subtitle
- publisher
- city of publication
- most recent copyright date
- edition (if there are several)
- editor, translator, or reviser (if any)
- number of pages

Most of this information will be found on the title page and the reverse of the title page (copyright page).

Use the information as you find it. Use the publisher's name as it appears on that book. Indicate only the first city listed.

Konrad Lorenz

On Aggression

translator: Marjory Kerr Wilson

Harcourt, Brace & World, Inc.

New York ©1963

Eng. trans. © 1966

306 pp.

For a _magazine or newspaper article,_ include:
- name of author (if any)   • title of the article
- name of magazine or newspaper   • the date
- volume and issue numbers
- the pages on which the article is found

John L. Wilhelm

"Solar Energy, the Ultimate Powerhouse"

in

National Geographic, March 1976.

pp. 381-397

Vol. 149, No. 3

If you interview someone, record the name of the person interviewed, relevant credentials, and date of interview.

```
Interview with
     James Thomson
  Former Chief City Planner
                  (1969-1974)


May 23, 1977
```

Also keep cards for maps, sketches, works of art, recordings, filmstrips, and any other material you use. Make notes of the relevant numbers, the location (such as "city hall"), title (if any), and anything else that would enable you or someone else to find that same item again.

Mark the source of any material you photocopy.

Information cards

Most of your notes will record information or opinions you encounter. You may find yourself making a considerable number of information cards from one source and very few cards from another. Some notes will record specific statements, others will summarize

ideas. Still others will contain brief quotations (*in quotation marks*). All cards should show the author's name and the page number (or numbers) from which the data was taken. If you are using more than one book or article by the same author, the title may substitute for the author's name. You have the full information for all these sources on your source cards.

Above all, each note should be written clearly enough for you to read it back with the same meaning you intended when you wrote it.

Some examples of information cards:

Hamilton   pp. 813-814

   The U.S. govt. is investigating the possibilities of energy from wind power, as well as from other sources. In 1976, govt. invested $12 million in wind research.

Hamilton   pp. 815-816

An Iowa farmer has independently
erected a wind generator. That
and storage batteries provide his
entire energy supply.

Hamilton   p. 816

"Nothing in the books says
a windmill has to look like
a windmill..."

See illustrations

Kiefer

Even if fertility falls to replacement level (2.11 children per woman) zero population growth would not take place immediately. More women are now of childbearing age than there were in 1960. So there would be an increase before any leveling off.

Brown + Wray: pp. 322-323

Improved nutrition may be the most important reason for decline of death rate.

Much of what you learned in your research will not
be taken in notes. You will be forming ideas about the
topic and the manner in which you intend to pursue it.
Before you reach the end of your research, you should
be able to prepare an outline that will show the final
plan of the paper you will write.

Outlines, formats, and style

Just as a substantial building needs a strong framework, a substantial research paper needs a good outline. A well-written paper is based on a well-balanced
outline. In the finished product, the framework may be
obvious or hidden, but it must be there.

A good outline has a structure of major divisions
and subdivisions.

I. Roman numerals (I., II., III., etc.) mark off the major divisions of ideas in the paper.

  A. Capital letters (A., B., C., etc.) are used to subdivide ideas within each Roman numeral group.

    1. Arabic numerals (1., 2., 3., etc.) subdivide the ideas within each capital letter group.

      a. Lower-case letters (a., b., c., etc.) form the subgroups within the arabic numeral divisions.

It is not necessary to subdivide each topic. No topic, however, should have an **A.** subhead without also having a **B.** subhead. Similarly, if there is a **1.**, there must be a **2.**; if there is an **a.**, there must be a **b.** In other words, there should be at least two subdivisions within a category.

The subdivisions within an outline should be balanced. All **I** topics should be as important as **II** and **III** topics. Within each further division, there should also be balance.

Let us examine some possible outlines for the subject "What will the world's population be in the year 2000?" Note that in each example below, the title and the basic point of the outline in the paragraph following the title have been restated to suit the particular subject eventually chosen.

Outline 1

PLANNING FOR AN OLDER POPULATION

All evidence indicates that the proportion of old people to young people in society is increasing. The shift will require new planning for the future.

I. Evidence of the shift
   A. The declining birthrate
   B. The changing death rate
   C. Population profiles for the future
      1. Profiles based on current rates
      2. Profiles based on various predictions for the future
         a. same birthrate, lower death rate
         b. lower birthrate, same death rate
         c. lower birth and death rates

II. Implications of the population shift
   A. For work and retirement patterns
      1. Current patterns
      2. Prospective patterns
   B. For government planning
      1. Government income
      2. Government services
      3. Need for public institutions
   C. For people planning careers
   D. For industries

III. Planning for the future
   A. Fitting current data into planning schemes
   B. Monitoring future changes

IV. Steps to begin to take now

The outline above was written in phrases. The same outline can be written out in full sentences. It is often advisable to do so.

Outline 2

PLANNING FOR AN OLDER POPULATION

All evidence indicates that the proportion of old people to young people in society is increasing. The shift will require new planning for the future.

I. Evidence of the shift in the ratio of older people in the population is available in our present statistics.

    A. The birthrate is declining. Fewer children are born to the average woman.

    B. The death rate is decreasing. More people are reaching a greater age.

    C. From present statistics we can provide a profile of future population ratios. All profiles will suggest an older population.

        1. We can project the profiles by assuming the same birthrate and a lower death rate.

        2. We can assume a lower birthrate and the same death rate.

        3. We can assume both lower birth and death rates based on current trends.

II. The shift to an older population has implications in various areas.

    A. The pattern of work and retirement will be lopsided or will have to change.

1. Current work and retirement patterns are based on previous life expectations. If current patterns continue, a smaller proportion of the population will work and a larger proportion will be retired.
2. Patterns of work and retirement may change in the future to adjust to the new population expectations.

B. Government planning will have to be altered to adapt to the new population proportions.
   1. The government's income from taxes may be reduced by the existence of a smaller working population and a larger retired population.
   2. The government will have to provide more services to older citizens and will need to provide fewer services to children and young people.
   3. Government will need to build fewer schools and perhaps recycle school buildings to suit the needs of the elderly. More institutions will have to be created to assist the older population.

C. People who are planning careers should think in terms of the needs of the population ten and twenty years from now.

D. Industries will have to adjust their production to adapt to new population patterns.

III. We can begin to plan for the future by examining the new statistics.

    A. Current data can be used to plan for the population of people who have already been born.

    B. The government and individual companies can begin programs to monitor the proportions of future populations.

IV. It is essential to begin to take some of these steps now. Reasons are given for the urgency of current planning to avoid severe future problems.

The outline in sentence form is much clearer than the phrasal outline. A sentence outline can often help to clarify thinking about a subject. It will reveal the strengths and weaknesses of the structure better than a phrasal outline will.

Below is an example of another outline (and a different title) based on similar subject matter.

Outline 3

IS THE WORLD'S POPULATION OUTGROWING ITS RESOURCES?

The potential for population growth seems to be infinite. The world's population is doubling in shorter periods of time. The potential for developing the world's resources seems to be finite. Some people

claim that we are rapidly approaching our population limits. Others claim that the crisis will not occur.

I. A historical look reveals the accelerating rate of population growth, food production, and energy growth and consumption.

    A. Patterns and rates of population growth have varied in specific periods of the past.

    B. Food production has increased in the past, but not always in step with population growth.

    C. Our need for energy has increased and our sources for energy have decreased.

II. Experts do not agree on the prospects for the future.

    A. Pessimists argue that we are overpopulating the world and cannot forever expect to provide the resources for the people.

        1. They project growth charts that indicate evergreater numbers of people.

        2. They cite statistics that indicate limits to our capacity to feed people.

        3. They indicate that we are demanding more and more energy and are unable to continue to provide energy in the amount required for an unlimited time.

    B. Optimists argue that although there is a theoretical limit to the number of people the world can support, we are not in danger of reaching that limit.

1. They cite evidence of a leveling-off of population growth—with a possible zero population growth at some time in the future.
2. They believe that we have not tapped all our food-production facilities and that we have the capacity to provide far more food than we now provide.
3. They believe that there are new sources of energy that can provide us with an infinite energy supply.

C. There are areas of general agreement among virtually all experts.
1. It is theoretically possible to overpopulate the world.
2. Present food-growing techniques will not serve a greatly increased population.
3. Present energy technology cannot serve our future needs.

III. Whether you believe the optimists or the pessimists, prospects for the future are most hopeful if the rate of population growth slows and the resource potential is expanded.
A. Several charts are provided to indicate possible future population patterns.
B. Various new food-producing systems have been successful or unsuccessful. Reasons are examined.

C. It is too early to evaluate new sources of energy.

Outline 3 differs from outline 2 in many respects. Outline 3 is subdivided to the same extent as outline 2, and the items in outline 3 are balanced to an unusual degree.

An outline will take various shapes depending on the nature of the data and the way the writer assembles the data. By the time the outline is prepared, the writer should know that the data is available. Sometimes the outline will reveal the need for further data in a particular area.

Relation of information cards to outline

Each writer has a distinct style of relating the information cards to the outline. Some people prepare the outline itself by arranging the cards to create a pattern. Other people develop a mental image of an outline as the research progresses. Then they arrange the cards to suit the outline.

Whatever system is used, at some point the cards will have to be organized to fit the outline. It is advisable to make notes of the subtopic on an upper corner of each card.

A finished paper should never read like an assortment of cards. The data on the cards will be used indirectly in some instances and directly in other instances. Sometimes a card will be no more than a way of reminding you to include an idea. Some cards

may be irrelevant to the final topic. The notes may have been made before a final outline was drafted. Do not hesitate to eliminate irrelevant information. It is important for a writer to develop a sense of what is relevant and what is not.

Format

What will the final paper look like? Will the **I, A, 2,** and **a** divisions of the outline be obvious in the paper? Sometimes they will and sometimes they will not. Subdivisions may show on a long paper, but not a short one. The decision is the writer's.

When the subdivisions do show, subheads are used to indicate the divisions. When this system is used, all headings of one kind should be typed in a similar fashion. For example, if the **I.** head is centered, the **II.** head should be centered. Both should be underlined, or neither underlined. The same amount of space should be allowed above the **II.** head as was left above the **I.** head. The patterns of capitals and lower case should be the same for each. This follows for all heads of a particular category. The category should be treated identically.

If heads are not used, the framework should be apparent because the finished work has a logic to it and a natural sequence of thoughts. Some other format considerations are:

1. It is customary to type a cover page with the title, the name of the writer, the date, and the number

and name of the class (if the paper is written as a school theme) or the department or company (if the paper is written as a job assignment). The title is repeated on page 1. Sometimes the writer's name is also repeated.

Often, you are required to follow a specific style. It is advisable to learn whether your institution does have its own style.

2. All pages should be numbered in the same position on the page. The upper-right corner is customary. Once again, you should learn if there is a format preference at your institution.

3. All margins should be kept uniform. And they should not be skimpy.

4. Any charts, graphs, or other figures should be numbered. A standard style for title and legend of figures should be maintained.

5. The paper should be double-spaced. Any quotations of five lines or more should be single-spaced and indented. Quotation marks should not be used for these. Legends on figures may also be single-spaced. Footnotes are single-spaced.

Style

It is not necessary to be a great writer to produce a good research paper. It is necessary to have a good grasp of the major ideas, good information, and a good outline. By the time you are ready to write, you should be familiar with any new words or terms used in the

field, and you should be capable of explaining them.

The most difficult part to write is the first paragraph. It should set the stage for what follows. A first paragraph may raise an interesting question that you will answer or attempt to answer later in the paper. It may, instead, propose an idea that will be examined. It may argue a cause, state a conclusion, or do any of a number of other things. At times, a first paragraph may begin with a quotation that will serve as a theme for agreement or disagreement. Above all, the first paragraph should be interesting and should be related to the rest of the paper.

If you are having trouble putting your first paragraph into words, find a friend (or even imagine a friend) to whom you can say, "This is what I want to say. . . ." It is surprising how often you will find yourself saying what you have been having trouble writing.

Keep your writing as simple as possible. Use unusual long words when they are the most appropriate words, but do not try to introduce learned words just to sound learned. If the subject you are dealing with has its own vocabulary, do use the appropriate vocabulary. Try to avoid sentences that must be read and reread to arrive at their meaning. Often such sentences can be broken down to their components and rewritten with greater clarity.

There should be a logical flow from sentence to sentence and paragraph to paragraph. One idea will flow into the next, and your writing will be per-

[5] Bob Woodward and Carl Bernstein, *The Final Days* (New York: Simon and Schuster, 1976), p. 77.

Further references:

[6] Woodward and Bernstein, *Final Days,* p. 283.

(Note that even though the authors have listed their names in reverse order on the second book, it is advisable to repeat the title in further references to avoid confusion.)

Footnote for a book with an editor, but no author

[7] Fred L. Israel, ed., *1897 Sears Roebuck Catalog* (New York: Chelsea House, 1968), p. 149.

For an article in an anthology

[8] John T. Hitchock, "Fieldwork in Ghurka Country," in *Being an Anthropologist,* ed. George D. Spindler (New York: Holt, Rinehart and Winston, 1970), pp. 164–165.

Further references:

[9] Hitchcock, p. 173.

For a signed magazine article

[10] Edwin S. Dethlefsen and Kenneth Jensen, "Social Commentary from the Cemetery," *Natural History,* June–July 1977, p. 34.

Further references:

[11] Dethlefsen and Jensen, p. 37.

For an unsigned magazine article

[12] "Estrogen Therapy: The Dangerous Road to

Shangri-La," *Consumer Reports,* Nov. 1976, p. 642.

Further references:
[13] "Estrogen Therapy," p. 644.

For a signed encyclopedia article
[14] Philip James, "Orchestration," *Encyclopedia International,* 1972, Vol. 13, pp. 464–466.

For a famous play
[15] *Much Ado about Nothing,* III, iii, 53–55.

The styles of footnotes used to add commentary or asides may vary. One example would be:
[16] The *Oxford English Dictionary* gives an obsolete meaning for *population* as "devastation, laying waste." Many who fear the effects of overpopulation might tend to support this definition.
(Note: the *Oxford English Dictionary* is a standard general reference. Unlike other references cited, it would not normally appear in a bibliography.)

Footnotes should be typed single-space at the bottom of the page. A short line separates the text from the footnote.

The works listed in the footnotes, as well as other works that might not be quoted directly, are listed in the bibliography. The format of the bibliography citations differs from the format of footnote citations.

Bibliography

Strictly speaking, a bibliography is a list of books or printed articles. If some research was based on materials outside of books (interviews, graphic works, filmstrips, etc.), a list of "Other Sources" should follow the bibliography.

Items in a bibliography follow a particular format. Note that the format is *not* the same as the format for footnotes.

1. *Author's name* is given last name first. If there is more than one author, all the authors after the first are listed first name first.

   All books by one author are listed before the books in which that author collaborated with another.

   A period follows the author's name.

2. *Full titles are given and underlined* if they are titles of books. Titles of stories, poems, and articles are given in quotation marks. A period follows the title.

3. City of publication, followed by a colon and the publisher (as shown on the book used) are given, followed by the copyright date.

4. For articles, stories, and poems, the pages on which they appear are given.

What do you list in a bibliography? Certainly, you list all books or articles that have been footnoted. Often you list other books or articles that proved useful as general background but not as a source of specific footnotes. Do not list books that were consulted but did not prove helpful.

Sample bibliography:

BIBLIOGRAPHY

Carson, Rachel. *The Sea Around Us*. New York: The New American Library, 1961.

———. *Silent Spring*. Boston: Houghton Mifflin Company, 1962.

Hamilton, Roger. "Can We Harness the Wind?" *National Geographic,* December, 1975.

Hitchcock, John T., "Fieldwork in Ghurka Country." In *Being an Anthropologist,* ed. George D. Spindler. New York: Holt, Rinehart and Winston, 1970, pp. 164–193.

Kahn, Herman. *Thinking about the Unthinkable*. New York: Horizon Press, 1962.

——— and Anthony J. Wiener. *The Year 2000*. New York: Macmillan Company, 1967.

Ternes, Alan, ed. *Ants, Indians, and Little Dinosaurs*. New York: Charles Scribner's Sons, 1975.

Note: If you list two books by one writer, the name may be replaced by a dash for the second reference.

Index

Alphabetical Key For Quick Reference

Houghton Mifflin Company
Dictionary Division

Editorial Director
Fernando de Mello Vianna

Supervising Editor
Anne D. Steinhardt

Assistant Editor
Carole La Mond

Contributing Editors

Bruce Bohle   Pamela Burton DeVinne   Eden Force Eskin
Matthew Gurewitsch   Linda Hodgkinson

Art Directors

Geoffrey Hodgkinson   Mark Mulhall

All correspondence and inquiries should be directed to
Dictionary Division,
Houghton Mifflin Company
Two Park Street, Boston, MA 02107

Library of Congress Cataloging in Publication Data
Main entry under title:
The Written Word.
   1. English language — Rhetoric. 2. English language — Grammar — 1950- I. Houghton Mifflin Company.
PE1408.W775 808'.042 77-10738
ISBN 0-395-26168-6

P9-CRM-808

THE WRITTEN WORD

Houghton Mifflin Company · Boston

Atlanta · Dallas · Geneva, Illinois · Hopewell, New Jersey · Palo Alto